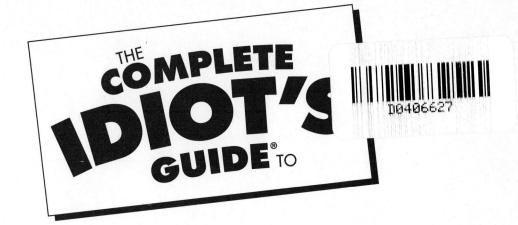

THE COMPLETE IDIOT'S GUIDE® TO

Starting an eBay Business

Second Edition

by Barbara Weltman and Malcolm Katt

ALPHA

A member of Penguin Group (USA) Inc.

This book is dedicated to all the eBay sellers, present and future, who prove that the entrepreneurial spirit is indomitable.

ALPHA BOOKS

Published by the Penguin Group

Penguin Group (USA) Inc., 375 Hudson Street, New York, New York 10014, USA

Penguin Group (Canada), 90 Eglinton Avenue East, Suite 700, Toronto, Ontario M4P 2Y3, Canada (a division of Pearson Penguin Canada Inc.)

Penguin Books Ltd, 80 Strand, London WC2R 0RL, England

Penguin Ireland, 25 St. Stephen's Green, Dublin 2, Ireland (a division of Penguin Books Ltd.)

Penguin Group (Australia), 250 Camberwell Road, Camberwell, Victoria 3124, Australia (a division of Pearson Australia Group Pty. Ltd.)

Penguin Books India Pvt. Ltd., 11 Community Centre, Panchsheel Park, New Delhi—110 017, India

Penguin Group (NZ), 67 Apollo Drive, Rosedale, North Shore, Auckland 1311, New Zealand (a division of Pearson New Zealand Ltd.)

Penguin Books (South Africa) (Pty.) Ltd, 24 Sturdee Avenue, Rosebank, Johannesburg 2196, South Africa

Penguin Books Ltd., Registered Offices: 80 Strand, London WC2R 0RL, England

Publisher: *Marie Butler-Knight*
Editorial Director: *Mike Sanders*
Managing Editor: *Billy Fields*
Acquisitions Editor: *Michele Wells*
Development Editor: *Julie Bess*
Production Editor: *Megan Douglass*
Copy Editor: *Ross Patty*

Cartoonist: *Steve Barr*
Cover Designer: *Bill Thomas*
Book Designer: *Trina Wurst*
Indexer: *Brad Herriman*
Layout: *Brian Massey*
Proofreader: *Aaron Black*

Contents at a Glance

Contents

Introduction

Once in a generation, a new idea takes hold to revolutionize our world. The car changed forever the way we get around. The computer ramped up the way we communicate. And eBay reinvented the way we do business.

eBay is the premier online auction site for buying and selling goods throughout the world. On Labor Day 1995, Internet enthusiast Pierre Omidyar launched what was to become eBay. Omidyar wanted to create a place on the web where people could buy and sell their goods on a level playing field, and he has succeeded.

Today more than 1.3 million people make a full-time living by selling on eBay, and more than 3 million others depend on eBay for income. By the end of the second quarter of 2007, there were 244 million buyers and sellers worldwide on eBay—185 million of them in the United States.

There were 559 million listings and, at any one time, there are more than 6 million items for sale, which is 300 times the number of items on all of Wal-Mart's shelves. In August 2006, the 2 millionth car was sold on eBay. In total, eBay is a $55 billion marketplace. No wonder eBay ranked 383 on the Fortune 500 list for 2007 and is one of the most successful stocks traded on NASDAQ.

eBay has opened up a world of possibilities for just about anyone who wants to make money. You don't need an advanced business degree from Harvard or Yale. You don't need millions of dollars in up-front capital to get started. You don't need any special skill or talent. All you need, besides a computer, an Internet connection, and something to sell, is a desire to succeed and an understanding of the steps you must take to accomplish your goal.

eBay is uniquely positioned to offer you an opportunity for financial independence. You don't have to let constant job insecurity drive you mad; you can become self-reliant. Whether you're currently worried about keeping your position, are a stay-at-home parent looking for a convenient way to earn extra cash, or just enjoy being on eBay, this book will help you build a business that can take you where you want to go.

This book is designed to help you start and run a profitable online auction business through eBay. Unlike many unscrupulous promoters who promise you instant millionaire status if you buy their system, we can assure you that, like running any type of business, it takes time, attention to detail, and hard work to succeed on eBay. You can't put up a house before laying the foundation any more than you can construct a business that can withstand the ups and downs of the marketplace without a solid understanding of what it takes. There's no quick fix or magic formula to shortcut hard work, imagination, and determination. But if you're willing to devote the necessary resources—both personal and financial—to your business, you're bound to achieve your dreams.

We want to caution you that the rules for running your business on eBay will change constantly—the eBay fee structure is always being adjusted, categories for listing your items come and go, and new features appear all the time. This book does *not* address the special rules for selling cars and real estate on eBay. But for all other items you want to sell, you'll get the basics. Of course, you'll also need to stay tuned for further developments in this ever-changing online world of eBay.

How to Use This Book

Do you want to become a full-time seller on eBay or make money from a sideline eBay business to supplement your income? Of course you do; that's why you're reading this book. Thousands of new sellers will list their wares on eBay this year. But nearly 70 percent of listings never sell. Putting a listing for your antique teddy bear on eBay is no guarantee that it will sell or that your hoped-for business will succeed.

Certainly, not knowing the things that can trip you up will contribute to your failure. There's no point in devoting your efforts to selling items if you lose money on each and every sale—volume is not enough to succeed. You need to set goals and devise ways to achieve them.

This book will guide you, step by step, in creating the eBay business you've dreamed of. It will help you understand what's involved in running an eBay business and how to go about it. And it will provide directions on how to take your business to a higher level of success.

This book is divided into five parts. Each part covers an aspect of running your business.

Part 1, "There's No Business Like eBay Business," explains how millions are already working full-time on their eBay activities and how you can join them. Whether you hop in for the next Webkinz craze, sell surplus inventory, or find new items to market, you're bound to find a niche on eBay. In this part of the book, you'll see why eBay is so great and learn the basics of how to get started.

Part 2, "Your Stock in Trade," guides you through the intricacies of deciding what to sell, how to price it, and where to find it. This nuts-and-bolts part of the book is vital to your success. You have to know what items are selling. It's up to you to do the research on hot items and learn how to price them right.

Part 3, "Making It Work," is all about selling—in the United States and abroad, which is the core of your eBay (or any other) business. You must make yourself stand out from the crowd on eBay by creating great listings and using marketing techniques. And, of course, you want to be paid as quickly and effortlessly as possible. To do so, you'll have to see that customers receive their items.

Part 4, "So Now Your eBay Business Is Growing!" No matter how enjoyable conducting your sales activities on eBay is, running a business isn't all fun and games. At some point, you have to get down to the mundane chores of keeping your books and records and paying taxes. You have to make sure that you're doing everything by the book and keeping things legal. You also have to think about protecting your business in the case of catastrophe and avoiding frauds targeted at you, the eBay business owner.

Part 5, "Taking Your eBay Business to the Next Level," is all about expanding your business. This includes making it to PowerSeller status and reaping the benefits this entails. You also want to use multi-channel selling to expand your customer base. You may need to hire employees or join with other people to run your business if you want to grow. You'll also need to rely on software and online tools to perform your eBay activities, because you won't be able to do things manually anymore. You may need to raise money to buy more inventory or equipment to increase your profits. And, of course, you must always keep up with new developments that can enhance your eBay business opportunities.

Road Signs

As you go through the pages of this book, you'll see special guideposts or boxes that will help you avoid problems, understand technical lingo, gain a leg up, and learn something new and helpful.

Power Point

These boxes contain tips, such as an idea or a website that can help you do things better or easier.

Auction Alert

These boxes contain warnings about things you should avoid if you want to stay out of trouble.

def•i•ni•tion

These boxes contain definitions of terms and expressions used on eBay and by general business owners everywhere that may be new or confusing to you.

An Educated eBay Seller

These boxes give you eBay facts and figures, and explore the fun of running an eBay business.

Acknowledgments

We acknowledge with appreciation all the people who shared their eBay stories with us and allowed us to share them with you. We're especially grateful to our acquisitions editor, Michele Wells, who helped to develop the book.

Special Thanks to the Technical Reviewer

The Complete Idiot's Guide to Starting an eBay Business, Second Edition, was reviewed by an expert who double-checked the accuracy of what you'll learn here to help us ensure that this book gives you everything you need to know about running an eBay business. Special thanks are extended to Lissa McGrath, who added special insight into the topic.

Trademarks

All terms mentioned in this book that are known to be or are suspected of being trademarks or service marks have been appropriately capitalized. Alpha Books and Penguin Group (USA) Inc. cannot attest to the accuracy of this information. Use of a term in this book should not be regarded as affecting the validity of any trademark or service mark.

Part 1

There's No Business Like eBay Business

eBay is a marketplace like no other. In 2006, eBay broke into the ranks of the Fortune 500, attaining 458—after being in business for only 11 years! By 2007 it had jumped up to number 383. Why this success? Because eBay has created a great arena in which you can connect with customers to sell your wares and run a successful business.

To make it on eBay, you don't have to be a genius or have an Ivy League education. You don't need thousands of dollars to launch your business. You don't have to start full-time. All you need is a good understanding of the fundamentals about selling on eBay.

In this part, you start off with the basics of setting up shop in your home to run your business.

Why Start an eBay Business?

In This Chapter

◆ Setting realistic expectations

◆ Turning your hobby into a business

◆ Selling on eBay full-time

◆ Buying a fully loaded eBay business

eBay may be your ticket to financial freedom. You can start selling for profit on a shoestring and build your business into something to be proud of—a business that can supplement your income or become your main revenue stream. However, before you go off in a million directions with unrealistic expectations, take a deep breath and collect your thoughts.

In this chapter, you'll learn to set realistic goals for your eBay activity, whether you want to make eBay your part-time or your full-time business. You'll find out how you can transform your hobby or passion into a money-making activity. You'll focus on some realities to face in making eBay your full-time business. You'll also assess whether you want to rely on the information in this book and your own abilities or use businesses-in-a-box to get started.

Becoming an Instant Millionaire Takes Time

Winning the lottery or coming into a huge inheritance may be a way to become an instant millionaire, but starting an eBay business is not. You may be able to build up your business so that one day you're doing sales in seven figures. One diamond seller grosses over $8 million annually, a stereo dealer sells more than $5 million a year, and a couple who sell fishing tackle gross over $2.5 million. The title of a recent book *The eBay Billionaires' Club*, suggests that the sky's the limit. But don't expect instant success on this scale.

What does it take to turn eBay into a successful enterprise? Like any other business venture, expect to put in time, imagination, and some money.

◆ **Time.** The amount of time you devote to eBay activities is entirely up to you. It can take a great deal of time just to find an item to sell, post a listing (which includes determining value, photographing the item, and writing a description), answer questions from interested buyers, follow up with the winning bidder, collect payment, and wrap and ship the item. This brief job description of a single eBay sale does not take into account all the other aspects of incorporating this sale into a business, such as record keeping, ongoing promotion (including soliciting positive *feedback* from buyers), and meeting tax responsibilities.

def•i•ni•tion

Know the sound that blasts back when someone's too close to a microphone? On eBay, **feedback** is the rating and comments that buyers and sellers give each other—positive, negative, or neutral, as well as scores on a 1 to 5 scale for sellers on specific aspects (item description, communication, shipping time, and shipping and handling charges). This information is posted (just click on the number next to a member's name) to enable other eBay buyers and sellers to decide with whom they wish to deal.

◆ **Imagination.** You need a plan of attack for launching and growing your business. You also need creativity in finding things to sell and posting your auction listings in the most favorable way. With competition fierce on eBay, your imagination may be the single most important factor in determining your business success.

◆ **Money.** This includes your investment in the items you sell and related expenses (for example, your Internet access costs). You can usually start your business for next to nothing, but if you want to grow, you'll need to put in real money (for example, to buy special software to track sales and inventory).

Figure 1.1

eBay's homepage.

eBay Businesses Are Like No Other Businesses

Doing business on eBay is unique; there's nothing like it anywhere else. This is because eBay, the world's largest online marketplace, has its own lingo (which you'll see throughout the book), its own set of rules (eBay policies and rules are explained in detail in Chapter 13), its own currency (PayPal, a payment method available through eBay, is covered in Chapter 8), its own communication system (Skype, covered in Chapter 2), and its own community of millions and millions of committed and highly competitive buyers and sellers.

One more feature makes doing business on eBay unique: it is possible for just about anyone, anywhere, to start a business, as long as you have something to sell and the equipment to do it. This is why stay-at-home parents with small children tugging at their shirts, seniors who've left the 9-to-5 rat race, the disabled who need to work from home, downsized employees, and others by the droves have ventured onto eBay to make money. You can, too.

An Educated eBay Seller

According to research from the Association of American Retired People (AARP), more retirees are starting their own businesses, and the trend is expected to accelerate as Baby Boomers head into retirement. Now 16.4 percent of the workforce who are 50 or older are self-employed. A report from the Ewing Marion Kauffman Foundation shows that those age 55 to 64 are the most likely to start their own businesses. And eBay reports that about 20 percent of all eBay users are age 55 or older. While there's no breakdown of how many of these are eBay sellers, certainly there is a growing opportunity here.

You probably don't need to raise seed capital as you would with a storefront business. You may already have whatever you require to put your toe into the business waters and begin to see revenues come in your door. All you need initially is …

- **Something to sell.** This could be an item you find in your attic, basement, or garage—perhaps vintage clothing, old toys, or costume jewelry. You can even sell something you've made, such as afghans or potholders. Or you can purchase new items for resale, starting with small (affordable) lots and increasing in size as your revenues permit.

- **A digital camera to photograph your item.** While there's no law that you must display a photo of your prized possession listed for sale, you'll probably have little success if interested buyers can't see what it looks like (cameras are discussed further in Chapter 2).

- **A computer.** Without a computer, how could you write your ads and post them on eBay?

- **An Internet connection.** Without being connected, you can't get onto the eBay website.

You don't need to stick with a 9-to-5 schedule. You can run your eBay activities at your convenience—at 3 A.M., if this works for you. This feature permits you to integrate your eBay selling into your personal routine. You can schedule auctions to run at optimal times so your work hours are convenient to you. Night owls have as much chance to reach buyers as early-bird risers. Stay-at-home parents can develop an independent livelihood between their children's nap schedules and school activities. Caregivers to infirm or elderly parents can put in hours at the computer and still have time to accompany parents to the doctors.

Used Versus New Items

eBay started out as an online flea market for people to clean out their attics and sell to collectors. While many people still use eBay for this purpose, it is more common today to use the eBay venue simply as an online marketplace to sell just about any item you can think of.

Today, 16.6 percent of eBay sales are from collectibles—old treasures found at garage and yard sales, in basements, and in attics. The bulk of eBay sales now are new (unused) items purchased for the purpose of reselling them on eBay.

An Educated eBay Seller
eBay sales today are very different than they were at the company's inception. The opportunity to sell online in the eBay marketplace has brought collectibles out of the woodwork. And as the law of supply and demand dictates, the prices of many types of collectibles have dropped dramatically as the number of items for sale has exploded. Here's what this means to you: decide at the start what type of eBay business you want to run—selling used items or new inventory. Then find specific items to sell, such as handbags, video games, or children's books. It's called selling in a niche, and it is the best way to succeed on eBay.

Moving from a Hobby to a Real Business

To sell a thing or two on eBay doesn't take much time or commitment on your part. Just list an item, follow the auction, and ship it to the winner. But if you want to transform your hobby into a real business, be prepared for the time you'll need to spend and the new things you'll want to learn about in order to succeed.

You can start things off as a hobby, but don't assume that this makes you qualified to run a business. Being in business means following the rules, including keeping good books and records, employing marketing strategies, accepting payment in more diverse ways than simply a buyer's personal check, and continuing to educate yourself and grow your business.

To cross the line from hobby to business is a matter of mental adjustment. You don't need to do anything special to actually be in business—there's no required eBay registration for a business, and there's no minimum number of sales you need to make each month or revenues to receive in order to be a real business. What you need is the devotion to the activity with an expectation of making a profit, and following through on recordkeeping and all the other boring business chores.

 Power Point

There is a specific business registration on eBay that allows business owners to use their business name and have authorized users, such as employees. Sellers can either register as a business right from the start, or modify their account through My Account in My eBay and change the Account Type from Personal to Business. Modifications can also be made when an authorized employee leaves, so they can no longer access the account. This modification takes about 20 seconds to do, and doesn't affect any other part of sellers' accounts.

Being a Part-Time Seller

There's no rule that requires you to be a full-time seller. You can devote as much or as little time as you want. But the more time you're willing to spend, the more money you stand to make.

The great opportunity that eBay presents is flexibility—you decide when and to what extent you can devote resources (time and money) to your business. You can put in a full eight-hour day as you would in any office job, or merely schedule a few hours at a time when it's convenient for you to run your eBay business.

You can intend for your part-time activities to be a sideline business, supplementing your day job. Or you can use part-time selling to test the waters for your business talents, with the goal of growing your eBay selling into a full-time venture.

Even if you're a part-timer, selling on eBay takes time. Just to give you a flavor of some of the activities you'll need to handle when selling (which you'll learn about in detail throughout the book), look over the following list of tasks. Of course, only you know how long it will take to do them all. And with practice, some of the following tasks may become a snap:

- Finding an item to sell
- Photographing the item, including uploading images to your computer and editing them for your ad
- Estimating value so you know what price to list the item
- Writing an ad
- Answering questions from potential bidders
- Following up on the winning bid, including sending an invoice along with a congratulatory e-mail that contains information about shipping and handling expenses
- Collecting payment and depositing it into your bank account
- Packing the item
- Shipping the item, which can entail a trip to the post office or a UPS pickup
- Requesting that the buyer provide positive feedback to boost your ratings, if he or she is satisfied with your service

Given the time you put in, it's not hard to feel like you're receiving less than minimum wage for your efforts. You may spend hours to complete a single listing and make only a few dollars on the sale. Take heart—as your listing skills and business savvy escalate, you're bound to start seeing a real return on your investment.

Finding a Space in the Crowd on eBay

While the rewards of selling on eBay can be great, don't assume it will be easy. The marketplace has become crowded as the popularity of eBay has grown. This means more competition for you.

Power Point

Continually experiment with selling different items in order to test the eBay waters before you invest a lot of money in inventory. You want to see what items are in demand, what competition you face, and what talent you have in marketing different things. You'll find more advice on selecting your inventory in Chapter 4.

The challenge in making eBay work as a business for you is *finding your niche and exploiting it fully.* It can be done. Someone in Ohio whom I'll call Jane has managed to carve out a highly lucrative place on eBay selling new clothing items to large-size women. She buys up brand name blouses and other apparel at local stores on sale (usually waiting for final sales at rock bottom prices) and then markets them to women who, because of their size, may have difficulty getting out to shop.

Making eBay Your Full-Time Business

It's been estimated by eBay CEO Meg Whitman, that there are now approximately 1.3 million sellers who make eBay their full-time business. Some of these sellers are corporations, but the vast majority are individuals just like you.

Just because there are more than a million sellers doesn't mean that there isn't room for one more. You can join the ranks of these dedicated eBay sellers to make a full-time livelihood from your online auction activities.

Once your activities start to be substantial, you may merit the title of eBay *PowerSeller*, which is a designation from eBay that you've achieved a certain amount of sales.

Achieving PowerSeller Status

Becoming a PowerSeller entitles you to a range of things that can be parlayed into even more sales for your business. Here is a sampling of the perks you get for being a PowerSeller:

◆ **Special PowerSeller icon.** You can use this icon on all your listings and even display it on your personal website. It's a great marketing tool to give buyers confidence in who you are and what you sell.

◆ **Special help from eBay.** You can get problems resolved and questions answered by access to special e-mail and, if your sales are large enough, by phone and even by a PowerSeller support team member assigned to your account.

◆ **Access to special promotions and discussion boards.** Get cut-rate listing fees and entry into the "secrets" shared by the PowerSeller community on eBay discussion boards.

def•i•ni•tion _____

Once your eBay sales reach a critical mass—more than $1,000 a month or you achieve some other benchmark—eBay rewards your success, inviting you to be a **PowerSeller**. This status entitles you to certain benefits that are not available to sellers who are less successful.

An Educated eBay Seller

Bronze, Silver, Gold, Platinum, and Titanium are PowerSeller categories. You can move up the power scale as your sales grow. For more information about the PowerSeller program, go to http://pages.ebay.com/services/buyandsell/welcome.html.

◆ **Access to wholesalers.** Find inventory at favorable prices from wholesalers who market exclusively, or at least more favorably, to PowerSellers.

◆ **Attend special events.** Exclusive activities at eBay Live!, the annual convention, and other meetings are restricted to PowerSellers.

◆ **Use fringe benefits.** Health coverage (in some but not all states) and other low-cost benefits are offered through eBay solely to PowerSellers.

◆ **Unpaid Item Insurance.** eBay is currently testing a new feature for PowerSellers that will refund listing upgrade fees (bold, subtitle, Featured *Plus*, etc.) if the seller has to file an unpaid item claim with eBay. This test will run through the end of December 2007 and then eBay will make a decision about continuing it.

The ins and outs for PowerSellers are discussed in Chapter 17.

Financial Considerations

The great thing about starting an eBay business is the modest financial commitment required. Registration to sell on eBay is free. As mentioned earlier, you may already have the items in your possession to get started. You may already own a computer and a digital camera to list your wares. What more do you need?

You've probably heard the expression "It takes money to make money." eBay is no exception. In the long run, you probably can't make a living only selling what you already own (unless you happen to own Filene's Basement or Tiffany's). You'll need money to buy inventory. And you may want to invest money in marketing activities to promote your sales.

Money becomes a key factor in how successful you can be in growing your eBay business to the next level. Money determines what you have to sell and whether you can afford to take on employees. These and other money matters are discussed throughout this book.

Setting Up Your Business

To get started on eBay, you don't need to take any legal steps to formalize your business. You don't need to form a company. There's no law that you must take any special action to open up shop.

But once you see eBay as a full-time, long-term commitment, you may want to take steps to protect your business. This can mean formalizing your business enterprise (see Chapter 13), insuring your property (see Chapter 15), and taking other measures.

Working from Home

If you've spent your working career in an office or store, you're used to having people around all day. Working from home can be a shock. You may be alone a good part of the day. Before you commit to this work arrangement, be sure you understand both the good and bad.

Advantages to working at home include:

◆ **Costs.** Overhead is already covered. Unlike a brick-and-mortar business, you don't have to pay extra rent, utilities, and other expenses when you run your eBay business from home—you're already paying the rent (or the mortgage).

- **Flexibility.** You don't have to punch a clock to collect a paycheck. You control your schedule and can arrange your time to fit your lifestyle.

- **No commute.** You don't have to pay money or put in time just to get to work—you're already there. As we tell people, our commute is down the stairs and to the left.

- **No barriers to the disabled.** If you have a condition or handicap that makes getting around a problem, then working from home may be ideal

Disadvantages to working at home include …

- **Solitude.** Not everyone is cut out to work from home—the lure of office gossip around the water cooler may be too much to give up. Of course, for other people, the lack of interruptions from co-workers, office meetings, and other structured activities is a blessing—giving them more time for work (and play).

- **Distractions.** A crying baby, barking dog, or nagging spouse can make working from a home a challenging experience. Juggling the demands of family isn't easy when everyone is in the same space.

Auction Alert

Set boundaries for your eBay business if you want to separate your business from your personal life. Fix time limits on when you'll work (and when you won't). Otherwise, you can quickly burn out from the 24/7 challenge that working from home presents.

- **Loss of space and privacy.** Depending on where you live, what you opt to sell on eBay, and other operations decisions, running the business from home can cost you dearly in terms of space and privacy. You have to reallocate your living space to accommodate your business needs.

- **Constantly open for business.** Working from home can be challenging from a time-management perspective. You're never closed—the temptation or need to work is always there.

Don't Quit Your Day Job too Soon

If you must depend on the money you bring in from your eBay activities, consider testing the waters first before deciding to quit your day job and become a full-timer. Your day job gives you …

- **Security.** You know for certain how much money you'll earn each month, with eBay revenues being gravy.

◆ **Capital.** Your salary, which already goes to cover your living expenses, can be used to finance your eBay activities. You can spend part of your paycheck to build up inventory and promote your sales.

◆ **Fringe benefits.** You may enjoy benefits, such as medical coverage or life insurance, through your employer. If you need these valuable perks, don't give up your day job until your eBay business has reached a level that can support paying for needed benefits (some of which may be available to PowerSellers who want to pay for them).

Power Point _____

If you have a spouse or significant other with whom you share expenses, you may have more flexibility in deciding whether and when to make eBay your full-time business. For example, if you enjoy health insurance through a spouse's employer, you may be able to quit your day job sooner to pursue your eBay dreams.

Selling for Others

One variation on the eBay business theme is becoming a seller for someone else. Your neighbor may clean out his garage and discover "treasures" he'd like to sell on eBay but doesn't have the time or ability. If he knows you're an eBay seller, he may ask you for help.

You can supplement your own selling activities by becoming a seller for other people. If you're doing a friend or relative a one-time favor, you may do this work gratis. However, if there are several items and you make a habit of selling for others, be sure to charge for your services. Here are your options:

◆ **Charge a flat fee.** Charge a fixed rate for each sale, regardless of whether the item sells and the final price it fetches. Make sure the person you're selling for bears all the cost of listing and selling (including eBay fees).

◆ **Charge a percentage of the sale.** Charge a fee based on a portion of each sale. Typical percentages range from 25 percent to 40 percent or more of the winning bid (30 percent is certainly an acceptable rate). Remember, you're investing your time and energy and should be compensated for your efforts.

◆ **Use a combination of the above.** You may charge a flat rate for certain aspects of selling, such as picking up items from a buyer, and also collect a percentage of the winning bid.

Power Point

Protect yourself—make sure an attorney reviews the terms and conditions for the eBay Trading Assistant agreements you make with your customers. For example, be clear who bears the risk if the item is broken or the buyer reneges on the purchase.

If you want to make selling for others a key component of your business or perhaps your exclusive activity, consider becoming a certified *eBay Trading Assistant*. There are now more than 30,000 Trading Assistants, many of whom make serious money. This allows you to be listed in the eBay Trading Assistants Directory for free, announcing to others that you're available to handle their online auctions for them. It's entirely up to you to negotiate your fees and set your selling terms. Interested buyers find you by searching the Directory according to zip code and what they need help in selling, such as household items. To learn more about being an eBay trading assistant, go to http://pages.eBay.com/tradingassistants/learnmore.html#requirements.

def•i•ni•tion

As long as you've sold at least 10 items during the last three months, have a feedback score of 100 or higher, and have more than 97 percent of your feedbacks positive, you can create a special eBay account called an **eBay Trading Assistant**. This status enables you to sell for others. It doesn't make you an eBay employee or its independent contractor. You can display the Trading Assistant logo on all of your listings. A **Trading Post** is a Trading Assistant with a drop-off location or storefront that has regular hours. To become a trading post you need a feedback score of 500 or higher and monthly sales on eBay averaging $25,000.

Don't get in over your head without understanding the ramifications of becoming an agent. Did you know, for example, that you're legally obligated to pay eBay fees because, technically, you're the seller? If you become a seller for others, be sure to consult with an attorney to determine any state laws you may have to deal with. For example, if you're selling cars online, special local laws may apply.

Buying a Packaged eBay Business

People are always looking for shortcuts and the easiest way to make money. To help these people, there are packaged programs designed to instruct would-be sellers on how to create an eBay business from scratch. Whenever there is a real economic opportunity, you'll find con artists trying to get you to go for this easy way. They take your money, and, in return, you receive information that you could have found on your own at a fraction of the cost. In effect, you lose both your money and the time you could have devoted to developing your business on your own.

Not all promotions for eBay business kits are fakes; some contain valuable information. How can you recognize a scam? Like any other fraud, if it sounds too good to be true, it probably is. You may receive e-mail solicitations promising that you can get your eBay business up and started and learn everything you need to know simply by buying a CD-ROM, a book, or DVD. The costs—from $39.95 and up—may seem reasonable. But ask yourself what you get for your money. Certainly, no more information (however many "secrets" the products promise to reveal) than you will get from reading this book or through other legitimate products. Save your money and your energy so you can invest in yourself.

Power Point _____

If you fall victim to a scam—you don't get what you pay for or the sales come-on is deceptive—report this to the Federal Trade Commission on a complaint form at https://rn.ftc.gov/pls/dod/wsolcq$.startup?Z_ORG_CODE=PU01. This may not help you, but you can take comfort in knowing that you may have prevented someone else from being another victim. You can also report the event to eBay. More scam alerts and remedies are discussed in Chapter 14.

Of course, you can use many valuable products and tools in your business to help you maximize your eBay efforts. These options are discussed in Chapter 20.

What about buying a franchise to sell on eBay? There are a number of franchises, such as QuikDrop (www.quikdrop.com) and eAuctionDepot (www.e-auctiondepot.com), which are storefronts where consumers bring their wares. Franchisees sell the items on eBay and keep a good chunk of the winning price.

As with owning any franchise, there are substantial up-front costs to buying into the business, as well as ongoing costs paid to the parent company. As a general rule, franchises tend to do better as start-ups than nonfranchises because processes have been formalized and there are marketing advantages. But the added cost of eBay-related franchises may not make sense because of the labor intensity of selling items and small margins that can be realized for these services.

Auction Alert _____

In June 2007, over 60 of the 100 iSoldIt (www.i-soldit.com) franchises sold had already folded and there was a buzz that the entire operation could go bankrupt.

Now there's another way to go—multi-level marketing on eBay. Like Tupperware and Avon parties, you can host get-togethers where acquaintances bring items for you to sell. As with any multi-level marketing, you can make money from these direct sales (you charge a percentage of the final price) as well as by recruiting other sellers (you get a percentage of their revenues). For more information, see Chapter 18.

Don't Go There

While you can make a nice living by selling items for other people, you won't make any real money by paying others to sell for you. You need to be the seller.

And you probably won't make money by becoming a seller for an online "club." Here's how this type of operation works: you join a club and list a company's items for it. It doesn't cost you anything other than your time and effort to start working for the company. After a sale, the company ships the item directly to the buyer and pays you the difference. This is called drop shipping. Sounds great in theory, but in practice, you may put in many hours of work on items that never sell. The reason: the club grows so that there are many people trying to sell the same thing, diluting the market so you can't make a profit.

The Least You Need to Know

- An eBay business is easier to launch than just about any other type of business and just about anybody can do it.

- eBay can be your business on a part- or full-time basis, depending on the time and resources you are willing or able to devote to this activity.

- eBay isn't a get-rich scheme; it requires a strong commitment to learn the ropes and put in the hours to succeed.

- Don't fall for promotions promising immediate eBay success or secrets; they are probably just scams that will cost you money and waste your time.

Barebones Startup

In This Chapter

- ◆ Setting up your home office for efficiency and comfort
- ◆ Connecting to the outside world
- ◆ Equipping your business properly

You don't have to lease office space in a high-rise downtown building or open a storefront in a suburban mall to run your eBay business. You can operate from the comfort of your own home. But you still need the right location within your home to operate comfortably and efficiently. And you need to have the right equipment to support your activities.

In this chapter, you'll learn about physically setting up your business office to operate your eBay business. You'll find out where to put things and what things you'll need to get started properly and run well.

Space in Your Home

Whether you live in a mansion or a one-bedroom apartment, you can conduct a worldwide business out of your home. But you have choices to make. Where will you be most comfortable conducting your activities? A spare bedroom? The den? The kitchen table? Keep in mind that you'll probably be spending a lot of time in your work area, so you want to make it as workable (and comfortable) as possible.

Take the time to lay out your office space in your home. Doing this will provide the following key benefits:

- **An efficient work space.** This is the place where you can best run your business.

- **A home office deduction for your business.** Tax rules come into play in your choice of locations. Unless you follow these rules, you won't be eligible for a deduction, as explained in Chapter 16.

- **A cost-effective setup.** With some ingenuity, you can make an existing space serve your needs with little new money added. If you don't think ahead, you may run into problems later, such as needing to bring in new electrical lines, which can cost you big bucks.

Finding a Place for Your Computer and Inventory

To pick the best location in your home from which to operate, you need to balance the space you have available against the space you need to accommodate your equipment—your computer, photography setup, and perhaps storage for your inventory.

Look around and decide what works for you. Maybe you can convert an attic, basement, or garage into office space. Perhaps you already have an extra room waiting to be set up as your new office.

Power Point _____

Small as your business may be, consider having a satellite office—your laptop, Blackberry, or cell phone connected to the Internet through wireless (Wi-Fi) technology. Your satellite office becomes whatever space you're in at the time—Starbucks, an airline terminal, or another location in which you can use your device. This office away from home is useful in monitoring your auction activities.

Think about how much space you require. Ask yourself what equipment you intend to have in your office. Do you plan to store inventory at home? Where can you best photograph your items? Where can you pack shipments most easily? Clearly, you don't have to do everything in the same place; you can do your listings from a spare bedroom, store your inventory in the garage, and pack boxes on the kitchen table.

Exploring Space-Saving Strategies

If space is limited, as it is for most people, consider some space-saving strategies:

◆ **Buy equipment that takes up less space.** For example, instead of having separate machines for printing, scanning, photocopying, and faxing, use an all-in-one machine for these tasks. You'll save money as well.

◆ **Store inventory offsite.** You can store inventory with a self-storage company. Find one near you so you can easily access your items when you need them. With the expansion of these self-storage companies nationwide, you can find competitive monthly rental fees. The more space you take, the more you'll pay. Find a self-storage facility in your area in your local Yellow Pages or through SelfStorage.com (www.selfstorage.com).

◆ **Use a fulfillment company.** Instead of handling your inventory, let a pro manage your inventory for you. A growing number of *fulfillment companies* cater to small business e-tailers, including Innotrac (www.innotrac.com) and FFP Global (www.fulfillmentplus.com), or you can get quotations from five fulfillment companies through VendorSeek (www.vendorseek.com/fulfillment_services.asp). Even if you think your space can house your merchandise now, think ahead; as you grow your eBay business, you may outgrow your space.

def•i•ni•tion

Companies that warehouse your goods and then package them and ship them to your customers are called **fulfillment companies**. They may also provide 24-hour customer support and processing of merchandise returns. These are different from drop shipping companies because you already own the merchandise that the fulfillment company ships out.

◆ **Ready your wares for sale.** If you create your items or buy fixer-uppers to refurbish, you need a workplace for this activity.

◆ **Let employees telecommute.** Suppose you have or expect to have workers or friends on your payroll to help you run your business. They don't have to be physically present in your home; they can work from their own homes and connect to you through e-mail, voice mail, or just a loud shout out the window.

Have Any Connections?

In e-commerce, you may never need to talk with a living soul by telephone. But even though most of your business is conducted online, it's highly unlikely that you won't need to use the more than 125-year-old technology called the telephone.

What's more, to connect you to the Internet, you may have to rely on your telephone lines. Think about connections for:

◆ Personal conversations by telephone.

◆ Connections to the Internet.

Phone Lines

You're not *required* to have a landline (a telephone line to your home) in order to run an eBay business; just about everything you need to do can be done through your computer and the Internet (although you may use your phone lines for dial-up access to the Internet as well as collecting payments). But as a practical matter, you probably want to reach out and touch your customers and vendors by telephone (even if it's a cell phone or computer-based connection), at least on some occasions.

Is your family phone usable for your business? There may be nothing wrong with your five year old answering the telephone when a neighbor calls. However, as your business grows, you may want a dedicated phone line for business. Instruct family members that this number is off limits for personal calls. Alternatively, you can use a distinct ring tone for business calls and teach family members not to answer these calls.

Do you need an 800 (or 866, 877, or 888) number for customers? Probably not, since communications are conducted primarily through e-mail. However, if your eBay activities are only a component of a larger business, you may want to have a toll-free number. You don't need a separate line for a toll-free number, and can use any phone line for this purpose (we use a dedicated fax line as a toll-free number for under $10 a month).

Power Point

Add a Skype button to your listings so buyers can contact you—at no cost to you or them—quickly with last-minute questions about your items.

You can also make phone calls through your computer. For example, use Skype (www.skype.com), a company now owned by eBay, to talk with customers at no cost if they have Skype (you can also use the service for $29.95 to make unlimited calls within the

United States and Canada). Download the necessary Skype software through its website or from eBay (http://pages.ebay.com/Skype).

Internet Connections

To do any business on eBay, having a computer is only one half of the equation—you also need to connect to eBay through the Internet. For this, you need equipment and an Internet service provider.

There are three basic ways to connect to the Internet: through your telephone line, with the same cable used for television reception, and with a wireless connection (based on satellite technology). The one you use depends on how much you are willing to spend, how fast you want to connect, and what's available in your area.

As you may recall from the old days of the previous decade, connecting through a telephone line was the first way to get onto the Internet. The speed for opening web pages and downloading or uploading files was painfully slow in retrospect.

Today, however, your phone line can provide you with speedier connections and always active service using a digital subscriber line (DSL). In an increasing number of locations, you may also have access to Fios, a high-speed method of access through newly-installed fiber optic phone lines (you don't need to have a home phone line for Fios; use your cell and still get high-speed access to your home). If you're doing a lot of buying and selling on eBay, you'll need high-speed Internet access.

Or your local cable company may offer its own high-speed access through the cable line. To connect in this way, you need a special cable modem. If the cable company doesn't give you a modem for free, you can purchase one from a computer store, online, or directly from your cable company.

An Educated eBay Seller

Fios or cable? If you're starting from scratch and both options are available, which one should you choose? Consider speed, cost, security, reliability, and usability. Both provide high-speed access, but Fios may be more reliable because cable won't run when the electricity goes out (Fios access can continue for up to 4 hours after a power outage, assuming your laptop can run for this period). Fios claims to be faster, but with wireless access the speed differential to cable access may not be noticeable. To help you make a choice, read some of the blogs online (do a Google search for "Fios versus cable").

If you have a laptop and you are on the go a lot, wireless technology enables you to connect to the Internet from just about anywhere. All you need is a wireless LAN PC card in your laptop and access to a "hot spot," an area from which you can tap into the Internet through wireless technology (called Wi-Fi). There are a growing number of hot spots around the country. In addition to office buildings, airports, convention centers, and government buildings, many Internet cafés provide not only coffee, but are also wireless hotspots for Internet connections. For rankings of the best Wi-Fi metropolitan areas, see the Novarum Wireless Broadband Review at www.novarum.com/Rankings.htm.

It'll cost you to connect to the Internet—usually, the price is linked to speed (the more you pay, the faster you go).

- Telephone connections are available through your telephone company. You can also connect using AOL, MSN, or other such private companies that link up through telephone lines.

- Cable access is available through your local cable company or via a satellite dish.

- Wireless connections for your laptop on the go are available through the same companies that provide service to cell phones. For example, T-Mobile HotSpot service connects you up to 50 times faster than a dial-up connection. If you want wireless connections at home, you'll need a broadband router that works off your main provider.

Tools of the Trade

A doctor needs instruments to practice medicine, and you need certain technology to ply your eBay trade. You don't need to have the biggest and best to run your business. You can always start with what you already own and then obtain better equipment as your business thrives and your needs grow.

You can't run an eBay business without two things:

- A computer
- Internet access

Depending upon what you're selling, you also need a digital camera to run your business well.

Desktop or Laptop?

The computer has made eBay possible; without it, there would be no online auctions. The type of computer you use is entirely up to you. Some eBay sellers rely solely on their desktops; others use laptops. And some use both—they take their laptops with them because they can't stand to be far from their listings.

Hardware is one thing you may already have, but do you also have the software it takes to run your business? You don't need to buy any special software to list your items and run your auctions on eBay; you can rely solely on what eBay provides for free or for a monthly charge. But you may want at some point to use software that isn't provided on eBay and you'll need to buy it.

Successful eBay business owners use a wide range of commercial software for various purposes. Just to give you a taste of what's available to ease your burden (auction-management tools are discussed in greater detail in Chapter 20), here's some of what you can do:

- ◆ **Conduct online auctions.** You can automate many of the steps in the auction process by relying on software designed for this purpose. The software can help you complete your listings more efficiently, track your auctions, send customized notices to winning bidders, and do more. eBay provides a number of solutions—some are free and some have a modest monthly cost. For example, Turbo Lister is a free listing tool that eBay provides. Designed for medium- to high-volume sellers, it enables these sellers to upload thousands of items in bulk and easily schedule listings in advance. Unlike the Sell Your Item form, you do not have to be connected to the Internet to work on your auctions in Turbo Lister. So if you're on a slower Internet connection, this may be a better option for you. The only time you need to connect is when you are ready to launch the auctions. My eBay is another free tool that lets you track your auctions—those you are conducting and those you are bidding on, as well as those you may simply be watching. Fee-based tools are explained in Chapter 20.

- ◆ **Keep books and records.** Remember that you're in business and should be keeping a good account of your business activities. You want to follow your inventory, log in sales, and know what you're spending in your business. This can be done most efficiently with commercial software for this purpose. Software programs to consider are listed in Chapter 12.

Picture This

No matter how rich in description your ad copy is, a picture of your item can say more than a thousand words. Fortunately, buying a digital camera to meet your needs is relatively cheap, and operating it is easy.

Digital cameras start at around $85 and can cost more than $2,000. What's adequate for accurately capturing images of your items? It's the number of pixels that count. You can swing for models now offering more than 10.0 megapixels—Canon, Nikon, Olympus, and Sony each offer models with these pixels in the $500 range. But a 4 to 5 megapixel camera will usually suffice.

The more pixels you have, the sharper your images will be. At the same time, the more pixels you have, the more computer loading time is required for potential buyers to view your pictures. For web purposes, you can use a 5 megapixel point-and-shoot camera such as the Canon PowerShot a460, which sells for under $100.

There is also a Wi-Fi camera from AuctionCamera (www.auctioncamera.com) that enables you not only to shoot good photos, but also manage inventory. The camera, which costs nearly $1,000, can scan bar codes and help you organize your photos.

Power Point _____

According to the Consumer Electronics Association, more than one third of U.S. households already have digital cameras, and by 2010, 80 percent will have them. If you're one of them, start with what you own and see if it will do for now. Remember that digital technology is continually changing, so if you don't get the latest and greatest today, you'll be able to get the newest and best tomorrow. For updated reviews of digital cameras, go to www.pcworld.com. For price comparisons, go to www.pricegrabber.com.

The camera may not be the only equipment you need to get the pictures you want. Other items include:

♦ **A close-up lens.** You need this lens if you're photographing small items, such as jewelry or flatware, or want to capture seals and signatures on prints and your camera won't enable you to do this. Some models have macro capability and a good optical zoom built in.

♦ **A tripod.** You need this three-legged device to hold your camera steady. A table tripod can help you get great pictures no matter how unsteady your hand is.

- **Lights.** Today's cameras don't require professional lighting, but if your home is dimly lit, you may want to use a lighting device or two. You don't need professional photography lights; you can use two or more bulbs and a reflector to increase your lighting.

- **Background material.** To offset your items to their best advantage, you may want to place them on something other than your kitchen table. A piece of black felt, for example, lets your silverware shine. A big roll of colored drawing paper is another useful backdrop. If you want to get fancy, consider a light box, which, as the name suggests, is merely a box featuring overhead lighting and a background that makes shooting your images easier. Or you can purchase a portable photo studio that sits on a tabletop and has a choice of various reflective backgrounds to illuminate your object when you use a flash (for example, the D-Flector from SharPics at www.sharpics.com); prices start under $70. Some of them fold flat, too, which can help conserve some space when not in use.

- **Software to help you edit your photos.** For example, Adobe Photoshop is the premier software to improve the quality of your images. Cost: $649 for the professional version. But you don't have to use this sophisticated product to capture images that will more than adequately display your items. Consider more basic programs, such as Adobe Photoshop Elements or Photoshop Album, which enable you to fix common problems, such as lighting and focus, in a flash. Cost: $99 and $49, respectively.

- **Software to enhance your photos for display.** You can use SlideTour (www.slidetour.com) to upload, display, and manage your images. (It's worth a view of the site to see what this software can do for you—there's an online audio/video tour of the product.) Cost: either 50¢ per image or various price plans (e.g., $24.95 per year).

You don't have to be a pro to take great pictures, but a little knowledge won't hurt you here. Talk with the experts at your local camera shop to discuss the type of equipment you'd want to capture great images of your items. Buy a book on digital photography and lighting principles to learn even more.

Other Useful Business Items

Barebones startups may get by with just a computer and maybe a telephone line—and, of course, pictures of your children to decorate your office. But to run an eBay business effectively, you may want or need other things, including …

- **Furniture.** Your kitchen table may not work well as a desk that you plan to be at for many hours in the day—where will your family eat while you track your auctions? You'll want a desk, bookshelves (to store books on your specialty, records, and so on), and a comfy chair.

- **A printer.** You may need to print pages off your computer—for your records, to track values of items, or to learn about developments in e-commerce. You probably don't need a color or laser printer; a basic inkjet printer for less than $50 will do (it may even be included with the price of a new computer).

- **Good lighting.** One simple overhead in the middle of the room you're using as your office may not work well for close viewing and reading both on- and offline. Make sure you have sufficient light, from windows and fixtures, to avoid eye strain.

- **Supply cabinet.** To keep your home from looking like a warehouse, you may want to stash shipping labels, paper clips, and other supplies neatly in a conveniently situated cabinet.

All of these items will make for a more productive work environment.

The Least You Need to Know

- Set up your office for comfort and efficiency, remembering that you're going to be spending a lot of time there.

- Get the right computer and telephone equipment to run your business.

- Connect to the Internet in the fastest way you can afford (from the options available in your area).

- Outfit your office with all the accessories needed to run your business smoothly and efficiently.

The ABCs of eBay

In This Chapter

- ◆ Registering to buy and sell on eBay
- ◆ Getting a feel for the eBay landscape
- ◆ Selling basics
- ◆ Doing post-sale management

If you're brand new to eBay, take a little bit of time to get to know the lay of eBay land—what the site looks like and how to maneuver through it. Becoming a buyer is a great way to learn to become a seller, by paying attention to how other sellers conduct their sales. If you are already buying on eBay and now want to sell, just jump right into the selling section to learn how to get started making money.

In this chapter, you'll learn how to use eBay, including registering and choosing your User ID. For eBay newcomers, you'll see how to browse, search, bid, and buy and sell on eBay and acquaint yourself with the eBay culture. Take as much time as you need to experience eBay. You'll also find out what it's going to cost you when you sell your items. Finally, you'll get an overview of how to manage your sale after the bidding is over so you can collect your money.

Enlisting in eBay

Like every 18-year-old male in the United States who must register with the Selective Service System, anyone who wants to buy and sell on eBay must register. Once you have registered here, you will join the more than 233 million other registered eBay users. *Signing on is free* and only takes a few minutes. If you've already registered so you can buy items, you don't need a separate registration to sell. And if you've been selling an item or two, here and there, you don't need a special registration for an eBay business.

Browsing, searching, bidding, and buying on eBay are also free (other than what you pay the seller for your newly purchased item).

If you use a free e-mail service such as Hotmail or Yahoo! mail, you must give eBay your credit card or ATM card for address verification purposes only. Don't worry—nothing is charged to your card. If you use an e-mail address provided from your Internet service provider (ISP), eBay accepts this as address verification, provided the ISP is not on a spam list. eBay does not ask for your Social Security or tax identification number, although this could change in the future if tax law requires it (eBay-Australia has begun tax reporting).

eBay has a privacy policy that you will want to read if this concerns you. eBay uses the personal information it collects from you when you perform a transaction on the site to help it run more efficiently. Rest easy—eBay does not sell your personal information to third parties.

Registering to Buy and Sell

Registration is simple and takes only a few minutes. You can complete your seller's registration at the same time as your buyer's registration or wait until you are actually ready to start selling. Your seller's registration needs to include your checking account information and an ATM or credit card number (again, nothing will be charged to these cards at the time of registration). You then decide how you want to pay your seller's fees: either from your credit or debit card on file with eBay, or directly from your checking account, called "Direct Pay."

You can update your registration information at any time. For example, if you move, you can change your address with eBay registration.

You can also change from an "individual" account to a "business" account at any time without losing your feedback or changing any of your other settings.

You do not rack up any eBay fees until you list your first item for sale. And there is no monthly charge for eBay. You pay only when you want to sell your merchandise on eBay.

You can register with eBay using the Register button in the Welcome to eBay section on the home page (see the following figure).

Power Point _____

If you plan to make eBay a full-time business, it is a great idea to open a separate bank account, to keep your personal transactions separate from your business life. Fund the business account with a small amount of money, to get you started. Also obtain a business credit card to be used solely for your eBay business activities.

Figure 3.1

Click the Register link to register with eBay.

What's in a Name?

Are you happy with the name your parents gave you? You can use it or any other name you dream up to use as your eBay user ID (also referred to as a member ID or username). This is the name that others see when you bid on or sell an item. This must be a name not already being used by someone else, and it can't be your e-mail or website address.

User IDs are important on eBay, especially as a seller. Who do you want to be known as by the eBay community, and what do you want your eBay business to be called? Make the name catchy so that other users will remember it. Many eBayers who are only buyers choose a user ID that reflects something about them. For example, it might include something about where they live, their profession, their collectibles interest, their personality, or even their religion.

As a business owner, your user ID should reflect your business. If you are already an established entity, it can be your current business name. If you are just beginning your business venture, choose something that you like and that will be easy for your buyers to remember. If buyers cannot remember your name, they will have a difficult time finding you again when they want to place another order with you.

Power Point _____

If you're going to sell only motorcycle parts, an easy name for repeat business might be motorcycleparts4you (if the name's not yet taken). The negative aspect of choosing this business name is that if you branch into other areas of selling, it limits you quite a bit. Bertsparts might be a better choice because "parts" can refer to numerous things. And because you will sign all of your e-mail with "Bert," your name will become associated with your business.

eBay has rules about what your user ID may and may not include. It may contain a combination of letters (*a* through *z*), numbers (0 through 9), and many symbols, and it must be at least two characters long. It can't contain spaces; be obscene, profane, or hateful; or be an e-mail address or a URL.

Your user ID can't include any of the following items:

- The @, &, <, or > symbols.
- URLs (for example, xyz.com).
- Consecutive underscores (__).
- An underscore (_), dash (-), or period (.) at the beginning of a user ID.
- Spaces or tabs.
- The word *eBay*. Only eBay employees may use *eBay* in their user IDs.
- The letter *e* followed by numbers (eBay reserves these IDs for testing purposes).
- A term that is similar to, or could be confused with, a third-party's trademark or brand (for example, you can't use harleydavidson as your user ID).

You can change your user ID once every 30 days (though you don't want to do this on a whim because you waste any brand identity you've created thus far). But you may want to change your user ID if you expand your product line and want a name that's more representative of what you sell. Buyers are more wary of sellers with recently changed user IDs (easily identified by the icon after your user ID) so you may see a temporary decline in sales until the icon disappears (after 30 days have passed).

Completing the Registration Process

Your user ID is your name. But you also get security protection by selecting a password. This can be anything you choose, as long as it's a minimum of six characters. Select a password that's easy for you to remember but difficult for someone else to figure out. For tips on selecting your password, visit Syracuse University's Information and Technology Services at http://its.syr.edu/accounts/psswdsug.cfm.

Power Point _____

Are you always forgetting your password at different sites? At eBay, there's help available. When registering, you're asked the answer to an ordinary question of your choosing from a pull-down menu (such as what street you grew up on or your mother's maiden name). If you forget your password, your secret answer to the question of your choosing will allow eBay to remind you. Better yet, write down your passwords somewhere near your computer or keep it in a file for passwords on your computer for easy access.

Once you complete the registration form, eBay sends you an e-mail that you must respond to in order to finalize the registration process.

If you lost your registration e-mail or it never arrived, eBay can resend the e-mail. If you still fail to receive the e-mail within 24 hours, try re-registering with the same e-mail address. If you still do not receive the registration e-mail, check with your Internet service provider to see if there are any technical glitches, such as a full inbox for e-mail. Also, check your junk mail folder to make sure that the e-mail was not viewed as spam. When all else fails, go to the Register page and click the Help link.

You can change your password whenever you want. To prevent identity thieves from hacking into your eBay account, you may want to change your password routinely—say, every week or every month; it's up to you. You also are instructed by eBay to change your password when your account has been compromised (for example, someone has tried to hijack your account). Each time you change your password, you will have to come up with one you haven't used before. eBay keeps a record of your old passwords and will not let you use it again.

Creating Multiple Accounts

Okay, so you've followed all the steps to registering on eBay. You're not finished yet. You may want to set up more than one account, using each one for different purposes. Ellen did this for her handmade jewelry business. In fact, she set up three accounts. She used one for purchasing supplies, a second one for selling her finished products, and the third for selling off slow movers that she wanted to dispose of.

Power Point

Be sure to link each account to PayPal. You can use the same PayPal account for all your eBay accounts. Go to the Profile section in PayPal to add your different e-mail addresses for each eBay account. PayPal will accept up to six e-mail addresses.

The advantage to multiple accounts is that you create separate feedback accounts so that your potential buyers can't view your purchasing records. They won't know that you bought the items you're now selling and then research what you paid for them. For example, if you have a single account in which you buy a camera on eBay for $100 and then list it for sale at $200, bidders can view your feedback section to research the sales you won and discover what you paid for the item.

The disadvantage to multiple accounts is that your feedback numbers are not added together. Usually, this is a drawback until you achieve at least a dozen ratings within each account. Once you've passed this threshold, the disadvantage disappears.

Using My eBay

Have you always dreamed of having your own personal secretary, someone who keeps track of all your activities and all of your data in an organized fashion? Well, eBay helps make this dream come true by giving you your own personal eBay secretary, otherwise known as *My eBay* (see the following figure). Best of all, you don't have to pay any salary or fringe benefits—My eBay is free.

Your My eBay pages are there whether you use them or not. Each folder or page keeps track of all your eBay activities. If you want to follow the auction of a particular item, click the Watch This Item link, and, like magic, it appears on your list of items you are watching in your All Buying page. All of the items you bid on appear there, too.

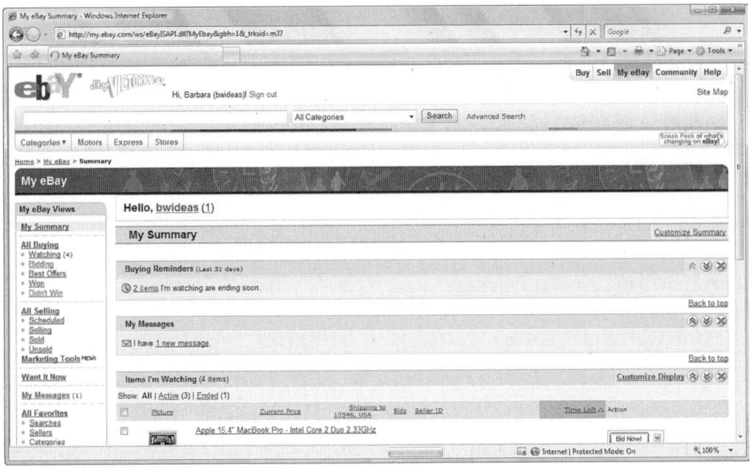

Figure 3.2

My eBay is your personal account manager.

Every time you list an item, it is logged into your selling page, along with all of the information concerning the starting price, the current bid price, and the *reserve price*, if you have one.

"Reserve not met" appears underneath the bid price until the bidding reaches the reserve price.

def•i•ni•tion

When an auction has a **reserve price**, it means that the seller is not obligated to sell the item unless the bidding meets this price. The reserve price is set by the seller and is hidden.

Once the reserve price has been met, the words disappear and no future bidder will know that there was ever a Reserve on the auction. At this point, the seller is obligated to sell the item to the highest bidder.

Figure 3.3

Until the bidding price matches the hidden price set by the seller, bidders will see "Reserve not met" beneath the current bid.

My eBay also keeps track of when auctions start and end, how many unique bidders you have, how many people are watching your items, and much more.

From Listing to Selling

As the New York Lottery commercial says, you have to be in it to win it! It's the same for eBay: you have to post your items for sale and follow certain steps in order to successfully dispose of your items and make money.

The first step is putting your items up for sale, which is called listing them for auction.

Listing Your Products

The listing process can be as easy as one, two, three—if you take things one step at a time. We'll run through the steps to give you a quick overview of the listing process. Each step is amplified throughout this chapter and in greater detail in Chapter 7.

1. **Prepare your listing.** This means writing a title and description of what you are selling. It also includes photographing the item, if necessary. And it means selecting the category in which you'll list your sale. Do this with care—if you include your new designer blouse under Antique Clocks, you won't get a single bid because no one will be able to find your listing.

   ◆ **Write a title the eBay search engine will love.** With 19 million items up for sale at any one time, how will yours be found? Title (the name of your item) is everything. You have up to 55 characters for the title; you can't use *HTML*, asterisks, or quotation marks. Use as many important words in your title as you can that you think buyers might search by. "Sony CD Mavica 300 Digital Camera, NR" has the brand name, a generic keyword, and "NR" (no reserve), indicating that this auction will be sold to the highest bidder, no matter what the bid. By contrast, "Cool Sony Camera, you'll love it," uses a lot of characters and doesn't say much. The only word that would be picked up by the eBay search engine is the word *Sony*. Don't waste any of your 55 characters on adjectives and superlatives—words like beautiful, unusual, the greatest, or unique—because they won't be picked up by the eBay search engine.

def•i•ni•tion

HTML is an acronym for Hypertext Markup Language. It's the special coded language for translating ordinary text into website documents.

Use the singular rather than the plural in your title because the eBay search engine distinguishes between them and most buyers only enter the singular form of the item they're looking for. Use an "&" instead of spelling out "and" to save two of the 55 characters if necessary.

◆ **Provide a detailed description**. The description and pictures for your item are the meat of the listing and deserve some thought and often some fine-tuning to get great results.

The description, which should probably run no more than 500 words, can be detailed, fancy, and colorful. Or it can be basic, plain, and short. It must, however, tell honestly and clearly what it is; state size, color, and dimensions; say whether it's new or used; and disclose any flaws. A good rule of thumb is to describe what bidders will see when they look at the picture. If you have dates, historic perspective, or personal information, or know about previous owners (called provenance), include a paragraph about them; most bidders appreciate those extras. Be sure to list dimensions in both inches *and* centimeters, if appropriate (remember that buyers in countries on the metric system aren't familiar with inches, feet, and yards). You can use the HTML that you already know, or you can use the eBay HTML editor, which gives you simple options to give your auctions some zing.

You can always add to your description if your item does not yet have any bids and there is at least 12 hours to go before the auction ends. A tip-off that you may need to add more information is if you're receiving a number of inquiries about your item that a better description would have answered.

Power Point _____

If you are a member of an organization related to what you are selling, be sure to say so. This gives you credibility with bidders. For example, if you're selling a military medal and you belong to the Orders and Medals Society of America (OMSA), add this information to your listing. The same goes for any personal expertise you may have that relates to items you sell—include this information in your listing.

◆ **Set your price.** The psychology of pricing is nothing to take lightly—it takes up all of Chapter 5. As studies have shown, bidders are more likely to get involved and buy if the starting price is low. Hundreds of auctions start at a penny, and rarely do they stay at that price. Another popular price to motivate bidders is 99 cents. Sellers like this price, too, because it is the highest price allowed in the lowest insertion fee band, so they pay less in eBay fees and generate more bidder interest at the same time. If you've got an item that is monetarily valuable but not necessarily popular, it would be wise to use a reserve auction. You'd hate to sell something at a very under-valued price—and, remember, the buyers and sellers are legally bound to complete the sale.

♦ **Add a picture.** Pictures are the rule for eBay sales. Only if you have tickets or something intangible for sale should you *not* necessarily include a picture. You can use eBay Picture Services. eBay's service hosts your pictures and gives you your first one free in any auction. You have choices for lots of different options to display your pictures, including a slide show. There are other picture-hosting services which are less costly than eBay. A couple of popular ones are www.photobucket.com and www.Inkfrog.com. If you use an auction-management service, picture-hosting is usually included in the cost.

Power Point _____

If you want to host your own pictures, use the URL link of their location. You can insert as many as you want for free using eBay Basic Picture Services.

♦ **Add the extras.** Spruce up your listing with options; it will cost you because there's a charge for listing upgrades, but using them may pay off big in the long run. You can fancy up your listing by adding one of the eBay sharp-looking designer templates, such as a film strip for your camera, baby decorations for your baby items, or just an abstract border for color.

Other advertising items you may want to include are options that increase your item's visibility, such as having your picture in the gallery, indicating that it's a gift with a cute icon, or putting your item title in bold. Anything that says "featured" means it will show up on the page first. Featured items increase bidding by 65 percent.

eBay now permits the use of embedded videos, as long as they are from an eBay-approved video source, such as Onstream Auction (www.auctionvideo.com) or YouTube (www.youtube.com). There's no additional eBay listing fee for adding video to your listing; however, you might have to pay the video hosting company a monthly fee. You can also choose to include a link to the video rather than embed the file in the auction. If your buyers are on a slower connection, an embedded video could take a long time to load and they may lose interest and go elsewhere.

Power Point _____

A Gallery picture is a must. It's the picture you see next to the title on the listing page, and it makes your auction stand out from ones that don't have a gallery picture. It costs just 35¢ and eBay claims it can increase the final price by 14 percent. Some buyers just scan the gallery pictures before they'll even read the listings!

2. **Decide on the type of auction you want to use.** For example, you may use a regular auction with a reserve (such as your cost for the item). Also set the auction period, the number of days you want the auction to run (discussed in more detail shortly).

3. **Describe your terms of sale.** This includes posting the methods of payment you accept (for example, personal checks, PayPal, or credit cards). Include your return policy. Complete the seller form.

Power Point _____

If you are selling a collectible item, it's a good idea to describe how you verified authenticity, or that you are not an expert and are listing the item in as is good faith but can't verify any authenticity. This will avoid any claims after the sale that you misrepresented the item. Hopefully, this practice will ensure that you receive only positive feedback for your selling efforts. Offering a money-back guarantee helps here, too.

Maximizing Browsing Factors

With more than six million items for sale every day, your goal is to make your auction stand out from the crowd. One way to do this is to make the eBay Browse feature work for you. The Browse feature enables bidders to stroll through categories they are interested in—from art or books to tickets or video games.

When you click Buy, you'll see categories to browse. Whichever category you select will display featured auctions first. The other listings are also there, but it may be many pages before they display.

The cost for a featured listing (called Featured Plus) is high: $19.95 per listing. And there's a special featured listing

def•i•ni•tion _____

If you want to give your listing special status, you must pay to have it treated as a **featured auction**. This entitles you to be listed first when a buyer browses within a specific category.

that appears on the eBay home page (called Home Page Featured): $39.95 per listing for a single-item and $79.95 if it is a multiple-quantity auction. As you can see, these options are pricey and not worth the money for your run-of-the-mill listing. However, the special featured listings can be useful for certain higher-priced items, and sometimes necessary if you're selling in a category where most of the listings are featured (such as the laptop computer categories).

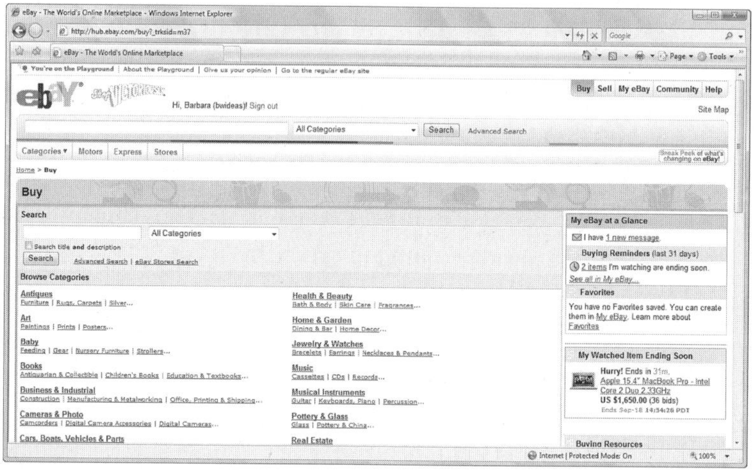

Figure 3.4

Searching on the Buy screen.

The Auction Process

The principles of selling on eBay are the same as selling magazines door to door, sending out catalogs, or opening a store in a mall. You need to have quality products readily available, market them well, and be a responsible seller that buyers can trust.

However, selling through an auction involves certain procedures that are not the same as other selling methods. Take the time to understand how the auction process works.

Aside from the process of the auction, using this selling method has one key difference from other ways of selling: you don't know at the start what your final selling price will be. If you sell a blouse in a storefront, the price you receive is the amount you put on the price tag. In an auction, the price you receive is the highest bid when the auction closes. This may be more or less than you anticipate.

Going, Going, Gone

The auction format adds a special dimension to selling. It's exciting because of the surprise element of not knowing until the auction closes what the final outcome will be.

Regular eBay auctions can run from 1 day to 10 days; 7-day auctions are the most common. If you want maximum exposure to your rare antique, a 10-day auction is the ticket (there's an extra charge for this long auction). If you have hot items that get bid on heavily, turn them over in 3 days. Very time-sensitive items, such as events tickets, tee times, and food, might move best in a 1-day auction. Whichever timeframe you select, the highest bidder at the end of the auction wins (unless the final bid doesn't meet the reserve price you set).

Take care to time your auctions so that they end at a time of day when buyers are online. While some buyers may be online at any time of night or day, it's usually not a great idea to have the final selling time be in the middle of the night; 6:00 P.M. Pacific time is a better time.

Power Point _____

The eBay community debates the best day to list (and end) an auction, with little consensus. Many believe that ending an auction on Sunday is optimum because the largest audience may be viewing listings on that day. However, keep in mind two points: eBay is worldwide, so Sunday in New York is Monday in Tokyo. Also, because eBay is based in San Jose, California, auctions run on Pacific time—7:30 P.M. is 10:30 P.M. in New York.

Auction Alternatives

Ordinary auctions aren't your only selling option on eBay. If you're selling multiple items that are exactly the same, you can use a Dutch auction to sell all of them in one fell swoop. Here's how a Dutch auction works. You set a minimum price, and bidders bid that price or higher. If there are more bidders than items for sale, the items go to the highest bidders, but at the price bid by the lowest successful bidder.

For example, suppose you have five items offered at $1. The first two bidders bid $1. Then four bidders bid $1.25. Two more bidders bid $1.50. The highest five bidders win (the two bidders who bid $1.50 and three of the bidders who bid $1.25). Note, when there are multiple bidders who bid the same price, the earlier bids take precedence. The first two bidders and one bidder of the second group lose. All of the winners each pay $1.25. Remember, it's the lowest successful bid.

If you're a nail-biter who can't stand the uncertainty of the auction process, you can use Buy It Now auctions to sell your items at a fixed price, just like in a store. Alternatively, you can use Buy It Now as an added feature to a regular or reserve auction, to give buyers the option of how they want to acquire your piece.

> **Auction Alert**
>
> If a regular auction has Buy It Now, this option disappears after the first bid. In a reserve auction, the Buy It Now feature disappears after the bidding meets the reserve price (although eBay is currently testing whether to leave it throughout the auction). To use Buy It Now on an individual auction, you must have a feedback score of at least 10 or be ID verified, where a third party (such as Equifax in the United States) works with eBay to confirm who the seller really is.

The Buy It Now price is usually higher than what you might set for a reserve price, but not as high as an item could achieve through bidding. If this sounds like it has excitement built in, it does. Some buyers don't want to wait until an auction closes, and Buy It Now is a perfect opportunity to make sure they don't lose out on that item they've always wanted. As a seller, you make a quick sale, something that may be worth the cost of not achieving the highest possible price that you might have realized if you'd allowed the auction to proceed.

Buy It Now can be combined with a Best Offer option. This allows the potential buyer to make a counteroffer to the Buy It Now price. The seller may accept or reject it.

The Sell Your Item Form

The Sell Your Item form, shown in the following figure, is what you complete to post your item for an auction. The following instructions are based on the comprehensive Sell Your Item form. At the time this book was prepared, eBay was rolling out a one-page form for casual sellers, with many fields already filled in.

The Sell Your Item form has been streamlined for fast listings. It remembers personal information that remains the same, such as your city, region, and sales tax rates, so no retyping is necessary each time you list an item. Provide the required information:

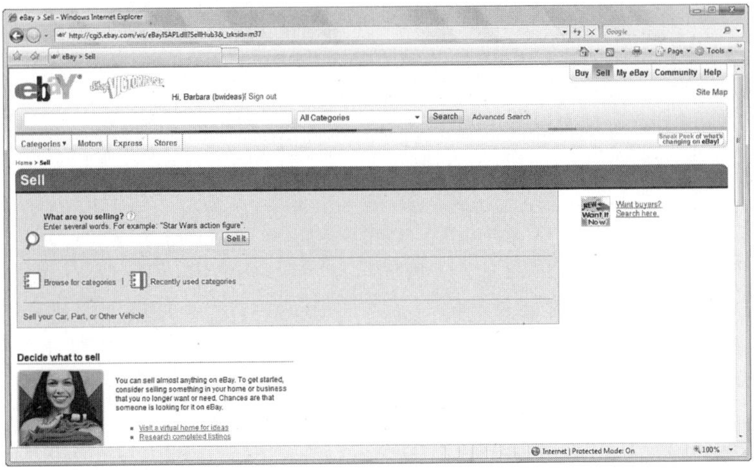

Figure 3.5

Use this form to complete your auction.

1. Choose the category for listing your item. With more than 50,000 categories, subcategories, and second level subcategories, this can be a daunting task. If you know exactly in which category you belong, go ahead and select it using the Browse for Categories link. Alternatively, when you start to create a listing, eBay gives you a list of suggested categories to choose from. This is determined by the keywords you enter about your item. You can use one eBay recommends or reject them all and browse for your own category. When you list future items, your past listings template will remind you of the categories you've used. If you want more exposure for your item, list it in two categories, such as a ski suit in skiing apparel and snowmobiling apparel. There's an extra cost for listing in multiple categories—if you list in two categories, you'll double the cost for insertion and most listing upgrade fees. But you'll pay only one final value fee. According to eBay, using the List in Two Categories feature increases final values by up to 17 percent.

2. Describe your item. This includes the title, subtitle, items specifics, and your uploaded pictures.

3. Design your listing. Use a listing designer, which is essentially a template to create the "look" for your listing. Add here a visitor counter if you want one.

4. Choose the format you'll use for this auction. Fixed Price is a Buy It Now auction that has no other option (i.e., there is no starting price included with the Buy It Now price). These can be single-item or Dutch auctions. Auction denotes auctions with a starting price and bidding as an option. These can also have a

Buy It Now price and can be single-item, Dutch, and may have a reserve price if you wish. If you also have an eBay Store, you will see an option for Store Inventory. If you don't have an eBay Store, you won't see this option.

5. Payment methods you accept. This can be limited to PayPal, for example, or include any and all methods acceptable to you—cash is not allowed.

6. Shipping terms. Be clear about who will pay the shipping costs (almost always it is the buyer), where in the world you will (or won't) ship to, and what the shipping charges will be (including insurance). For your convenience, there is a self-service shipping calculator integrated into your auction page. You select the package type, weight, and up to three shipping services you are willing to offer (Priority Mail, First Class, UPS Ground, etc.). When the buyer enters his zip code, it will show exactly what the shipping cost will be. You can add a handling fee if you wish (the buyer will only see the total cost, not the breakdown). Many sellers, however, prefer to set a fixed rate that will closely approximate the actual charge in order to simplify the process. Doing this may result in slightly higher charges for some buyers and lower for others versus the calculated shipping, depending on their location. As a seller, things will probably average out for you in the long run. One option is the Priority Mail Flat Rate box. This is not weight or destination specific, so it's really easy to use so long as your item will fit inside one of the sizes. They're also available co-branded with eBay's logo which looks quite professional (and they're free packing material).

7. Your return policy. Reading the policies of others sometimes helps to formulate your own policies. Being clear and leaving no doubts or questions will help to protect you in case problems arise.

8. Listing upgrades. Here you can add features to enhance your listing (for added eBay fees). These features include a border, bold face type, and a gift icon.

The final job in filling out the Sell Your Item form is to review it for errors or changes. Once you're happy with the form, click the Submit button and you've got yourself an auction! You'll know if you missed something really important if you start getting e-mails about details you forgot. If you discover that your auction needs revision, don't worry—there's a way to do that, but the sooner you do so, the better.

The Sell Your Item form also includes the title of your item, a description, photos, and your starting price (pricing is one of the keys to success on eBay and is explained in Chapter 5).

eBay Fees

Think of what it would cost you to sell the conventional way—to stock inventory, open a store in a mall, advertise your wares, and spend time away from home (which entails such expenses as child care, transportation costs, and work clothes). On eBay, you can reap as much as you would the conventional way, but avoid all of these up-front costs.

eBay does charge sellers to use the amazing website, which is a platform on which to sell goods to the worldwide marketplace. But you can sell items, collect payment, and ship them out without ever leaving your house. What do you pay for this luxury? There's a sliding-scale commission that eBay charges only when you sell your item (there's no added fee for shipping right from your home).

There are three types of eBay fees:

◆ **Insertion (listing) Fees.** These are fees for listing your items for sale. Insertion fees range from 20¢ to $4.80 per item, depending on the cost of your item. Insertion fees are nonrefundable. The following table lists the standard insertion fees.

Insertion Fees

Cost	Insertion Fee
$0.01 to $0.99	$0.20
$1.00 to $9.99	$0.40
$10.00 to $24.99	$0.60
$25.00 to $49.99	$1.20
$50.00 to $199.99	$2.40
$200.00 to $499.99	$3.60
$500.00 and up	$4.80

Power Point

Since the break points for Insertion Fees are at whole dollar amounts, you'll save money by setting your starting price, opening value, or reserve price just under the break point. For example, instead of setting a reserve price of $25 (with an insertion fee of $1.20), set the price at $24.99 and save half the Insertion Fee (just 60¢).

♦ **Additional fees for optional services.** If you use Buy It Now or certain other optional eBay features, you'll pay a cost for the privilege. For example, the first picture is free, but there's a 15¢ charge for each additional image. If you want to supersize an image, there's a 75¢ fee. Don't worry if you don't know what these features are yet—in Chapter 7, you'll learn about them in more detail and can evaluate whether they're worth it.

♦ **Final Value Fees.** These fees amount to a small percentage of the winning bids. You pay these fees only if the auction is successful. The following table lists the Final Value Fees.

Final Value Fees

Closing Value	Final Value Fee
$0.01 to $25.00	5.25 percent of the closing value
$25.01 to $1,000	5.25 percent of the first $25 ($0 to $1.31), plus 3.25 percent of the remaining closing value ($1.31 to $31.69)
Over $1,000	5.25 percent of the first $25 ($0 to $1.31), plus 3.25 percent of the next $25 to $1,000 ($1.31 to $31.69), plus 1.5 percent of the remaining closing value (1¢ and up)

Auction Management

You've listed your item. What's there to do while you wait for your auction to end? If you're lucky, not much but watch the price rise on your auction.

Chances are, though, you'll have to answer a few questions by e-mail. You may even have to revise your auction listing to make it clearer or more detailed, or to add something.

If someone e-mails you, that person probably needs clarification or wants answers about your item. Always check your e-mail a couple of times a day and answer politely and as soon as you can. The first e-mail from each person goes through eBay, but after that you and the other person have each other's e-mail addresses, and you can communicate directly. If you receive e-mails again and again about the same question, you may need to revise your auction listing or you can automatically post the question and your response on your listing. You can also set up Frequently Asked Questions to show when a buyer clicks Ask Seller a Question. These can be answers to questions you are routinely asked, but that you already covered in the auction description. Sometimes buyers just need to see it again.

If you decide your auction listing needs to be revised, it's not difficult to do. Just find your listing in your My eBay section, and use the drop-down menu to the right to select Revise. You then can edit each section individually, but there are some restrictions.

 Auction Alert _____

> Beware of e-mails asking you to end your auction early or make a deal outside eBay. This is against eBay policy, and neither buyer nor seller is protected by eBay if such a deal goes bad. Any seller has the option to end an auction early (though not during the final 12 hours if there are bids), but any and all bids must be canceled before doing that. And if this becomes a pattern, buyers' trust in you as a responsible seller is affected.

You don't want to be spending your time redoing your work over and over again. Make your initial listing as complete and correct as possible; it's better to take time up front to get it right than have to put in more time later to revise the listing. If you add information after there is already a bid, that bidder has the option to withdraw her bid if the revised information significantly changes the item. So, for example, if you said a laptop had a DVD burner, but then realized it was actually just a CD burner and added a correction to the listing, the buyer would be more than justified to withdraw her bid.

Post-Sale Management

When the bidding is over, your work isn't over. On the contrary, you may have to do as much or more *after* the sale as you did to obtain it. You need to take four key steps after the auction has closed (assuming there has been a winning bidder):

- ◆ Contact the winning bidder within three days to inform him or her of the auction results.

- ◆ Arrange to receive payment from the bidder.

- ◆ Pack and ship the item, if it's in your possession (or inform the company holding your item to ship it).

- ◆ Solicit positive feedback and a favorable Detailed Seller Rating from a satisfied customer.

Contacting the Winning Bidder

Now is not the time to be sending Valentine's cards through the mail—time is of the essence here, so contact the winning bidder as soon as you can. Do this by sending an invoice, a process automated through eBay (you merely click on the "Send Invoice" button on the item page), or by personalized e-mail.

Key points to cover in your e-mail include these:

- ◆ Offer congratulations on being the winning bidder.

- ◆ Restate the amount of the winning bid.

- ◆ Discuss payment options you are offering the buyer (the options you included in your listing).

- ◆ Remind the buyer of the cost of packing and shipping (including insurance, if any), which is usually called shipping and handling or S&H. This amount should have been included in your listing description and should come as no surprise to the buyer.

- ◆ Remind the buyer of any sales tax (and whether it applies to the S&H charges). Again, this information should have been included in your listing description.

- ◆ Obtain shipping information—the buyer's address and, where necessary for shipping, his or her telephone number.

- ◆ Ask the buyer to leave you positive feedback and a favorable seller rating.

Other communications with the bidder can be held later. These are covered in Chapter 8.

Arranging Payment

Now it's time to show you the money and collect payment for the sale you've made. There are several options on how to get paid—some are quicker than others.

The subject of getting paid is discussed in Chapter 8.

Power Point _____

If you don't receive payment, you can request a final value fee credit. Reasons for the credit: the bidder did not respond to you after repeated attempts and more than 7 days have passed, the check bounced, the buyer backed out or returned the item to you for a refund. The credit isn't automatic; you have to ask for it and it takes about 7–10 days to process.

Packing and Shipping Your Items

Our basement is stocked with bubble wrap and bags of peanuts (the Styrofoam shipping kind), as well as boxes of all sizes, packing tape, and labels—all the supplies we need to send delicate porcelain across the country without breakage.

You may not need to be concerned with shipping if your inventory is kept with *drop shippers* or *fulfillment companies* that can mail out items for you. In this case, your only responsibility here is informing your vendor to make a shipment and where it goes.

def•i•ni•tion _____

A **drop shipper** is a company that owns inventory you sell; the drop shipper sends the item to your buyer per your instructions. A **fulfillment company** arranges for inventory—to collect it, store it, and ship it. You buy merchandise from a vendor who delivers it to the drop shipper. The drop shipper stores it until you've sold it. At that time, per your instructions, the drop shipper mails out the merchandise to your buyers.

The topic of packing and shipping is covered in detail in Chapter 9.

Soliciting Feedback

How can people trust you as a seller? One way is to look at your feedback score, a rating system established by eBay to let the bidding public know about you.

A buyer of your auction can enter a positive, neutral, or negative rating. Then eBay displays the total of all feedbacks and calculates a feedback rating. Here's how the score is figured: subtract the number of negative feedbacks from the positive ones, and then divide this number by the total number of feedbacks. This gives you a percentage. For example, say you receive 2,854 positive feedbacks and 2 negative ones. Your score is 99.9 percent ([2,856 total feedbacks – 2 negative feedbacks] ÷ 2,856).

Your feedback score (the number in parentheses after your user ID) is calculated by assigning all unique feedback a score. Only one rating per user counts (so if a buyer bought five items from you and left five positive feedback comments, it would still only count as one for the purposes of the feedback score calculation). Positive feedback is assigned a +1 rating, neutral feedback is 0, and negative feedback is –1. Your feedback score is simply the total of all of these ratings.

The buyer can also leave a rating, from 1 to 5, about four specific aspects of the transaction: item description, communication, shipping time, and shipping and handling charges. The average is displayed on your feedback profile page. These are called Detailed Seller Ratings.

Your goal is to raise your feedback score as high as possible; the higher the score (and rating) is, the more confident bidders will be to buy your items. Buyers aren't required to leave feedback—you must ask for it. They can be induced to leave you positive feedback if you do the same for them. Obviously, the more positive feedbacks you can solicit, the higher your score will be. You can work to get negative bids retracted and take other steps to increase your feedback score.

The feedback system is discussed further in Chapter 14.

The Least You Need to Know

- Register and pick your eBay name to get started buying and selling on eBay.
- Familiarize yourself with the auction process by browsing items for sale and bidding on things you like.
- Listing your items is a multistep process.
- Following the close of an auction, you must complete the sale process.

Part 2

Your Stock in Trade

You have the desire to sell, but what will you sell? eBay may have started off as an online garage sale where people were able to sell junk from their attic and basements, but today things are different. Collectibles account for only a small percentage of eBay sales. The vast number of items offered today on eBay are new items, including clothing, jewelry, DVDs, and electronics.

You have to decide what to sell—a decision that takes research to know whether the things that interest you will also interest eBay customers. Once you know what you want to sell, you have to find your merchandise and keep a steady supply of it coming in.

In this part of the book, you'll learn how to research the types of items that are selling and which ones are not. You'll also learn how to find your merchandise and how to price it right so it will sell.

Chapter 4

Deciding What to Sell

In This Chapter

- ◆ Deciding what types of merchandise to sell
- ◆ Finding selling opportunities you can exploit
- ◆ Doing market research

Knowing how to list an item on eBay and complete a sale is great, but you first must have something to sell. Something old? Something new? Something blue? If you start out selling items in your attic that you want to get rid of, you'll soon run out of merchandise.

In this chapter, you'll learn which type of seller you want to become and what you'll sell. You'll discover opportunities in the eBay marketplace that you can use to your advantage. You'll see why and how to do market research.

What Should You Sell?

Antiques to video games and everything in between are being sold on eBay today. What you decide to sell is entirely up to you. Sell the crafts you create, dispose of Aunt Em's Hummel collection, or buy new merchandise for the sole purpose of selling it on eBay.

It's usually a good idea to specialize in a particular category of item. Like the strippers in *Gypsy*, you gotta have a gimmick to really make it on eBay, and specializing is step one. This allows you to become an expert in a particular area. It also saves you time because you get to know prices well and become familiar with terminology used in creating listings.

Depending on the type of items you sell, you can make money, as long as you understand the economics of the situation. You can be a low-volume seller who lists one or just a few items at a time, each with high-profit margins, or a high-volume seller who conducts many auctions at the same time—typically more than 10 simultaneously. However, each sale generally has a low-profit margin.

> *Example:*
>
> Geraldine lists a rare Frederick Remington small bronze sculpture of a bronco buster with a Buy It Now price of $9,500. She inherited the piece from her great aunt, so it cost her nothing. Whatever she receives is, in effect, profit to her. George sells R&B CDs for $5 a pop; they cost him $3 each. He has to sell nearly 4,800 CDs to reap the same profit as Geraldine. This means George may have to run thousands of auctions, whereas Geraldine makes the same money running a single auction.

Despite the sale of cars and real estate on eBay, keep in mind that the average eBay buyer spends less than $50 per item. This dollar limit may influence what type of items you want to sell.

Item Restrictions

eBay has some rules on what you can sell. Violate eBay policies and you can have your listing canceled and forfeit listing fees, your account may be suspended, and you can lose PowerSeller status. You can't under any circumstances sell any of the following items, which are currently included in the eBay list of prohibited items (the list can be changed at any time).

> *Prohibited Items:*
>
> Alcohol
>
> Animals and wildlife products
>
> Catalog and URL sales
>
> Counterfeit currency and stamps
>
> Counterfeit items
>
> Credit cards

Drugs and drug paraphernalia

Embargoed goods

Firearms (and any individual part that is needed to fire a gun)

Fireworks

Government IDs and licenses

Human parts and remains

Links

Lock-picking devices

Lottery tickets

Mailing lists and personal information

Plants and seeds

Postage meters

Prescription drugs and medical devices

Recalled items

Satellite and cable TV descramblers

Stocks and other securities

Stolen property

Surveillance equipment

Tobacco

Travel (unless you become an eBay verified travel seller). For details on obtaining this verification, go to SquareTrade at www. squaretrade.com/sap/jsp/ ebayTravelChoose.jsp.

In addition to this extensive list, you can't sell items that infringe on copyrights or trademark protection, such as beta software and movie prints you've made. eBay is constantly monitoring items for sale and may add to this list at any time.

Some items are not automatically prohibited; they are classified as questionable and can be sold only under certain conditions. The following list shows items eBay deems as questionable.

Questionable Items:

Artifacts

Autographed items

Batteries

Auction Alert

Why did your listing disappear? eBay will yank the listings of any item that's prohibited, even if you want to dispose of it for free. eBay relies on members of the eBay community to inform it of prohibited listings.

Catalytic converters and test pipes

Charity or fundraising listings

Contracts and tickets

Electronic equipment

Events tickets

Food

Freon

Hazardous materials

Imported and emission noncompliance vehicles

Mature audience items

Offensive material

Pesticides

Police-related items

Presale listings

Slot machines

Used airbags

Used clothing

Used medical devices

Weapons and knives

Wine

Auction Alert

Even if the item can be listed on eBay, some manufacturers and suppliers are now banning their items for sale on eBay. The reason they give is a fear that sales on eBay damage their brand image.

For example, wine is a questionable item because only preapproved sellers can list it for sale. Used clothing is questionable because you must thoroughly clean it before selling it—no used underwear can be sold, no matter how clean it is. When selling items overseas, be sure to know what's legal there. For a complete listing of the conditions for selling questionable items, go to http://pages.ebay.com/help/policies/items-ov.html.

Finding Your Fit—Finds and Fads

Some people look great in tailored suits; others can wear tie-dyed clothing. It's all about knowing what looks good on you. The same is true about what items to sell on eBay. You need to find the items that you'll be best at selling.

◆ **Sell items you like.** You're going to be spending a lot of time finding out about them, researching their value, and writing descriptions, so you might as well enjoy yourself by sticking to items that interest you.

◆ **Sell items you know about.** If you already have some familiarity with antique dolls, for example, because you've been a collector yourself, you have a leg up on someone starting from scratch. You already understand the item, and you may even know about prices. Obviously, not every type of item requires expertise.

If you're going to be a reseller, a bottle of Shalimar perfume is just a bottle of perfume, and expertise isn't a prerequisite. Consider carefully those items that do require expertise, though.

◆ **Sell what you can afford to acquire for sale.** If you are starting with a limited budget, you probably won't be going into high-end jewelry right off the bat. You can start with things you already own, such as inherited items you don't particularly like or have room for in your home. Or you can start buying wholesale lots for resale that are modestly priced. When you have the money, you can start to build an inventory of items to sell. We'll tell you where you can find your inventory in Chapter 6.

You may want to run with the crowd and stick with the most popular categories, or take the road less traveled. Use eBay Pulse (http://pulse.ebay.com) to view the ten most popular categories each day. On May 22, 2007, Webkinz topped the list, followed by Wii, Xbox 360, and Apple iPod. You can use eBay Pulse to check the top listings within a certain category as well. For instance, under the category of Antiques, furniture topped the list, followed by Victorian, art deco, and silver.

Experiment with Different Items

One thing often leads to another—you start off selling a box of Tinker Toys you found in your parents' attic, and before you know it, you're selling all kinds of toys and games. You become an expert in the field. Bidders in the eBay community eagerly await your next sale. Or you start selling digital cameras and expand your line to include camera accessories, such as camera cases, tripods, and lights.

A dream or a realistic scenario? It happens all the time. eBay becomes a fixation: you're driven by the fun of the auction and the reward of the sale to add to your listings. To do so, you must expand the number of items you have for sale.

This can entail entry into new arenas. These can be related to what you're already selling—for example, from costume jewelry into estate jewelry. Or the arenas can be in completely new types of items—from the antique kitchen utensils you used to sell to new handbags that you find are more profitable.

There's no limit to your choices. Just remember that you may need to build up your expertise for new areas, something that takes time and an interest in learning. Have fun and experiment with new items.

Selling Leftover Inventory from Another Business

In the old (pre-eBay) days, when a business couldn't sell some items, they were often put on bargain basement shelves or sale bins to sell for pennies, or they were simply discarded. Today these items may find a good home through an eBay auction, bringing in prices that are nothing to sneeze at. Best Buy has learned the value of listing on eBay and is now selling off inventory that failed to move in its retail stores. They're certainly not the only major retailer on eBay.

Selling leftover inventory can be the core of your eBay business. Items can be inventory from another business you are already running or the inventory from someone else's business. Finding this inventory is discussed later in this chapter.

Being a Reseller

eBay isn't just an electronic garage sale in which old items dug out of attics and basements are disposed of instead of being junked. Today eBay is an online marketplace for the sale of new as well as used items of all kinds.

You can make a business of reselling new items that other businesses could not dispose of. Here's how it works. You buy out remainder lots from businesses disposing of unsold inventory—perhaps last year's models. Some people don't have to own the newest camera or the latest fashions. You then sell each new item for more than you paid for it.

One young man started buying up music CDs in bulk. He broke up the packages, assembled three CDs in a set, and resold the sets on eBay for huge profits. His business became so lucrative that he brought his father into the business to help.

Finding Selling Opportunities on eBay

In the early days of eBay, if you sold old jazz records, you may have been the only one (or there were only a handful of sellers) in your category. Today virtually every category on eBay has numerous sellers; fierce competition exists. It's important to discover untapped selling opportunities that you can exploit to make money.

You do this through researching what will and will not sell and learning what you can and cannot buy well. eBay gives you several ways to see what types of items are selling well—the items change all the time.

The first place to start is to look at the popular items featured on the eBay Buy page. You'll see the best sellers in various categories, such as DVDs, CDs, and books.

If you jump from the Buy page to any of the 34 top-level categories featured there, such as Collectibles or Jewelry and Watches, you'll arrive at the Category page. Here you'll see the top 10 selling items within the category.

Yet another place to look is at Seller Central, your source for the latest seller tips and tools (http://pages.ebay.com/sellercentral). Here you can find a What's Hot link on the left side of your screen. Hot items are listed by category.

Researching What's Hot, Hot, Hot!

The basic rule of the marketplace—supply and demand—applies to eBay. If there's a demand for a particular item, bidders will compete for it, driving up the price. Conversely, if there's no demand, you may not get a single bid. For example, in Collectibles, about 30 percent of listed items never get even one bid.

You have to know what bidders are interested in so you won't waste your money buying items that won't sell (or, at least, won't sell at attractive prices).

You must research the areas you want to list items in to see if there is demand. Check the *sell-through rate* within each category. The higher the rate is, the greater your chances for sale are. The average sell-through rate on eBay for all categories is about 30 percent, though individual sellers may experience much higher rates.

You can do this research simply by visiting listings that may relate to the items you plan to sell.

You can also use one of the following software tools that help you with market research:

def•i•ni•tion

Items that are listed may or may not sell. If they do sell, they are part of the **sell-through rate**. For example, if there are 10 items listed for sale and 3 items sell, the sell-through rate is 30 percent.

- ◆ **Hammertap3** (www.hammertap.com) gives you sell-through rates, average bids per item, average sales price per item, and much more. Cost: $19.95 a month, with a 10-day free trial period. *Note:* this is the leading seller for market research.

- ◆ **Mpire** (www.mpire.com) tracks items on many online sites—not just eBay— so you can determine what's selling and how prices are running. Many features on the site are free. You might have heard of Mpire before. They used to be an auction management company, but they refocused their business a couple of years ago.

- **TeraPeak** (www.terapeak.com) helps you find the hottest categories and sell-through rates. Cost: from $14.95 a month.

- **What's Hot** (www.vendio.com) reports on the hottest items selling in each category on eBay. Cost: $3.95 a month.

Another important aspect of research is valuing your items. This topic is covered in Chapter 5.

The Least You Need to Know

- Steer clear of trying to sell any items that are prohibited by eBay; items in gray areas may not be worth your efforts.

- Find items to sell that you know about (or are willing to learn about).

- Decide whether to sell new or used items.

- Do market research to determine what items are selling at good prices.

Valuing Your Items

In This Chapter

- ◆ Understanding the impact of value on bidding and insertion fees
- ◆ Figuring break points in fixing value
- ◆ Using current and prior eBay auctions to fix value
- ◆ Using online and offline tools to determine value

The price is right, if you know how to set it. Just because you bought low doesn't mean you can sell high. On the other hand, if you bought low, you may still be able to sell very high. Value isn't absolute; it's what the market says it is at any given time.

In this chapter, you'll learn about the importance of knowing the value of what you're selling. You'll see how to fix your prices and learn about tools—online and offline—you can use to help you. You'll learn about different options for new merchandise as well as collectibles and antiques.

Putting a Price on Your Items

Usually, *value* is what someone is willing to pay for something. Value changes all the time and involves a lot of both research and gut instinct on your part.

def•i•ni•tion

Value can have several meanings, so make sure you know which value you're determining. Wholesale value is the amount an item might sell for at the dealer level. In contrast, retail value is what an item might sell for in a storefront or gallery. On eBay, items are usually priced at wholesale value.

You have to know what your item is valued at in order to set the auction price, fix a reserve price, use a fixed price auction, or set a Buy It Now price.

- ◆ The **starting price** (or opening bid) is the place where the bidding will start. If you have a multiple item (Dutch) auction, the starting price must be at least 99¢.

Power Point

When selling something that you simply must receive some minimum amount for, then instead of setting a reserve price, start the auction at the price that would have been your reserve. You'll pay a higher insertion fee, but avoid the extra cost of using a reserve price.

- ◆ The **reserve price** is the lowest bid you'll accept. You aren't required to fix a reserve price; this is your option. Setting a reserve price serves two purposes: it helps to stimulate bidding to get the auction going (in order to at least reach this price), and it protects you from unusually low bids—you don't have to sell unless your reserve price is met. Setting a reserve price entails an additional eBay fee, from $1 for a reserve price of $0.01 to $49.99, to 1 percent of the reserve price (up to $50) for $200 and up; the fee is refundable if the item sells. You can't set a reserve price in a Dutch auction.

- ◆ The **Buy It Now** feature in an auction gives buyers an option to obtain the item without having to bid on it. They agree to pay a fixed price—the price you set to ensure that you get a fair price for your item. It costs you an additional listing fee of 5¢ to add the Buy It Now feature to an auction for items priced from $0.01 to $9.99; 10¢ for $10 to $24.99; 20¢ for $25 to $49.99; and 25¢ for $50 or more. To use the fixed-price auction for one item, you must have a feedback rating of at least 10 (if you accept PayPal as a payment method, your feedback rating only needs to be 5); for a fixed price in Dutch auctions, you must have a feedback rating of at least 30 (if you accept PayPal as a payment method, it only needs to be 15), alternatively you can become ID Verified and not be restricted by the feedback requirements.

How Low (or High) Can You Go?

The opening price you set for your auction is crucial. It affects both the interest you may generate in the auction and the insertion fee you pay to eBay to list the item for sale.

If your starting price is too high, you may discourage bidders from looking at your item or bidding on it. And, of course, you'll pay a higher insertion fee to eBay.

If your starting price is too low, this can be an indication to bidders that there's not much value here, and you may also discourage bidding. Opening bids of less than $1 usually are viewed as "junk" for most items and usually won't draw bidders to the fray.

Power Point

Review the table of insertion fees when fixing your starting price (see Chapter 3 for details). The break point is important: setting your opening bid at just one penny below the break point can save you money on eBay fees. For example, instead of setting the opening bid at $10 (for which the insertion fee is 60¢), set it at $9.99 (for which the insertion fee is 40¢). As the number of your listings grows, the savings mount up.

Some buyers may search by price or their budget and count you out at the low end. Pricing too low can cost you money in the long run (you won't earn what you could have, had you priced things more accurately). And you're spending a lot of time marketing low-end items with very little to show for your efforts.

What's the Break-Even Point?

Your price must be high enough to enable you to make a profit. In some cases, you may just want to move inventory to make space or raise cash and aren't focused on profit; still, you don't want to lose money on these sales.

You don't have to become an accountant to know what your rock-bottom price can be. You only need to understand how to figure your break-even point—what you need to sell something for in order to *not* lose any money after factoring in your costs as well as your time.

Of course, you can adjust your price to suit your objectives. If you are trying to simply move an item that is just sitting around, you may want to start low and be willing to accept less than items you value and can afford to wait for in terms of price.

Sometimes it is worth selling at below cost. Retailers will eventually do this when they absolutely have to shift the inventory. Think about it, if you have something sitting in inventory and not selling, it's not making you any money. Sometimes it's better to cut your losses and sell it for less than you paid for it and reinvest the money into something that will sell. If you choose your replacement inventory wisely, you should make back the loss you took and be back on the road to showing a profit in no time.

Determining the Value for Your New Merchandise

Say you're selling DVDs or children's clothing. How do you know what price to set for an opening bid and what you can expect to receive on a sale? You're going to have to do some research on pricing. The better informed you are, the more money you stand to make.

Use eBay itself to help you fix an opening bid. Look up current sales of the item you are selling. With eBay auction volume today, there's bound to be at least one ongoing auction of the same thing you want to list. For example, if you want to sell the DVD *Harry Potter and the Prisoner of Azkaban*, search for this item by entering it in the search box on the eBay home page. (When we looked, there were 223 listings, with prices from as low as one penny to $25.)

Figure 5.1

Prices for items like yours.

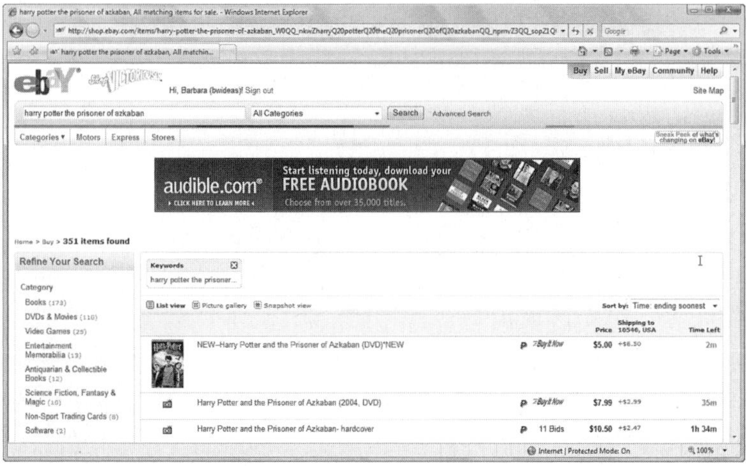

You can, if you wish, follow the listings of items over a week or two to see if there are price fluctuations you want to take into account.

Then look up winning bids for identical items on past auctions for the past two weeks by selecting the Completed listings check box in the left-hand Search Options area. (You'll have to log-in again to see this information.)

Power Point _____

Are you pricing hundreds or even thousands of items? Use an online pricing tool to help you. Vendio Research (www.vendio.com) is an online database that enables you to get average prices and number of eBay listings for items. This tool is designed to help you determine what starting and reserve price will get you the maximum selling price. Cost: $7.95 per month. Other options: HammerTap3 (www.hammertap.com) at $19.95 a month and PriceMiner (www.priceminer.com) at $9.95 a month for computer access or $14.95 for wireless access.

The following list provides alternative ways to determine price:

◆ Refer to online catalogs or catalogs that you receive through the mail from retailers and manufacturers; they clearly list the price of items. Don't toss those junk mail catalogs; keep them as part of your business library for future research.

◆ Shop local stores and discount outlets to see what things are going for. Keep in mind that the region you live in can affect pricing—prices in New York City stores aren't the same as in Little Rock.

◆ Use online research tools. For example, TeraPeak (www.terapeak.com) lets you search millions of eBay listings for free, so you can see the average sale price of your items. Other online research tools are mentioned in this chapter.

◆ Become an online shopper. Pretend you are on the hunt for the very item you're selling. See what you would have to pay for the item. For instance, if you have a Rosenthal china teapot to sell, what would you have to pay to buy it? Go to Replacements Ltd. (www.replacements.com), which has over 11 million items of china, stoneware, crystal, glassware, silver, stainless, and collectibles for sale—what are they charging for your item? Check other online sites, such as Craigslist (www.craigslist.org), as well.

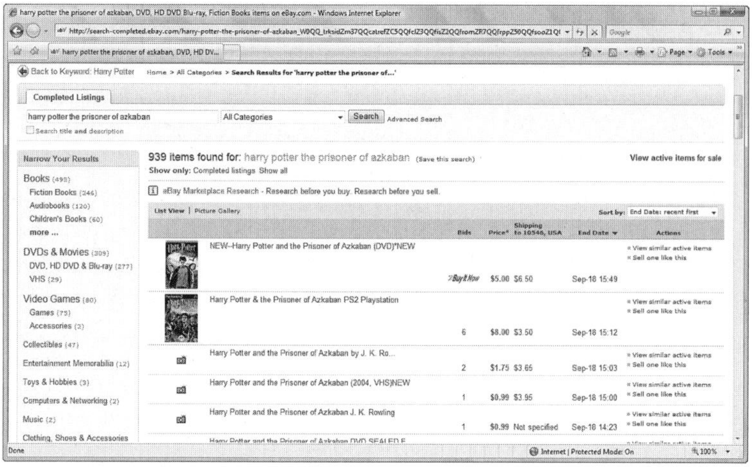

Figure 5.2

Current listings for items like yours.

Valuing Collectibles and Antiques

For real estate, it's location, location, location. But for collectibles and antiques, it's condition, condition, condition. The same item can be worth $10 or $10,000, depending on its condition.

> **Auction Alert**
>
> Forget any sentimental feelings you may have toward an item. The fact that it was your grandmother's wedding dress and was precious to your family has no bearing on determining price. Remember that bidders won't have the same attachment to the item as you do. Although an interesting backstory can help sell an item.

Because collectibles and antiques are often one of a kind, it's difficult to check around for the price of the same or a similar item. You can't bring all your items to the *Antiques Roadshow* every day to get an expert appraisal for free. You must use the resources available to you—offline and online—to narrow the price range to arrive at your starting bid price.

It is helpful if you specialize in an area of collectibles, such as Steiff teddy bears or U.S. posters from World War II. As you gain expertise in a particular type of collectible or antique, your valuation skills will improve and you'll be able to easily set your price.

The Past Is Prologue—Using Past eBay Auctions

The advent of eBay has changed the valuation landscape of antiques and collectibles by bringing them out of the woodwork. Greater supply usually means lower prices; many dealers in antiques and collectibles will tell you that prices in the past several years for many objects have plummeted. On the other hand, eBay has drawn more buyers into the game, creating greater excitement on auctions and helping to maintain prices. That said, it is still important to determine the current price of items you put up for sale—and here's how.

Auctions held in other forums besides eBay, such as local auctions and other online stores (such as Amazon.com), can provide you with valuable information on value.

National trade papers, such as *Antiques*, *The Arts Weekly*, *Antique Trader*, and *Maine Antique Digest*, contain breaking news on antiques and collectibles, including what's hot in the marketplace and recent sales prices.

For sales of antiques and collectibles, you can also use current and past eBay auctions to find a clue to pricing. For current auction listings, search for the item you're listing on the current eBay listings to see pricing for the item. Just go to the eBay home page and enter the item you are researching in the search box. For example, if you're selling a Nippon humidor, enter "Nippon humidor" in the search box and click Find It for a current listing.

Auction Alert

When you are researching prices on items currently listed for sale, be sure you are comparing apples to apples. Remember that condition can greatly affect the price of an antique or collectible. Be sure to carefully examine the condition of the items listed as well as your own item.

You can also check the completed sales of an item from eBay auctions during the past several weeks. For example, look at past auctions of Nippon humidors. After searching for current listings of these items to buy, simply click the Completed Listings check box under Search Options on the left side of the page. Here you'll find the winning bid in green (or the starting price/highest bid on an item that didn't sell in red), the date, and the number of bidders.

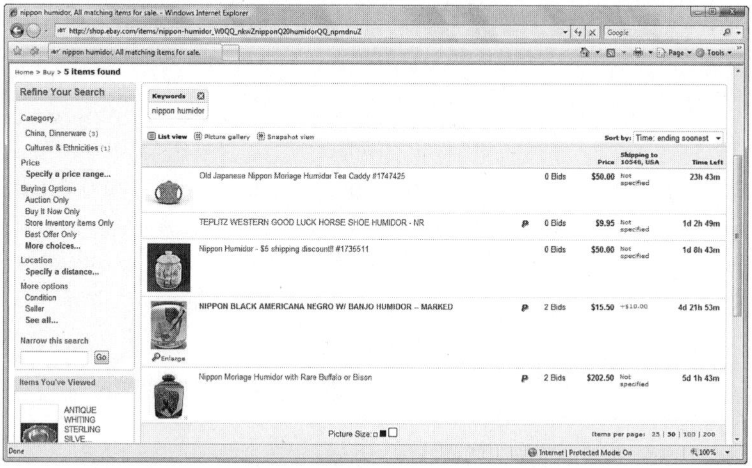

Figure 5.3

Current auction listings of your item.

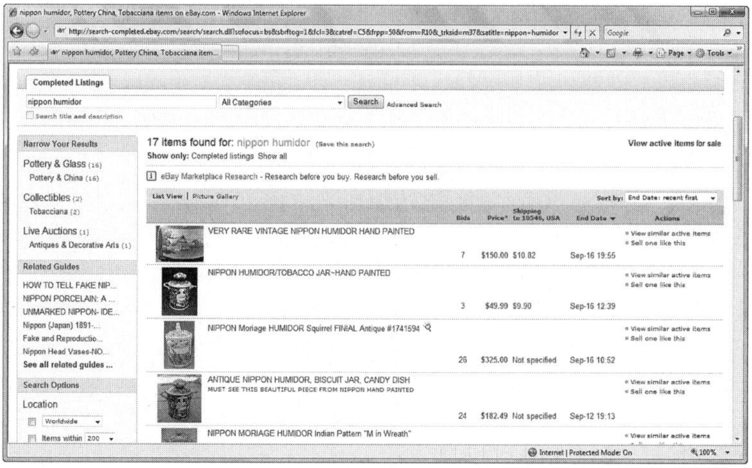

Figure 5.4

Completed sales of items like yours.

Price Lists and Guide Books

Name the antique or collectible, and there's bound to be a book on the subject. Often these books include price guides. There are books and price guides to all types of antiques and collectibles. Price guides are a good starting point to find out about the value of your treasures, but they are not the last word. The most popular general price guides, which are usually updated each year (so get the most recent edition), include these:

◆ *Antique Trader Antiques & Collectibles Price Guide,* by Kyle Husfloen

◆ *Collectibles Price Guide,* by Judith Miller

- *Kovels' Antiques and Collectibles Price List*, by Ralph Kovel and Terry Kovel

- *Schroeder's Antiques Price Guide*

- *Warman's Antiques and Collectibles Price Guide*, by Ellen T. Schroy and Tracy L. Schmidt

There are also some online price guides. Most of the online guides are free but may require you to register at the site:

- Kovel's Online (www.kovels.com)

- Collect.com (www.collect.com)

- Maine Antique Digest (www. maineantiquedigest.com), click on Prices Database

- Price Miner (www.priceminer.com)

Power Point _____

You may be able to purchase these guides through eBay. The New and Used Books category may include price guides as well as general reference books on the type of antiques and collectibles you are selling. Just make sure you know which edition you are purchasing.

Price guides are a great help in determining the value of your items, but they aren't the final word. Rather, they are a good starting point. You need to consider other variables—the condition of your item, recent sales on eBay (that may not yet be reflected in the guides), and the economy in general. Also, different types of antiques and collectibles move in and out of favor with the marketplace—something that may have been hot last year may be a slow seller today (and might require you to adjust your price accordingly).

More Ways to Set Prices

If you have a very valuable antique, don't even think about listing it for sale on eBay until you know what you've got. In this case, you may want a formal appraisal. Expert appraisers typically charge between $75 and $250 an hour to extensively research your item and provide a detailed analysis supporting the value they suggest. They require an in-person view of your item, so you'll probably need to find a local expert.

Auction houses, such as Sotheby's and Christies, also have appraisal services. Using these services is best reserved for high-end items.

For just about anything else, there's a less costly way to go. Some online services can appraise your items or provide second opinions so you don't underprice (or overprice)

An Educated eBay Seller

To find an appraiser in your area, check your local telephone directory, or contact the American Society of Appraisers (www. appraisers.org), Appraisers Association of America (www. appraisersassoc.org), or the International Society of Appraisers (www.isa-appraisers.org).

them. You describe the item, its condition and origin, and other information, and you receive an appraisal from experts. You usually can receive the appraisal within a day to a week. Here are your options:

- Antique Appraisals Online (www3.sympatico.ca/ appraisers). Cost: $9.95 per appraisal. There's also an "Ask the Expert's" service, which can give you a preauction valuation. Cost: $3.95 per item.

- InstAppraisal.com (www.instappraisal.com). Cost: Free.

- WhatsItWorthToYou.com provides appraisals for each item you submit (www. whatsitworthtoyou.com). You can get an eBayOpinion, which tells you what the item is worth on eBay (this service is not provided by eBay, but by the WIW2U group). Cost: $9.95 per appraisal.

The Least You Need to Know

- Setting the right opening bid for an item can affect the bidding interest you'll draw and determines the insertion fee you pay to eBay.

- Pricing an item must take into account your costs so that you don't lose money.

- The value of new merchandise can be figured using past auction information, as well as general good shopping skills.

- The value of antiques and collectibles can be figured using past auction information, as well as price guides and appraisals.

Chapter 6

Where to Find Inventory

In This Chapter

- ◆ Finding new merchandise to resell
- ◆ Using eBay to stock your inventory
- ◆ Hunting for bargains on used items
- ◆ Using drop shipping to avoid warehousing inventory

Ask just about anyone selling items on eBay what the number one challenge is in running a business, and the answer will be sourcing. Sourcing is the umbrella term for finding merchandise to sell. Where you look for items depends on what type of items you're selling; you won't find vintage clothing in an outlet store, and you probably won't find new DVDs in a thrift shop.

In this chapter, you'll learn what sourcing is all about. You'll see where to find new items for resale—both locally and online. You'll see how eBay can be both your store for selling and your location for buying your merchandise. And you'll find out where to look for preowned items, including antiques and collectibles.

Buying New Merchandise to Resell

Today the vast majority of eBay sales (based on volume) consists of new items; the early days of eBay when collectibles dominated the website are long gone. Obviously, the cheaper you can buy items to resell, the more profit you stand to make. But where can you find items to sell? You can pursue many avenues.

You may find new items in your own backyard if you know where to look. You can also locate wholesale lots for resale online through a number of sources.

You want to look for the following:

♦ **Closeouts.** This refers to inventory that merchandisers, manufacturers, or distributors want to get rid of in a hurry, usually because they cannot sell it in the normal course of business.

♦ **Government surplus.** This includes items purchased by the federal, state, or local governments that are no longer wanted. Government auctions are discussed later in this chapter.

♦ **Sales.** This includes items that are marked down to practically nothing. These items can be found at discount clubs, outlet stores, or just about anywhere else. Some places mark down items over and over again; wait for final markdowns. If you can get onto the mailing list for some companies, you'll receive special discount coupons in the mail. Use these during the sales to get even better prices.

Neighborhood Resources

Start locally to build up your inventory. Use your imagination to ferret out items you can list on eBay. One eBay seller collects new books that college professors have on hand in their offices at the end of each semester (they get them from textbook publishers). The professors are glad to clean out their space, and the seller has obtained product for free!

Check your local free weeklies, such as *PennySaver* and *Thrifty Nickel*, to see what's available in your area. You can even advertise for products, using Wanted to Buy and Cash Paid ads to solicit offers of merchandise for sale.

Contact local merchants who may be eager to dispose of inventory that won't sell. They may lack the time or interest to sell the inventory themselves on eBay. You may get inventory for next to nothing, particularly if it's not a chain-store.

Find wholesalers who can give you good prices on items for resale. If you don't have an uncle, a cousin, or even an old high school chum in business who can sell items to you wholesale, you can find wholesalers in your local telephone directory or through the Internet.

Major retailers have stores in outlet centers across the country. Usually they sell last season's merchandise at discount prices. They may also sell *seconds*, which are items with slight imperfections (imperfections you should certainly disclose when you list the items on eBay). Look for final sales and closeouts to get the best buys.

Shop discount clubs, such as Sam's Club, BJs, and Costco, to look for bargains. If you can buy something right, you may be able to sell it for a profit.

> **Power Point**
>
> You can locate outlet centers nationwide using OutletsOnline, at www.outletsonline.com/pages/outlets.html.

Attend trade shows where wholesale merchandise is featured. For example, ASD/AMD (www.merchandisegroup.com) hosts mega-events nationwide, drawing up to 50,000 attendees at any one show looking for wholesale lots in just about any category of product you can imagine. The ASD/AMD Variety Merchandise Show in Las Vegas each year is the number one variety, discount, and general merchandise show in the nation (check dates at www.merchandisegroup.com/merchandise/index.jsp).

Become a seller for local artisans who lack the time or ability to sell their creations online. Make contacts with artisans at street fairs and craft shows in your area.

Online Resources for Deals and Steals

You can explore other online avenues for sourcing. Some will lead you to overseas markets where items are being manufactured for resale. Here are some resources to help you get started:

♦ **GoWholesale** (www.gowholesale.com, owned by Liquidity Services, a public company) provides very extensive sourcing for a wide range of products, including specialty items, items for the home, and electronics. Wholesale411, the world's largest wholesale directory on the Internet, is now part of GoWholesale.

♦ **Government surplus** (www.usa.gov/shopping/shopping.shtml) enables you to buy office equipment, furniture, and industrial equipment that the federal government no longer needs. This site is a gateway into buying surplus from the government. You can also find government surplus sold through auction at Liquidity Services (www.govliquidation.com).

- ◆ **Worldwide Brands, Inc.** (www.worldwidebrands.com), founded by Chris Malta (the product-sourcing expert for eBay Radio), offers a wholesale directory, updated daily, of light bulk wholesalers, drop-shippers, large wholesalers, and more. You can buy affordable quantities, generally less than $500 per order, from many of the wholesalers listed. Access to the OneSource Directory costs $299, which is a one-time fee only.

- ◆ **Wholesale Distributors Net** (www.wholesaledistributorsnet.com) calls itself the center of the wholesale universe; 34,000 businesses visit each month. This site is another directory to domestic and imported wholesale lots.

- ◆ **Overstock.com** (www.overstock.com) is an online outlet for clothing, electronics, and more. Check the clearance bins for buying opportunities.

- ◆ **Ubid** (www.ubid.com), another online auction place, may be a bargain hunter's dream site. Here you can often buy cameras, stereos, and other items at very attractive prices.

Finding Inventory on eBay

eBay isn't just a place for selling your wares; it's also a great source for sourcing. You may buy items on eBay and other auction sites for resale if you can obtain them at attractive prices and then market them properly for a higher resale price.

Wholesale Lots

eBay has a special corner called Wholesale Lots at http://pages.ebay.com/catindex/catwholesale.html where you can find wholesale items offered by merchants and distributors selling off excess merchandise and end-of-life products (last year's models). Here you can find all types of items for sale—art and books, business and industrial, clothing and accessories, health and beauty, jewelry and watches, sporting goods, and much more. The site currently has 27 main categories of wholesale lots.

Check the size of the lot on which you are bidding—you must take the entire lot and can't simply sample an item before buying the lot. Most wholesale lots for sale on eBay are small or medium-size, making them affordable to you. The lots may be small—say, a dozen—or they may be larger (as in 500,000 gemstones for sale). A lot may be quoted in terms of dozens (for example, two dozen pairs of silver earrings), or it can be an odd lot (for example, 56 Disney videos). The price you are bidding covers the entire lot. Check on how the lot is offered—a random quantity of 50 videos, for example, may give you 50 of the same videos or 50 different videos.

Figure 6.1

Wholesale Lots might have the bargains you are looking for.

Misspelled Items

One man's loss is another man's gain. If someone misspells the name of an item, bidders can have a hard time finding it. There may be few, if any, bidders. If you can ferret out spelling errors, you may be able to snatch up items at very good prices; there won't be much, if any, competition on the bidding.

Misspelling can easily happen with designer name items posted by rushed sellers who fail to check spelling carefully (and spell check won't necessarily pick up misspelled names). For example, Donna Karan's name may be misspelled as Donna Karen, Dona Karan, or any other combination of errors your imagination can create.

Power Point

Use software to help you find misspelled items. For example, the Lost Auction 6.2 has over 13,000 eBay categories to search (www.vbbitman.com) and helps you find auctions with little or no bids because of misspellings. Cost: free. eBay's search engine is also getting better at finding items despite misspellings and is recognizing international spelling (e.g., jewellery).

Misspelling also happens with basic language. You'll find listings for earings (instead of earrings), cutlry (instead of cutlery), and knifes (instead of knives). Take this as a listing lesson to you: when you write your listing, check your spelling in an old-fashioned dictionary so you don't lose out on sales opportunities.

How can you find misspelled items? Try your search using the asterisk trick. Say you want to find sports memorabilia for baseball great Roy Campanella. In the search, type in "Roy Camp*." The results will display items listed under Campanella, Campanello, Campenella, Campanela, Campanelle (some of the variations I found on eBay) and any other spelling variation to be found. For Joe DiMaggio, also search under DeMaggio.

Slow Weeks on eBay

Although eBay is a busy marketplace, sometimes things seem to slow down. These slow times may not be great for listing your items for sale, but they are opportunities for picking up bargains for your future sales. With fewer bidders, the prices remain low.

How can you determine if things are slow? eBay won't tell you this information. But you can find it through online sources, such as chat rooms, blogs, message boards, and discussion forums. You can tap into the eBay community by going to the Community section of the site map. Here you'll see links to forums, eBay groups, and discussion boards.

Generally, the slowest season is between June and September. In 2007, eBay actually reduced their fees during this period to entice sellers to continue listing items. Once the schools go back, buyers start thinking about Christmas and sales begin to pick up again.

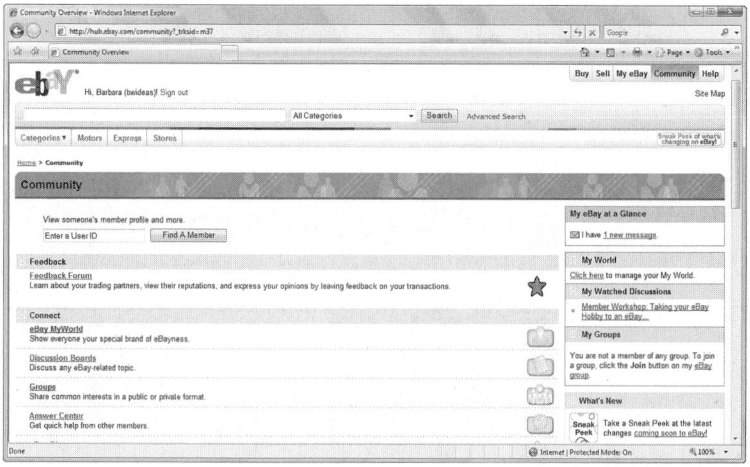

Figure 6.2

Get the inside scoop from the Community section.

Listen to what other eBay sellers are saying. For example, in the summer of 2007, there were a number of postings about the slow pace of sales on eBay. Was it summer? The economy? Stay alert to future slow periods so you can hunt for bargains.

Someone's Trash Is Another's Treasure

When eBay started up, it was called an electronic garage sale because most of the items for sale were used and old, the kinds of things you'd see in your neighborhood garage sale. Today eBay sales have shifted primarily to new merchandise.

But the brick-and-mortar type of garage sale is still a good source for finding items to resell on eBay. This is especially true if you're hunting for antiques and collectibles, such as vintage clothing and old board games, to resell. If you're a good bargain hunter, you may be able to find items, usually used but sometimes new, that you can resell.

A garage sale is also a great place to find fixer uppers—items you can clean up, repair, or refurbish and then resell on eBay. If you're in this fixing-up mode, garage sales can also be an ideal place to find parts needed for items you're working on.

Power Point

Use your imagination to find used items for sale. Two creative eBay sellers did just that when they advertised in their local *PennySaver*, seeking other people's gently used clothing and other items they could sell. The floodgates opened up as people cleaned out their attics and basements, sharing the profits with these eBay sellers.

Estate Sales

When a person dies and the relatives don't want the contents of a home or belongings, usually experts are brought in to conduct sales (typically auctions) of the furnishings and other items (such as jewelry, clothing, and other personal effects)—the relatives can then walk away with cash. Estate sales may run for a day or more (depending on the number of items to be sold). Typically, there is viewing permitted prior to the sale so that you can decide on items you want to bid on.

Where can you find out about estate sales? Check your local newspaper for listings in your area. Look for signs on lawns and elsewhere stating the event and time.

Flea Markets

People selling at flea markets are resellers just like you. But if you can buy well, you can then resell the items again through eBay.

Most flea markets have regular schedules, such as every weekend or the last Sunday of each month. Flea markets may be listed in your local telephone directory and advertised in newspapers.

Flea markets are also a good place to network with other buyers. They may share their sources for merchandise (and other secrets) with you after you've had an opportunity to get acquainted at the flea markets.

Garage and Yard Sales

You can always tell when it's spring—the yard sale signs come out. Here you can often find bargains when sellers don't know what they have for sale and price things very low. The problem is increased competition for these items (eBay sellers are everywhere!), so be prepared to arrive early before the good stuff is gone.

Yard sales may be conducted by homeowners or by professionals that they hire to run their sales. Often professionals will list the sales online (go to www.yardsalesearch. com and search by state).

One way of making sure you get the good stuff is to call the day before. Many times yard sales are posted on Craigslist with a sample list of items for sale. If you are interested in one of those items, you can ask the seller if there is any way you could come look at it the day before. While you're there, you can ask about anything you see in the garage (which will more than likely be set up ready for the yard sale). Most of the time the seller will sell you items that were going to be in the yard sale even though you are a day early.

Thrift Stores, Consignment Stores, and Pawnshops

Often run by nonprofit organizations, such as hospitals and religious groups, these stores stock both new and used items that donors no longer want. There are always bargains to be had.

Check in your local telephone book for thrift shop listings. Other resources for locating thrift shops include these:

- ◆ **Salvation Army Thrift Stores** (www.satruck.com/FindStore.aspx). Locate a thrift shore nearest you by entering your zip code.

- ◆ **Thrift Shopper** (www.thethriftshopper.com). Search over 7,500 charity-driven thrift stores, either by zip code or city.

- ◆ **Thrift Town** (www.thrifttown.com). Claiming to be the greatest thrift store in the world, it has 15 locations in four western states. (California, Utah, New Mexico, and Texas). Click on Locations to find the store nearest you.

Similar to thrift shops, you may find bargains at consignment shops. These are stores in which sellers place goods for sale—the store owner does not buy the items, but rather, gets a cut of the sales price when items are sold.

Pawnshops are like banks for the poor; people obtain loans by using their valuables as collateral. If they fail to repay the loan when due, the pawnshop keeps the collateral and can resell it. Here's where you come in. Because pawnshops pay only a fraction of an item's value, they can offer the item to you at highly attractive prices. For links to pawnshops nationwide, go to PawnShop.net (www.pawnshops.net/shoplist_us.html). GlobalPawn (www.globalpawn.com) aggregates the inventories of pawn shops around the country into a single database, enabling customers to purchase inventory online.

Government Auctions

The federal government, as well as states and municipalities, needs to dispose of items from time to time. Typically, the goods are used, such as old office furniture, but there may be brand-new items for sale as well.

Usually, government surplus is auctioned off through advertised sales. Government auctions are not all the same; they have different formats and terms. For example, at one agency's auction you may be required to buy an entire lot of identical items, even though you only want one. Some auctions need sealed bids; or in other auctions you may be required to appear in person.

Check with each federal department or agency for its ongoing sales. For example, look for sales from the Department of Defense at www.drms.dla.mil or the sales of seized property by the U.S. Treasury at www.ustreas.gov/auctions. You may be able to buy a Ferrari at a cheap price, as long as you don't mind the bullet holes on the side.

Buying Right

Whatever source you use to obtain your merchandise, the same principle applies: buy right or don't buy at all. There's no easy way to teach this skill. Just like shopping for food in a grocery store, after a while you gain experience with pricing, look for sales, and learn to pass up high-price items you can live without. The same is true when shopping anywhere—online or offline—for your eBay merchandise.

Power Point _____

When you buy items for resale in your state (whether in person or online from an in-state vendor), you don't have to pay sales tax on your purchases. To be exempt from sales tax, you must provide the seller with your resale number (which you obtain from your state tax, finance, or revenue department). Sellers may not ask for a resale number, so speak up!

It will take you time to gain the experience you need to be an astute buyer. While you may be willing to pay a little extra for something you plan to use yourself, you don't want to employ this practice when buying for resale—you'll cut your margins too tight and the profits you make won't be worth your efforts. To be a good buyer, you have to know what items cost.

Knowing when to negotiate a price is crucial to buying right. Depending on the sourcing venue, it may be common practice to bargain with a seller. For example, at a garage sale or flea market, always ask the seller for his or her best price or make a low offer with the expectation of further haggling.

The Drop Shipping Alternative

If you're selling new items and don't have the money to build up inventory (or perhaps the room to store it), you can use a selling technique called *drop shipping*. You arrange with a wholesaler, who is the drop shipper, to effectively work as a sales agent. You don't have to buy items; you have to pay for them only when you sell them.

def•i•ni•tion _____

A **drop shipper** is a wholesaler who sells items to you (the reseller), but stores the items and then ships them directly to your buyers once you make a sale.

Here's how drop shipping works. You arrange with a drop shipper to market a wholesaler's wares, which you list for sale on eBay (the drop shipper will provide you with item descriptions and photos so you can create your listings). When an item is sold, you give instructions to the drop shipper to send the item from the wholesaler (or a distribution center) to the winning bidder. You never physically touch the item; everything is handled for you. Hopefully, all goes well and you get not only the money from the sale, but also positive feedback.

Of course, there is a downside to drop shipping (you don't get something for nothing): you pay for the arrangement. You might have been able to realize a greater profit if you'd bought the inventory at a lower price. You are charged by a wholesaler, who drop ships an item for the wholesale price, plus shipping costs (because you pass the shipping costs on to the buyer, you're paying only the wholesale price).

Finding Drop Shippers

Google "drop shippers" and you'll get more than a million listings. How can you separate the good ones from the bad? It's going to take you time and considerable research to make your selections. Check out whether the drop shipper:

- Has the ability to handle business-level issues, such as dealing with state sales tax when necessary.

- Stocks the items they are drop shipping for you. If they have to obtain the items from another supplier, this adds to cost and can delay shipping time to your buyer.

- Sells directly on eBay. You don't want to be in competition with the drop shipper on the same items.

Before you select a drop shipper, check the buzz with the eBay community. A bad experience is bound to be posted, helping you to avoid a similar unhappy experience. Also view comments on drop shippers at the forum at Wholesale-Auctions.org (http://wholesale-auctions.org/viewtopic.php?p=969).

Another resource for finding drop shippers is ThomasNet (www.thomasnet.com), formerly ThomasRegister, which is a free search engine for finding manufacturers throughout the United States and Canada. Once you decide on what items you want to sell, contact the manufacturer to learn which drop shippers they deal with.

Some reliable drop shippers include:

- DropShipAccess (www.dropshipaccess.com)

- DropShippers (www.dropshippers.com)

- Ezdropship.com (www.ezdropship.com), which claims to be America's number one drop shipper

- Shopster (www.shopster.com) there's an annual subscription fee, but use the 7-day free trial first

Handling Drop Shipper Problems

Possible scams are only one problem with drop shippers. "Out of stock" is another. Say you run a successful auction of an item on eBay and, when it comes time to instruct the drop shipper about where to send it, you learn it's out of stock. What do you tell your buyer?

Auction Alert

Save your money by avoiding drop shipping come-ons. Don't pay for lists of drop shippers that are outdated. Only use lists from reputable companies, such as Worldwide Brands (www.worldwidebrands.com), or find your own free with a simple Google search.

Contact the drop shipper immediately; your item may be on hand after all (the out-of-stock notice may have been a warning against future listings). If, indeed, it is out of stock, find out when it will be available. Then call the winning bidder and inform her of the situation. Expect that the buyer may be upset, but will be less so if you promptly communicate this information (in the least, you may avoid negative feedback).

You should offer two options—cancel the bid so the buyer can look elsewhere, or offer some kind of incentive for waiting (reduced shipping cost, etc.). This will help appease most buyers and should save your feedback rating.

The Least You Need to Know

♦ Use both online and offline sourcing to find the items you want to sell.

♦ eBay can be a great resource for buying wholesale or picking up bargains when listings are misspelled or times are slow.

♦ Buying at flea markets, estate sales, thrift shops, and other similar venues offers significant bargain opportunities for stocking your inventory.

♦ If you can't buy something for resale at a good price, don't waste your money—you won't be adequately compensated for your selling efforts.

♦ Drop shipping avoids the need to purchase (and store) inventory; you pay only for what you sell.

Part 3

Making It Work

The number one job of any business is to sell. Without sales, you can't make money. You can have the greatest products and put in hours of your time, but if you can't move merchandise, you won't make it on eBay.

When eBay started, selling was like shooting fish in a barrel—you couldn't miss. But today the competition is stiff, and many people just like you are trying to develop eBay sales into a prosperous business. To succeed, you have to know how to attract customers and develop customer relationships as well as what sales techniques work and don't work on eBay.

This part of the book is all about selling, both in the United States and internationally. You'll learn how to create great listings to attract buyers and use other sales venues to increase your income. You'll also find out how to get paid promptly, get purchased items to your customers as quickly and safely as possible, and find and keep your customers.

Chapter 7

Running Auctions

In This Chapter

- ◆ Creating listings to attract viewers and stimulate bidders
- ◆ When and when *not* to use eBay listing enhancements
- ◆ Upgrading your images
- ◆ Managing more than one auction at a time to build your business

The key to making it on eBay is selling. You can have the greatest items for sale, but if you don't list them well or manage your sales properly, you won't make money. The competition is just too stiff these days.

In this chapter, you'll learn how to make your listing stand out from the crowd using the eBay tools available to you. You'll also find out how to manage multiple auctions, a vital step in growing your eBay business.

Optimizing Your Auctions to Make More

Your listings must accomplish a number of things: they must clearly and accurately convey the description of what you're selling, they must attract potential bidders to read them, and they must stimulate bidding to achieve successful sales. This is easier said than done.

In creating your listing, keep in mind that most buyers are in a hurry and don't want to wait for a description to be displayed (especially those who do not have high-speed Internet access). In my opinion, which is shared by many leading web professionals, most buyers probably don't want to hear music or see fabulous backgrounds or read about your family. They want to see the item (multiple images are best) and read a complete description, including the item's size and any defects, no matter how small or insignificant you might think.

Auction Alert

Don't waste time creating your listing online—you may feel pressured to work too quickly here. Do it offline using your word-processing program. Then copy and paste your finished work onto eBay.

You don't want to sell an item and have an unsatisfied buyer want to send it back to you because your description was inaccurate or your photos were misleading. This wastes your time and money and can create negative feedback for you. Honesty is the *only* policy for both the buyer and you.

Creating a Better Listing

A good listing is one that will attract potential bidders to read on and then bid for the item. There are three parts to a good listing: the title (the thing that pops up when someone does a search for a particular item), including a gallery picture of your item that provides buyers an image in one of the first places they look; the listing description, which must provide key details about your item; and boilerplate information on the mechanics of the sale, including shipping, payment methods you accept, and your return policy.

You can create a better listing using your ever-improving listing skills as well as some online tools discussed later. Here are some tips to follow in writing your title:

- **Get your title right.** The title is the keyword description of your item displayed by eBay when someone does a search. You have only 55 characters (letters and numbers) to hook a viewer to delve into your listing, so your heading must be great—and spaces count. Be descriptive, but don't waste letters on superlatives, such as *beautiful* or *fabulous*. *New* or *used* may be appropriate words to add. Use *&* instead of the word *and* to save characters.

- **Use as many keywords as possible.** Use many descriptive words in your heading that clearly convey what you are selling—these are words that may be found through the eBay search engine by a person looking for something particular. Check successfully closed listings of similar items to see what terms keep cropping up. This will help you see what gets buyers to click through to the actual auction page (your first challenge). Include your item's brand or designer name. For example, in Donna Karan apparel, most listings use both Donna Karan and DKNY in the heading (some buyers may look under the name while others search for the initials). Key words include not only the name of the designer and the type of item, but can also include design periods (deco or gothic) and material type (bone or sterling). For example, the seller of a silver-toned necklace that could also be used as a belt had the following heading: "Pink & Silver Carved Hoop Ring Chain Belt or Necklace" (53 characters with spaces).

- **Spell the name of your item correctly.** If you don't, it may not be found at all—or, at least, not by as many viewers as you'd like. For example, be sure you list porcelain as Wedgwood (the correct spelling), not Wedgewood. And, even if the item is found, a misspelling makes you look bad (some buyers won't deal with sellers they perceive as real idiots). We wouldn't buy from a seller who spelled accessories as "acceseris"!

- **Be on the lookout for changing keywords.** Take, for example, the Bakelite story. Bakelite (a molded plastic used primarily for jewelry in the 1930's) got popular and still is, but now some people have started using the word *catalin* (the same plastic as Bakelite but used primarily in casts) to stand out from the massive Bakelite search lists and to attract "those in the know" for their exceptional item. It all comes down to knowing your market, your customer, and your target community.

Don't know what to call your item? Look at similar items' closed listings to view titles that received high prices so you can follow suit. Once you have your title, you must write a description of the item. Here are some other tips to follow:

- **Make it complete and accurate.** Technically, there's no limit to the number of words you can use in your description. But as a practical matter, keep the description to no more than a few sentences—going over about 200 words can turn off a potential bidder.

- **Make it readable.** Avoid big chunks of text. Keep sentences short. Make it fun to read and not a chore for the viewer. Here's where practice pays off—the more listing descriptions you write, the better they become. You develop a knack for the language and learn what works for your listings. eBay's HTML editor gives you the option of using bullets, so make use of it. This is a great way to highlight features of your item in an attractive way that also breaks up the text.

◆ **Revise, revise.** Not just the number of listings, but the number of times you revise an individual listing before posting really pays off, just like any other kind of writing.

Auction Alert

New York has enacted a consumer protection law that requires online sellers to display their return policy or face a penalty.

Each time you list an item, include shipping, payment details, and your return policy. You don't want to have to retype this information each time you create a listing. If you don't use listing tools (discussed later in this chapter) that repeat this information automatically, then create your own boilerplate terms to include with all of your listings.

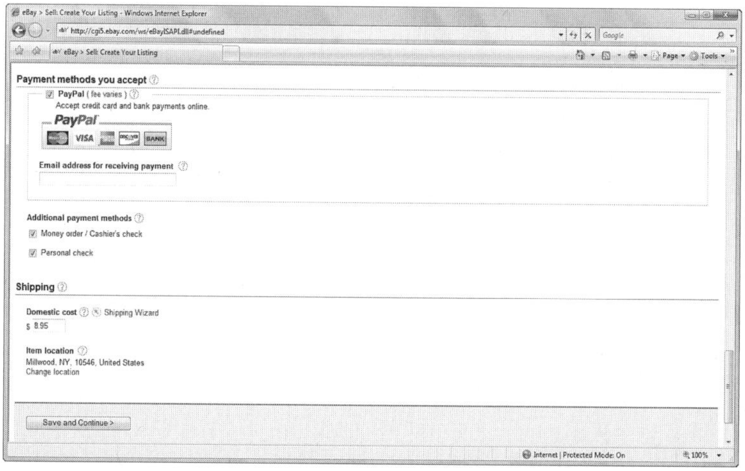

Figure 7.1

Boilerplate terms on shipping and payments.

Here are some tips for writing better boilerplate text:

◆ List each type of payment method you accept, such as PayPal, personal checks, money orders, and charge cards. Use the PayPal and charge card icons, which can be added automatically through PayPal, so they'll stand out and, of course, look more professional. You can download the icons from anywhere online and don't need permission from anyone to do so.

◆ Include a money-back guarantee, if you are willing to honor it. This reassures potential buyers that you stand behind what you sell. If you don't accept returns, say so by adding "This item is being sold as is. Although every effort has been made to describe this item accurately, the seller assumes no responsibility for the nature or condition of the item on arrival. No returns are accepted for any reason." As long as the item was described accurately, a seller won't be forced to accept a return in this case.

Using eBay Auction Enhancements

As competition on eBay mounts, you are always looking for an edge. eBay enables you to create an auction listing that stands out from the crowd. These options include …

- **Bold type.** Using boldface type helps to highlight your listing so buyers can easily see it. eBay says it increases the final sale price by 21 percent. Many experts say this enhancement is a waste of money.

- **Border.** Add a colorful purple border around your listing or your gallery view.

- **Buy It Now.** This feature enables a buyer to pay your fixed price to purchase your item and end the auction. But when a regular bid comes in, the Buy It Now (BIN) feature disappears and the auction proceeds normally. In some categories, however, the BIN price remains throughout the auction, even after the first bid is placed.

- **Featured Plus!** Get your listings seen first in your category. Your item will appear in the top of the page it belongs on. eBay says this increases bidding by 76 percent. You must have at least 10 feedbacks to use this option.

- **Gallery.** This is a thumbnail photo of your item that's included with your listing. It appears on the left of your auction title in the search results of your category. Buyers see your gallery picture when they are searching. eBay says it increases your final sale price by 12 percent.

- **Gallery featured.** With this option, a picture of your item appears in the special featured section above the general Picture Gallery.

- **Gallery plus.** When a buyer places her mouse over your gallery picture on the search results page, a large pop-up will open with a larger picture of your item.

- **Gift services.** This displays a little gift box icon. The gift services are gift wrapping, gift card, and/or express shipping directly to the gift recipient.

- **Highlight.** This feature highlights your item by backlighting it in a contrasting color.

- **Home page featured.** This is the way to get your listing maximum exposure within the featured area of the listings. eBay rotates the featured listings, so yours won't be displayed continuously. eBay says it increases bidding by 58 percent.

◆ **Item subtitle.** This adds an extra line under your title (for example, Title: 1 CT diamond ring Tiffany setting, GIA, Size 6; Subtitle: G color, VS1, emerald cut, 2 trillium side stones). It's been reported that using a subtitle can increase by 18 percent the likelihood of selling an item. But be aware that the subtitle is not searchable, i.e., if the bidder searches for "G color" and it is only in your subtitle, it will not show up in the search results. It will only show up if the buyer clicks Search Title and Description.

◆ **List in two categories.** If an item fits in two distinct categories, you can have it listed in each so that a search will direct bidders with different interests under each category. eBay reports an average 17 percent increase in sales when using this feature.

◆ **Listing designer.** Add background color and themes to your listing description—you don't have to know HTML to use this feature.

◆ **Scheduled listings.** This enables you to start your auction at a specific time.

◆ **10-day duration.** Auctions typically run for seven days; they can be as short as one day. But you can pay to have them run for as long as 10 days.

eBay enhancements aren't free—in most cases, you pay for each one you use. The following table lists the upgrade fees.

Listing Upgrade Fees

Listing Upgrade	Listing Upgrade Fee
Bold	$1.00
Border	$3.00
Buy It Now	$0.05 to 0.25 (sliding scale based on item's price)
Featured Plus!	$19.95
Gallery	$0.35
Gallery Plus	$0.75
Gallery featured	$19.90
Gift services	$0.25
Highlight	$5.00
Home page featured	$39.95 (single quantity); $79.95 (quantity of two or more)

Listing Upgrade	Listing Upgrade Fee
Item subtitle	$0.50
List in two categories	Double the insertion and listing upgrade fees (excluding Scheduled listings and Home page featured)
Listing designer	$0.10
Pro pack (five listing features at a combined reduced price)	$29.95
Scheduled listings	$0.10
10-day duration	$0.40
Value pack (gallery picture, subtitle, and listing designer)	$0.65

Stay alert to changes in eBay enhancement options by subscribing to Power Up from eBay Seller Central. You'll receive alerts to changes as well as listing opportunities, such as free listing days and feature discounts (http://pages.ebay.com/sellercentral/newsflash.html).

Should You Use Listing Enhancements?

As you can plainly see, each thing you do to upgrade your listing costs money. All these dimes, quarters, and dollars add up to real money. To make money on your eBay sales, you need to minimize your costs wherever possible. Of course, you may have to spend some money to make more money—it's a balancing act. Are listing enhancements worth the money? Which enhancements should you consider, and which ones should you pass on? Ask a dozen eBay sellers, and you probably will get several different opinions. Here are ours:

 ◆ **Things to use.** Using the Gallery is a must. When potential buyers don't see a picture, they usually pass by the listing without even reading it.

   Buy It Now is also a great feature if you can price your item well. For example, you buy a designer handbag for $100 and price it for $150 as a Buy It Now, wouldn't you be happy with a 50 percent profit if it sold quickly? This enables you to turn over your merchandise rapidly and recoup your capital, plus a profit.

◆ **Things to avoid.** Bold typeface listings don't necessarily stand out much more than regular typeface to justify the $1 cost. The picture of the item usually draws a potential bidder to read on. Do your own test by viewing a group of listings, and see whether the boldface means anything to you. For example, one listing feature—border—is pricey at $3 and probably not worth the cost.

Of course, there are always exceptions to the rule, and you may want to buck the tide for some of your listings, but for most inexpensive items, it doesn't make financial sense to use the home page featured option; it's just too costly. Why sell something for $200 that costs you $39.95 *extra* to list?

Listing in two categories could make sense for some items. Suppose you have a Nippon humidor with a horse vignette. You might list this item in both Nippon and Horses to attract bidders interested in each category. This is called a crossover item—something that appeals to buyers in more than one category. Remember that listing in two categories doubles your insertion fee as well as the fees for most listing upgrades. Paying extra for listings in two categories isn't necessary because when a buyer does a search in one category, the listing will contain the information for the other category (for example, Nippon humidor—horse-drawn carriage).

> **Power Point**
>
> Save money by not paying for a gift icon. Any item can be purchased as a gift, and you can always indicate your willingness to gift-wrap in your shipping and payment description. The only time Gift Services is a smart investment is around the holidays. Bidders can search by items offering Gift Services, and eBay heavily promotes this option around the holiday season.

The gift icon might be useful during holiday time if you're selling gift-type items. The 25¢ insertion fee covers only the gift icon—you still need to gift-wrap the item and enclose a card as the icon promises. The gift icon indicates that you offer some of these options: gift wrap/gift card, express shipping, and shipping directly to the gift recipient.

Scheduled listings, which enable you to dictate the time your auction starts, usually aren't necessary. After all, without paying for a scheduled listing, the listings start when you submit them and run for a sufficient time to attract bidders. You can time the auction to end when you want (for example, in the evening on a Friday) by starting them at the right time (for example, the same time the week before for a seven-day auction). But if you are going to be away without Internet access and want your auctions to proceed, this feature may make sense in this case. You can also do this using auction management programs discussed in Chapter 20.

The 10-day listing duration also is something that doesn't make sense in most situations. It may be useful when selling something exceptionally rare and expensive and you need the added time for exposure. In other cases, if something doesn't sell in the normal seven-day listing, an added three days won't help.

The highlighted feature is probably not worth $5 (even though some sellers use it); it's too pricey and doesn't add much to your listing.

The subtitle may make someone look at your listing, especially if you are selling a special item with a unique feature that collectors may go wild for. For example, in old phones, the title may be "Victorian Bakelite Stick Phone, fully restored" with a subtitle of "Original Kellog Mouthpiece, rare dial, serial 15388." But for most items, if the title and picture are done correctly, a potential buyer will look at your listing description without a subtitle. In your listing description you can provide any details you want *for free* to make the sale.

The listing designer may be superfluous if you can create your own look for your description.

> **Power Point**
>
> Use a free counter from Vendio.com and eBaycounters.com, for example, or eBay's own Visitor Counter to track how many people have viewed your item. Go to http://pages.ebay.com/help/sell/counters.html. eBay's tool is integrated into the Sell Your Item form. If you aren't getting many viewers, maybe something is wrong with your listing and you can revise it.

Other Listing-Enhancement Tools

You aren't limited to what eBay offers. Numerous companies provide help to upgrade your listings:

- **AuctionVideo** (www.auctionvideo.com) is an eBay-approved video hosting site from which you can add video to your listings. Cost: starting at $9.95 per month.

- **Boldchat** (www.boldchat.com) enables bidders to ask you questions through live chat. Cost: $29.95 per month for the basic plan; $49.95 per month for the Pro version.

> **An Educated eBay Seller**
>
> You can use many products to enhance your listings. For information on your options, see the Auction Software Review, your guide to eBay software and services, at www.auctionsoftwarereview.com. Some of the products are free; others have free trial periods, so explore your options as your business grows.

♦ **Skype** (www.skype.com), which is owned by eBay, is a way to communicate with your bidders by live chat or telephone. Both you and the person you want to talk to need a headset if you're using the voice option. Download the software for free. Usage cost: free for five minutes to anyone in 30 worldwide destinations; $29.95 per year for unlimited calls in the United States and Canada—and always free when communicating with other Skype users.

Power Point _____

You can add video to your listings through a number of free video hosting sites, such as YouTube (www.youtube.com).

♦ **Vhost SitePal** (www.sitepal.com) provides video and audio animated characters for your listing. Cost: starting at $9.95 per month.

Another key way to stand out from the crowd and create buyer confidence is to use seal programs. Like the Better Business Bureau seal, which stands for honesty in business dealings, there are now online seal programs that you can include in your eBay listings.

♦ **BBB OnLine** (www.bbbonline.org) is the electronic version of the Better Business Bureau. More than 37,000 websites now participate in the BBB Online Reliability Seal Program. Cost: pricing varies, depending on the size of business.

♦ **SquareTrade** (www.squaretrade.com) has a seal program used on three million eBay listings to denote that the buyer can be trusted. SquareTrade verifies you as a trusted seller and continually monitors your activities to see that you meet certain standards. Cost: $9.50 per month (30-day free trial period).

♦ **VeriSign** (www.verisign.com) is a seal program attesting that your site is secure. This gives buyers a sense of security when paying with a credit card. It probably isn't necessary if you rely solely on PayPal or checks sent to you through the mail. Cost: free trial period.

Say It with Pictures

Pictures are an essential part of just about every listing on eBay. You can (and should) include a picture with your listing heading.

And you should include as many pictures as necessary with your listing description to give buyers a good view of the item. For a sweater, one picture may do. For other items, such as an antique chair, you may need several pictures so the buyer can see it from different angles. To get great photos of your items, follow the do's and don'ts provided by eBay (http://pages.ebay.com/help/sell/photo_tutorial.html).

If you value your pictures, as well you should, be sure to copyright them to prevent someone from using them without your permission. Use the text-editing feature on the software program, such as Photoshop, that you use to edit your images to add the copyright symbol © and your User ID. Make sure the color you select for this text contrasts appropriately with your image so it doesn't get lost. If anyone uses your pictures without your permission, you can get eBay to help you seek redress through its VeRO program (for details, see Chapter 14). Some photo editing programs have a watermark feature specifically designed for this application.

Auction Alert

eBay suggests you use medium resolution for your images (for example, 1024×768 pixels). This provides excellent picture quality and results in a faster upload time, plus it is good for photo editing.

Getting Better Images

Because your pictures are a very important component in your sales pitch, make them as viewable and representative of your items as possible. The lengths you go to in order to accomplish this goal depend in part on the types of items you're photographing, your skill level, and the amount of money you're willing to invest in a digital camera and other equipment.

◆ **Use eBay Picture Gallery features** to help show off your images in the best light. For example, you can easily supersize your photos, a feature that enables viewers to click your smaller image to enlarge it. These supersize photos download quickly. Cost: 75¢ per image. For details, go to http://pages.ebay.com/help/sell/supersize.html. eBay's Picture Pack will save you money if you're displaying up to 12 images and they can be supersized. Cost: $1 for up to 6 pictures; $1.50 for 7-12 pictures.

◆ **Capture better images by using professional-type equipment—** a tripod to steady your camera, flood lights (halogen lights will do), and display props (backdrops and accessories, where appropriate). For example, if you are photographing vintage jewelry, your images may be better lit through the use of a table-top light tent, a box that sits on a table and provides focused

Power Point

Don't want to buy a light tent? Build your own light tent using tape and tissues, a pillowcase, or any other material that will diffuse the flash of the camera. There are a number of how-to articles on this subject (just enter "light tent" in a Google search).

lighting on your items for better image results. For example, Cloud Dome (www.cloudome.com) sells a tent for under $70. D-Flector (www.sharpic.com), a photo studio in a briefcase design, will produce professional-type photos. Cost: $69.95. You can get a complete tabletop studio, which includes a D-Flector, two compact tabletop studio lights, and a monopod to hold your camera, for $239.95. EZCube (www.ezcube.com) is a collapsible photographic light tent. Cost: $55 to $149.95, depending on cube size.

◆ **Fix up your photos using specialized software.** You can resize your images, crop them, change lighting, change backgrounds, and more with easy-to-use software that contains a number of editing tools. For example, Adobe offers two versions of its Photoshop: a basic and a professional version (www.adobe. com/products/photoshop/family). Cost: $99.00 for Photoshop Elements (basic editing) and $649.00 for Photoshop CS3 (professional editing). If you're a student or teacher, you can get reduced prices for Adobe software. The Photoshop Elements price is $69 and Photoshop CS3 is $299. Go to www.adobe.com/education for more information.

Figure 7.2

Supersize your image.

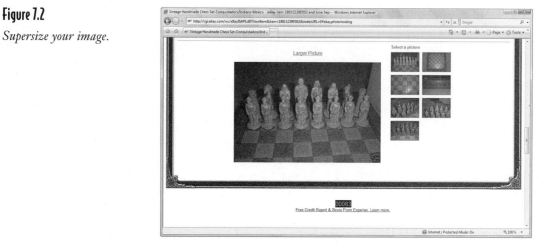

◆ **Change your picture display format.** Instead of a flat image that doesn't move, you can use software to enable the viewer to rotate the item, get a close-up, or magnify a particular part of the item. For example, Slidetour (www.slidetour. com) offers a slide tour format that includes magnification, combined with an audio presentation. Cost: free for up to 5 MB, with a sliding scale for more image storage. This is a Flash program, so your slideshow may take a little while to load on dial-up or other slower speed internet connections.

Storing Your Images

You have to keep your pictures somewhere so they can be used in your listings. You can use eBay Picture Services.

eBay Picture Services (http://pages.ebay.com/help/sell/pictures.html) enables you to upload multiple pictures at the same time, preview pictures before uploading, and do this all at faster upload times than previously available. There are two packages: Basic Picture Services and Enhanced Picture Services. Pricing is based on the number of pictures and your listing layout (the first picture in each listing is free).

eBay Picture Manager (http://pages.ebay.com/picture_manager) is an integrated hosting solution for your images. This service lets you manage your pictures online. Cost: depends on storage size (with reduced pricing for those with eBay stores).

Storing your images on eBay is convenient, but many eBay sellers also agree that it's expensive. Other companies will host your images for more modest prices:

◆ Auctionpix (www.auctionpix.co.uk). Cost: free.

◆ AuctionSuite (www.auctionsuite.com). Cost: from $1.50 per month.

◆ Deadzoom (www.deadzoom.com). Cost: $3 per month for 5 MB.

◆ InkFrog (www.inkfrog.com) and SpareDollar (www.sparedollar.com). Cost: $6.95 per month for 300 MB.

◆ Ranchoweb (www.ranchoweb.com). Cost: 50 MB for $11.95 per month.

 Auction Alert

As the number of simultaneous listings grows, you may no longer be able to handle things on your own. At this point, you may have to take on help if you want to continue to grow. This is explored in Chapter 19.

You can also store your images on a home computer if your Internet service provider gives you a static address (not all Internet providers do this), or on your own website if you have the storage capacity. This eliminates the ongoing image storage costs entirely.

Auction Strategies

"Going once, going twice, sold to the highest bidder" is the refrain from a live auctioneer. eBay's online basic auction format, which is the norm for most eBay listings, isn't much different—the seller lists an item, sets a starting price, and when the auction time expires the highest bidder is the winner.

This unadorned auction format isn't the only way to sell via an auction on eBay. You can use various options intended to increase the likelihood that you'll clinch a sale and receive at least a certain price.

Setting a Reserve

If you're selling things found around your home, you may not be concerned with the price you get—anything is better than nothing. But if you've paid for inventory, you probably want to at least recoup your costs. You can set a reserve price to ensure you receive a minimum amount.

The amount of your reserve price isn't posted for all to see (it's hidden and known only to you). Bidders discover the reserve price only when the bidding has at least reached this hidden number (some bidders may ask you in the course of the auction what your reserve price is, but it's considered unethical to tell). If the reserve price is never reached, you don't have to sell the item to the highest bidder.

Power Point

There are pros and cons to setting a reserve. It can mean you won't get a sale. If you simply must get a minimum, consider setting the starting price at the point you would have fixed the reserve.

You can't use a reserve for Dutch auctions (explained in Chapter 3). There is a service fee, which is fully refunded if the item sells (you don't get it back if the item fails to sell): $1 for a reserve price of $0.01 to $49.99; $2 for $50 to $199.99, and 1 percent of the reserve price for $200 and up (but this is capped at $50).

"Buy It Now"

Can't stand the suspense of the auction format? Give your bidders the opportunity to snatch the item off the auction block through the Buy It Now option. This allows bidders to buy the item at a fixed price and end the auction. (If no one opts for the Buy It Now feature, the auction proceeds as usual.) If you've set a reserve price, Buy It Now disappears once a bid meets the reserve.

The Buy It Now option can only be used if you have either a minimum feedback rating of 10 or are ID verified. Alternatively, you can use the Buy It Now option if you have a minimum feedback score of 5 and accept PayPal as a payment method.

Auction Alert _____

At the time this book is going to press, eBay is considering a change to the Buy It Now option. The feature would remain available on auction listings even after a bid has been received—so check whether this has become the rule. It's being tested in some categories now.

Relisting

Alas, not every auction on eBay is successful. eBay's sell-through rate—a comparison of items listed to items sold—averages about 30 percent (only 3 of 10 listed items sell). If your auction ends without a winning bidder (or your winning bidder fails to pay you), consider relisting the item.

It really doesn't cost you to take this step. If the item sells the second time, the second insertion fee is refunded. But don't delay: you must relist the item within 90 days of the closing date of the first auction. And be sure to tweak your listing title and copy to attract new bidders for your item.

Here are some requirements for relisting:

Power Point _____

Think long and hard before setting a reserve price in the relisting (assuming you can do this because you had one in the original auction). If the item fails to sell through the relisting, you won't get your second insertion fee refunded.

♦ You can only have one relisting of an item (subsequent relistings of the same item do not qualify).

♦ The starting price you set for the relisted item cannot be higher than that of the original listing (it can be lower).

♦ You cannot set a reserve price for the relisted item if the original listing didn't have one. If it did have a reserve price, then the reserve price for the relisted item cannot be higher than that of the original listing.

♦ You must use the Relist link either from the closed auction page or on the drop-down menu next to the listing in the Items Not Sold section of My eBay. If you just go to Sell and start a new listing, you will not get the relist fee credit (because eBay can't track that it was a relist).

Second-Chance Sales

There aren't many second chances in life. But eBay is the exception to this rule; you can get a second chance. If the winning bidder does not pay you, or your reserve price has not been met, a Second Chance Offer lets you offer your item to a non-winning bidder. Here's how: click on the Second Chance Offer (which you find on your My eBay page), which automatically sends a Buy It Now Price equal to the non-winning bidder's bid amount. For example, if the winner failed to pay, then send the Second Chance Offer to the next highest bidder at that bidder's final bid amount.

Auction Alert

Some sellers make their own second-chance-like offers to unsuccessful bidders. Doing this avoids paying eBay a final value fee for a successful sale. Of course, eBay frowns on the practice and strongly warns buyers against accepting offers from sellers outside of the eBay arena (buyers have no eBay protection for outside sales).

The great thing about Second Chance Offers—there's no extra eBay fee to do it! In fact, if this offer is accepted and you had a reserve price, you'll get your reserve price fee credited to you automatically. But you must act promptly, or lose this opportunity. You can send Second Chance Offers immediately after the listing ends; the maximum time to act is 60 days after the listing ends. The only restriction: you can't use a Second Chance Offer if you originally used a 10-day duration auction.

Managing Multiple Auctions

When you only run a few auctions at the same time, you can use a free tool to keep tabs on your sales. My eBay, which is a link on the top of each eBay page, lets you watch up to 100 items to track their status.

When you have a number of auctions proceeding simultaneously, you may feel like a juggler with three balls in the air at the same time. How many balls can you keep in the air simultaneously? Fortunately, running multiple auctions may be easier than juggling, with the help of various tools—through eBay and elsewhere.

eBay has recognized that medium- and high-volume sellers need help in managing their numerous ongoing auctions. Get help in listing your items, tracking your auctions, and handling your post-sale activities. Here are some eBay tools to help you (for a side-by-side comparison of features, go to http://pages.ebay.com/selling_manager/comparison.html):

- ◆ **TurboLister.** Designed for medium- to high-volume sellers, this tool enables you to easily create multiple listings. Use it alone or in combination with other software tools. Easily format your text and schedule your auctions. (This is only compatible with Windows 2000, XP, or Vista.) Cost: free. Download it from http://pages.ebay.com/turbo_lister.

- ◆ **Blackthorne Basic.** Create professional-looking auction listings with easy-to-use templates when listing 25 items or more. Insert information on shipping, tax, and payment terms. Create e-mail for customer correspondence. Cost: $9.99 per month (30-day free trial period). Subscribe at http://pages.ebay.com/blackthorne/basic.html.

- ◆ **Blackthorne Pro.** Get everything you have through Blackthorne Basic, plus many more features. These include scheduling listings, automating repetitive processes, tracking buyer information, printing labels, and submitting feedback automatically. Cost: $24.99 per month (30-day free trial period). Subscribe at http://pages.ebay.com/blackthorne/pro.html.

- ◆ **Selling Manager.** Also designed for medium- to high-volume sellers, this tool helps you manage the listings and post-sale activities. More specifically, you can use it to manage pending items to be listed on eBay at a future date; track active eBay listings; monitor unsold listings; and manage feedback, payments, and other post-sale activities. Cost: $4.99 per month (30-day free trial). If you manage a Basic-level eBay Store, Selling Manager is free. Subscribe at http://pages.ebay.com/selling_manager.

- ◆ **Selling Manager Pro.** Use this handy online tool to track your inventory; track your pending and active listings; relist unsold items in bulk; send invoices, e-mails, and feedback in bulk; track payments; and generate profit and loss reports. Cost: $15.99 per month (30-day free trial); free for those using Blackthorne Pro and Featured and Anchor Store subscribers. Subscribe at http://pages.ebay.com/selling_manager_pro.

- ◆ **File Exchange.** High-volume sellers can transfer their files from their computer to eBay, using files from Excel and other inventory software. Subscribe at http://pages.ebay.com/file_exchange. Cost: free for qualified sellers (registered on eBay for 90 days and have an average of at least 50 active listings per month for the last two months).

Growing pains can be eased by using applications readily available through eBay. eBay and third-party tools are discussed in Chapter 20.

Choosing Your Bidders

It's a free country, so you aren't required to sell to anyone you don't want to. You can, for instance, say you don't want to sell to anyone overseas (you don't want the hassle of shipping there).

You should block bidders you know will be trouble. This is something you can learn by checking bidders' feedback. If someone has, on multiple occasions, been reported as a "nonpaying bidder" (the person won an auction but didn't pay for the item), we suggest you block this individual from bidding on your items.

Learn about how to block up to 1,000 bidders at http://pages.ebay.com/help/sell/ manage_bidders_ov.html#blocking.

The Least You Need to Know

- Get the most bang for your buck in item headings by accompanying them with a photo in the Gallery and other listing enhancements.

- Make your listing description accurate, complete, and, whenever possible, fun to read.

- Develop your boilerplate on shipping and payment terms to save yourself repetitious writing.

- Handle multiple auctions with ease using eBay tools designed to assist you.

Chapter 8

Getting Paid

In This Chapter

- Getting your money up front before you ship
- Selecting your payment options
- Using escrow services
- Setting up a business bank account
- Getting satisfaction for nonpayment

Your auction has closed, so now it's time for the buyer to show you the money. But your buyer isn't there in person to hand it over. It's up to you to make arrangements so you can collect what's owed you (hopefully as quickly and with as little hassle as possible).

In this chapter, you'll learn about your payment options so you can choose the methods that work best for you. You'll find out about escrow services that can protect both you and the buyer. You'll also see why having a separate business bank account is a good idea. Finally, you'll learn what you can do when you've tried and tried with no success to collect your money.

Power Point _____

Make sure your listing includes a clear and complete statement of your terms of sale, to avoid any confusion later. Your description should include what costs the buyer must bear (such as postage and insurance), whether there is any sales tax, payment methods, and time frame for payment to be received.

Arranging Payments in Advance

In an eBay transaction between a buyer and a seller, someone has to make the first move. Either the buyer has to send payment and trust that the item will then be shipped, or the seller has to send the item and hope to receive payment. It's customary for the buyer to send payment before the seller sends the item. Of course, this custom often gives way to other business practices, as you'll soon see.

One payment from the buyer to you generally covers all. This means that the price you quote to the winning bidder includes not only the final value (the winning bid), but also shipping and handling, insurance (if any), and sales tax (if any).

Don't Ship Before Collecting

It's a well-established rule that, as a seller, you should wait to receive payment before you ship your merchandise. This means that if you are paid by a personal check, you wait until the funds clear in your account before sending the item to the buyer. Checks bounce all the time, and you don't want to be left holding the proverbial empty bag.

You can expedite the time it takes for a check to clear so that you can ship more promptly to buyers if you use a check-verification service (discussed later in this chapter).

Auction Alert _____

For credit card payments, don't ship to an address other than the billing address unless you've verified the alternative location. This could be a tip-off that the credit card used was bogus—after you ship, you could find that the credit card company removes the credit to your account, leaving you holding the bag—no goods and no payment.

Building Relationships with Customers

There's an exception to every rule. After just telling you *never* to ship your merchandise before receiving payment, you can ignore this piece of advice in one situation. If you already have an ongoing business relationship with a customer—someone you've done business with on numerous occasions before—you can make your own customized arrangements. However, just because someone has a great feedback rate is no green light to ship before receiving payment if you don't personally know the buyer.

For example, you may agree to ship immediately, with the customer promising to put a check in the mail. Or, for expensive items, you may set payment terms—a set amount immediately with the balance to be paid in two additional installments. Depending on how comfortable you feel with the customer, you may send the item now even though payment won't be received in full for a month or so.

 Auction Alert _____

Make sure that the person you think you're dealing with is really that person and not someone who has simply hijacked his or her identity. If you think Jim is the person who won your auction, contact the Jim you know by phone and have communication that establishes who Jim is. Be very wary if Jim asks you to ship the item to a location other than the one you're familiar with—this may be a clue that Jim is really Sally in disguise (using Jim's good name and reputation to acquire goods without having to make payment).

Paper or Plastic?

When bagging groceries, you have to decide between paper or plastic bags. You face a similar choice in collecting your money: paper (checks and money orders) or plastic (credit cards or other tech-payment options).

The more types of payment options you offer, the more customers you can attract. Some buyers prefer one type of payment option to another. As of 2006, eBay prohibits the acceptance of cash as a payment method unless the item is delivered in person and paid for at the time of delivery.

Checks and Money Orders

Checks come in all colors and sizes. Your bank's rules govern when a deposited check clears your account so that you can draw on the funds (and know that there's no problem with the check).

Under federal law, there are three holding periods for deposited checks:

◆ One day

◆ Two days for local checks

◆ Five days for out-of-state checks and ATM deposits

Power Point _____

Obtain instant verification that the check is as good as gold using an online service such as TeleCheck Check Verification Service from FirstData (www. firstdata.com), VeriCheck (www. vericheck.net), or Security Check (www.securitycheckllc.com).

Checks may take longer to become available to you under certain circumstances: if the bank has problems with its computer (and I don't have to tell you how often this happens!) or if you deposit more than $5,000 in a day, among other situations.

You can accept BidPay (www.bidpay.com), a payment alternative to PayPal (and other methods) that is free to the buyer (you pay 2.5 percent, plus a 50¢ transaction fee for U.S. buyers and 2.9 percent, plus a 50¢ transaction fee for buyers outside the United States).

BidPay does not have an actual "account" like PayPal. Buyers pay using their credit card, and the funds are deposited directly into your checking account. BidPay claims that adding this option to your listings increases sales by 15.4 percent. BidPay can now be integrated in your checkout offerings to give buyers a choice of using it to complete payment to you.

Plastic Is a Plus for Your Business

Let's face it; the United States is a credit card nation tethered to the small plastic cards that enable us to buy goods and services worldwide in an instant. MasterCard, Visa, Discover, and American Express are staples in our purchasing diet. You may want to offer this payment option to your customers. Here's what you gain if you do:

◆ **A wider customer base.** Some people like to pay only by credit card because it affords them buyer protection (they can work out problems directly with their credit card company if, say, goods aren't delivered).

◆ **Immediate cash.** The money charged by credit card is credited to your bank account the same day.

Of course, you aren't getting something for nothing. There's a cost to you (not the customer) for accepting credit cards.

◆ **Equipment fees.** If you don't want to call into the credit card company for every transaction, you may need an electronic tie-in to the credit card company. You can rent the necessary terminal (generally $20 to $80 per month), or you can purchase it for a one-time cost (usually several hundred dollars). You may be able to eliminate the need for the equipment if you process everything online, but you'll pay higher transaction charges if you do.

◆ **Per-transaction charges.** For every sale you make, the credit card company keeps a percentage, sometimes called the merchant fee. The amount varies with the volume of business you do and the credit card company you use. Usually, the per-charge fee runs between 1.5 percent and 3 percent of the amount of the charge. So, if you sell an item for $100 and there's a 2 percent fee, you'll net $98 (the credit card company keeps $2).

You Have a Friend in PayPal

PayPal is the number one way in which goods are paid for on eBay; there are more than 143 million PayPal accounts worldwide. More than 90 percent of all eBay merchants now accept PayPal and over one in three shoppers in the United States now has a PayPal account. PayPal is now in more than 190 countries and regions.

Think of PayPal, a wholly owned subsidiary of eBay, as a credit card. The buyer authorizes payment from his or her PayPal account to your PayPal account. It's not a bank, although you can earn some interest; you must actually transfer the funds from your PayPal account into your bank account or otherwise access your funds (the access methods are discussed shortly).

You can use PayPal to buy items on eBay for resale. Using PayPal does not require you to give your credit card information to a seller. You can also use PayPal to accept payment for the items you sell to others, and you receive payment immediately.

One of the best parts about PayPal is its fraud exposure protection. PayPal offers a Seller Protection Policy under which it will absorb *chargebacks* at no cost to you under certain circumstances.

def•i•ni•tion

When a charge is made to a credit card or PayPal by a buyer who later turns out to be no good (the buyer is bogus or is able to stop payment on his or her account), the money is subtracted from the money you thought you earned, which is called a **chargeback** (also known as a reversal).

Of course, there have been and will continue to be glitches in using PayPal. Many people have unfavorable tales of their dealings with this payment method. However, by and large, it seems to work very well and has become indispensable for any eBay seller.

One of the most important issues about using PayPal is security concerns. Payment Review, launched in the summer of 2007, will hopefully reduce fraudulent transactions. PayPal will identify risky transactions and keep them pending while it investigates them. Once the review is completed, sellers are 100 percent protected.

PayPal users can obtain an added measure of protection with a Security Key, a key-size device that generates a temporary 6-digit security code every 30 seconds.

Auction Alert

Never, ever respond to an e-mail purported to come from PayPal *unless* it is sent personally to you—this is merely a phishing expedition by an identity thief to obtain your account information. PayPal never sends e-mail to "PayPal account owner" or other impersonal term—it knows your full name and uses it for any communication with you.

Registering with PayPal

Registration is free, and the process is easy. Simply go to the PayPal site at www.paypal.com. You'll need to log in to access the site (a new user can register by clicking the Sign Up button at the top of the screen).

Then select the type of account—business instead of personal—by clicking the Business Account option and selecting, for example, the United States from the adjacent drop-down list box.

Figure 8.1

Sign up for PayPal.

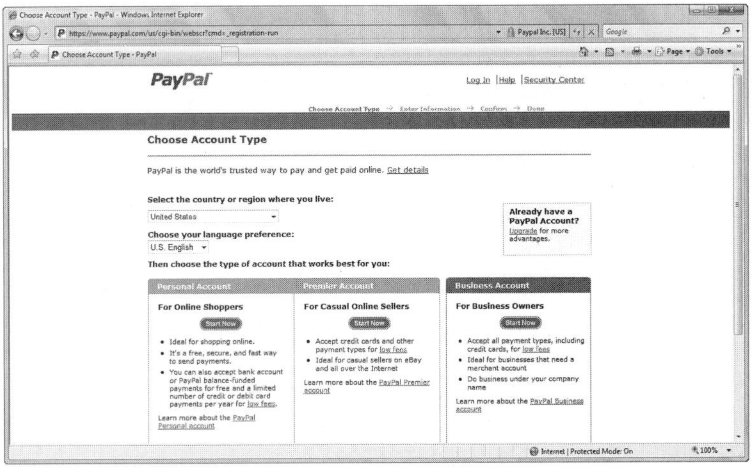

Figure 8.2

Select an account and country.

Click Continue to proceed to the next screen. Here you must enter all the required fields to complete your registration (the optional information boxes are clearly marked as such).

Then click Continue to complete the registration process.

To get you started, you're asked for your bank account information. This is the account that PayPal can tap into for payments you make through it. It is also the account into which you can transfer funds from PayPal.

Figure 8.3

Fill out the registration form.

Gauging the Cost of Using PayPal

While there's no charge to register for PayPal as a seller, you do pay to use it. There's a 30¢ charge for each PayPal transaction, plus a percentage of the payment amount (per transaction), as shown in the following table. These charges apply to domestic payments; different rates apply for cross-border payments. The rate you pay is determined at the beginning of each month, based on the volume of payments you received in the previous calendar month.

Fees for U.S. Payments to Merchants

Monthly Sales	Price per Transaction
$0 to $3,000	2.9% + $0.30
$3,000.01 to $10,000	2.5% + $0.30
$10,000.01 to $100,000	2.2% + $0.30
Over $100,000	1.9% + $0.30

PayPal offers different merchant solutions, so compare your options (and the pricing for each) by clicking on "Compare our solutions side by side" on PayPal's home page.

Making the Most of Your PayPal Account

It's easy to check the status of your account—how much money you've spent or accumulated. You simply go to the My Account page, shown in the following figure.

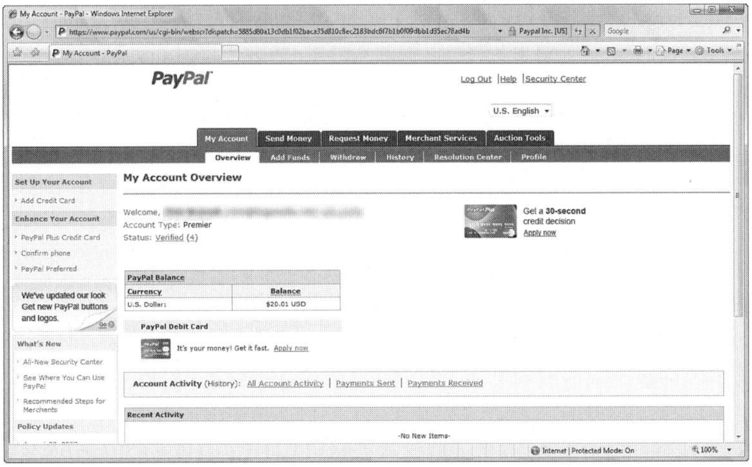

Figure 8.4

Manage your account.

If you're using your PayPal account to pay for items you're purchasing on eBay and the money is going out faster than it's coming in, you can add funds to your PayPal account. The money can be transferred electronically from a bank checking or savings account. Under Add Funds, you can easily transfer money from your bank account into PayPal. There's no PayPal fee for transferring money into your account. You'll earn interest (for example, in September 2007, the rate was over 5 percent on funds in PayPal accounts). Funds generally are available for you to draw on within three to four business days.

To withdraw funds, simply click the Withdraw link and then choose the payment method you want. You can withdraw funds from your PayPal account in six ways:

- ◆ **Transfer funds to your bank account.** There's no charge for this service. It may take three to four business days to show up in your bank account.

- ◆ **Receive a check.** There's a $1.50 charge per check. It takes a week or two until you receive the check by mail.

- ◆ **Shop with a debit card issued by PayPal.** As with any other debit card, you can access your money in PayPal instantly by using the card. You must request a card (one is not issued automatically), and this can take a few weeks.

Power Point _____

You get 1 percent back on every purchase you make with your PayPal ATM debit card (it is issued to you as a MasterCard and can be used wherever MasterCard is accepted). This 1 percent credit amount increases your buying power.

- **Get cash at an ATM machine.** Again, you need to obtain a debit card from PayPal. And you'll pay $1 for every ATM withdrawal.

- **Shop online with a PayPal virtual card.** PayPal creates a virtual MasterCard for you—it issues you a debit number to your PayPal account, and the number appears on your PayPal debit bar below your browser when you shop. To pay for online purchases, just enter your PayPal debit bar information, and the money is automatically subtracted from your PayPal account, at no charge to you.

- **Pay for purchases at PayPal stores.** More than 42,000 websites now accept PayPal, so you can shop till you drop, paying with the funds in your PayPal account. There's no charge for this payment method.

> **Power Point**
>
> Get monthly account statements to view the activity in your account (and make sure it squares with what you expect). You can get the three previous months' transactions in one convenient place—just click the "Show: All Activity; Within: Last Month."

You can check your account activity within the past day, week, month, or year. For example, if someone has promised to pay you, check the history for the day to see if the money has shown up yet. You'll also receive an e-mail notification when a payment has been received.

If you move, change the name of your company, or make other changes, you can edit your profile (the information that you've given to PayPal). This includes your account information (your company name, your e-mail address, the time zone you're in, and so on), your financial information (your bank account number, credit card information, and so on), and your preferences (instant notification, USPS shipping, sales tax information, include PayPal in all listings, and so on).

Offering PayPal Buyer Protection

Enhance your online credibility by qualifying to offer PayPal Buyer Protection. This promises buyers who buy from sellers displaying the PayPal Protection icon that they are covered up to $2,000 for items that are never received, or not as described in the listing. This protection covers all tangible items (not services or intangibles such as recipes). Buyers qualify for this protection on your sales if …

- You (the seller) have a feedback rating of 50 or more, 98 percent of which are positive.

- You are a verified member of PayPal with a premier or business account.

- You have a U.S. PayPal account or a PayPal account in one of 35 other countries.

Auction Alert

To activate PayPal Protection for a particular item, you must select PayPal as the payment option on the eBay Sell Your Item form. (Make the PayPal selection when you use bulk listing tools such as Turbo Lister or Blackthorne.) Alternatively, use the seller's preferences within PayPal to include this payment method automatically with all your listings.

You can also increase buyer confidence by using PASS™ (Payments as a Secure Service, www.passpayments.com) to provide greater protection against fraud and identity theft, serious concerns of many buyers today. There's no cost for using this service.

Offering PayPal Buyer Financing

If you're selling expensive items, you can offer an attractive financing through PayPal. This financing option can make it affordable for potential buyers to purchase high-end items from you. This financing option appears automatically with your listings when using PayPal.

If you are a qualified U.S. seller (i.e., you and your item would qualify for PayPal Buyer Protection), you can offer buyer financing for items of $50 or more. This allows buyers to defer payment for up to 90 days on items between $50 and $1,500. Credit approval is immediate and there is no interest or monthly payments if full payment is made within 90 days.

Alternative Online Payment Options

Dozens of companies offer handy payment options that you can use to cut the time it takes to receive payment and reduce the possibility that a purported payment will turn out to be bogus.

We can't cover *every* one of these companies, but we want to highlight one of them for you because they offer something a little different from PayPal.

Using an Escrow Service

Escrow isn't something you add to your salad; it's a payment arrangement that's designed to protect both buyer and seller. It uses a third party or intermediary to make sure that each party to a transaction does what is expected.

Let's take an example. Suppose you sell an expensive diamond ring on eBay. You don't want to ship out this $10,000 item until you've been paid. But the buyer may be reluctant to fork over these big bucks without receiving delivery first. So you both agree to use an escrow agent to meet you halfway. The buyer sends $10,000 to the escrow agent. When the agent is satisfied that the payment is good (for example, the check has cleared), you send the ring to the buyer and, upon receipt, the escrow agent disburses the money to you. If one party fails to live up to what's expected (for example, the buyer's check bounces), the escrow agent says the deal is off and returns the ring to you.

Power Point _____

The use of escrow in your listings adds an aura of reliability—you wouldn't agree to use this service if you weren't trustworthy. Even if you set limits on when you will use it, the fact that you have a practice of doing so at some sales threshold is proof of your good intentions.

Currently, only one escrow service is approved by eBay for sales in the United States (other services can be used for international sales, as discussed in Chapter 11): Escrow.com (www.escrow.com). The service is available for any purchase, but typically is used for purchases of $500 or more. But you can agree to use escrow for any higher threshold you set. For example, you can limit its use to items over $5,000, as long as you make this clear in your listing information.

Escrow costs money. There's a sliding scale starting at 3.5 percent on the first $5,000 ($25 minimum). The fee is 0.89 percent on amounts over $25,000. Higher fees apply to premier service, which includes additional buyer ID verification and fraud screening. The fee is based on the transaction amount, which is the price of the merchandise plus shipping.

Who pays the escrow fee? You can agree to split the cost, because escrow provides a benefit to both parties (although one party must pay for it and then receive a share from the other party). However, it is not uncommon on eBay for sellers to insist that buyers pay it all. If the buyer ultimately rejects the merchandise or cancels the transaction, the buyer is responsible for escrow fees, return shipping fees, and original shipping fee if the buyer agreed to pay them. The escrow fee and any original shipping fees are subtracted from the original payment made to Escrow.com.

Auction Alert

Beware of fake escrow companies that are becoming too common on the web. They pocket the money sent by buyers. Only use a reputable escrow company like the ones discussed in this chapter.

Using a Bonding Service

Another way that buyers can protect themselves and know that they're dealing with a reputable seller is to use a bonding service. This is a type of insurance that says the company will provide satisfaction if the seller fails to live up to his or her end of the bargain.

buySAFE (www.buysafe.com) is a bonding service for online auctions such as those conducted on eBay and in May 2007 reported its twelve millionth transaction. Large insurance companies—Liberty Mutual, Travelers, and ACE USA—guarantee protection to buyers up to $25,000 for any seller who has obtained bonding through buySAFE. Here's how it works: as a seller, you apply for bonding. The insurance company makes sure you are worthy of the buySAFE guarantee. Once you've passed an extensive and thorough background check, you may display the buySAFE logo on your website. Buyers have come to recognize the meaning of this logo—a true guarantee, which should increase the chances that they will do business with you. After all, there's no charge to buyers.

For sellers, there's no charge when applying for buySAFE. You pay only when and to the extent you use it. The cost is 1 percent of the final transaction price. If there is no winning bidder, there is no cost to you. You can select which auctions to affix the buySAFE logo to, reserving it for higher-priced items so buyers can gain comfort from the guarantee.

Power Point _____

BuySAFE and TRUSTe have partnered to create TRUSTe for Small Business, a program combining buySAFE's merchant performance certification process with TRUSTe's privacy certification process. Small businesses with monthly sales of $1 million or less can display the TRUSTe for Small Business Seal after passing a buySAFE certification process.

Banking on a Business Bank Account

When you started selling on eBay with an item or two, you may have been casual about where you put your profits. If you are now in an eBay business, you *must* set up a separate business bank account for your business funds. This action is important on many levels, such as financial reporting and your ability to borrow money to grow your business.

Power Point _____

To open a business bank account, you need an employer identification number (EIN) from the IRS. Even if you are self-employed, the bank may not let you use your social security number on the account and may require an EIN. You can obtain one instantaneously online at www.irs.gov/businesses/small/article/0,,id=102767,00.html. If you are incorporated, you must complete a corporate resolution form (the bank will give you one) and apply the corporate seal, authorizing this institution to be your business bank.

Keeping Everything Separate

When we're asked about the first thing someone should do when they decide to start a business (and we get this question very often), we always say to open a business bank account. This is a no-brainer to looking and feeling like you're really in business.

But just having the bank account isn't enough. It goes without saying that when you receive payment for things you sell on eBay, the funds should go directly into your business bank account (not your personal account). This creates a clear record of your gross proceeds.

Building Business Credit

Having a separate business bank account not only makes it easier to track your business progress and file your tax returns; it also helps to build up a business credit history. This becomes important if you want to grow your business and need commercial financing to do so.

As with your personal credit history, which is taken into account when you apply for a mortgage on your home, your business credit history is the underpinning of a small business loan. It shows the lender that you are fiscally able to repay what you borrow.

Nonpayment Recourse

Suppose you get stiffed. A buyer who wins an auction simply doesn't pay you. What then? Know your recourse so you can follow through immediately to limit or recoup your losses.

eBay Recourse

eBay does not guarantee anything on its site. Philosophically, eBay views itself as a marketplace, bringing buyers and sellers together. Its legal responsibilities end there.

But you have some options on eBay if things go sour:

- **Enter negative feedback on the buyer.** This will not help you recoup your losses, but it may help prevent it from happening to someone else.

- **Open an Unpaid Item dispute.** This alerts eBay to the events that have transpired. The nonpaying bidder is sometimes called an NPB (you may call the person an @X%?&!!). This must be done between 7 and 45 days after the listing has ended. If, at the time of the filing, the buyer is no longer a registered user or you and the buyer agree to mutually withdraw from the transaction, you can file a claim to recover your listing fees immediately.

◆ **Request a Final Value Fee (FVF) credit for a nonpaying bidder.** This won't give you the money you would have earned on the sale, but you can at least recover some of the fees you owe to eBay. To take this step, you must already have opened an Unpaid Item dispute (through the dispute console in My eBay) and then tried unsuccessfully to resolve the matter with the buyer for at least 7 days after filing that form. The FVF must be filed within 60 days after the listing has ended. Assuming you follow these steps, you can then receive a credit from eBay for the Final Value Fee it charged on the auction. However, in the case of Dutch auctions, you are limited to filing only one form per auction for as many bidders as necessary; you can't later resubmit for additional bidders. Filing an FVF does not prevent you from relisting the item for sale (and receiving the relist credit if it sells again). For information on the eBay Final Value Fee Credit Request Program, go to http://pages.ebay.com/help/tp/unpaid-item-process.html.

◆ **Recover listing fee upgrades if you are a PowerSeller who has filed an Unpaid Item claim.** Those who are not PowerSellers can only recoup their Final Value Fee in appropriate situations.

◆ **Block nonpaying bidders from participating in your auctions.** On your My eBay page, scroll down to the link to the Blocked Bidder list. Click the list to add the bidder's username. You can add several names at one time; just add a comma between user IDs.

Auction Alert

eBay does not bar a bidder from its site until three Unpaid Item Claims have been filed for that bidder. If you choose to do a Mutual Withdrawal From Transaction, this does not count against the buyer.

Legal Action

Just because you are selling on the Internet does not deprive you of any legal rights you may have in the normal marketplace. You have the same contractual and tort (civil) rights as if you are selling goods from a storefront.

Try to settle disputes using an online dispute-resolution (ODR) program. SquareTrade (www.squaretrade.com), which handles over 10,000 cases a month, offers two resolution options: direct negotiation or resolution using a *mediator* who can bring parties together in an effort to amicably resolve problems. Both parties must agree to the process. The mediator facilitates discussion; he or she is not a judge or jury. The direct negotiation process is free; the mediation process costs $29.95 to the party filing the case.

Auction Alert

Mediation is *not* arbitration or a court proceeding. The mediator cannot force either party to take action. The mediator is merely a broker of a peaceful solution.

As a practical matter, taking formal legal action may not make sense in most cases. Say you live in Nevada and a buyer from New Jersey stops payment on a check after you've shipped a camera costing $150. You'd have to go to New Jersey to sue him, something that would cost more than the money you lost.

On the other hand, if you've sold a forklift for $95,000, it may make sense to hire a lawyer in New Jersey and sue. Discuss your situation with a lawyer in your area to decide whether to pursue this course of action.

Government Action

Will your government help you if you have collection problems or fail to receive items you've purchased? Generally, the answer is no. However, when there is fraud or identity theft involved, some government agencies may be able to provide assistance (or at least go after the bad guys). Here are some resources to check out:

- Department of Justice (www.usdoj.gov/criminal/fraud)
- Federal Trade Commission (www.ftc.gov/idtheft)
- U.S. Postal Inspection Service (www.usps.com/postalinspectors)
- U.S. Secret Service (www.secretservice.gov)

As fraud and identity theft continue to plague the innocent, expect the government to be pressured into more aggressively pursuing wrongdoers.

The Least You Need to Know

- ◆ Don't send an item to the winning bidder until you've received payment (unless you have an established relationship with the buyer and feel confident that you'll get paid).

- ◆ Accept PayPal (exclusively or in conjunction with other payment methods) and learn how to use it to grow your business.

- ◆ Understand what steps you can take if you fail to receive payment.

- ◆ Report collection problems that may be the result of fraud or identity theft to the government.

Chapter **9**

Packing and Shipping

In This Chapter

- ◆ Making shipping arrangements with the buyer
- ◆ Wrapping your items for safe shipment
- ◆ Figuring the cost of shipping and handling
- ◆ Selecting your carrier
- ◆ Using fulfillment companies
- ◆ Making claims for damaged or lost items

You've completed the auction and collected your money. Now it's time for you to deliver your item to the winning bidder. How you handle this part of the sale process is very important—it can create appreciative customers who will leave positive feedback and do more business with you, or it can alienate them.

In this chapter, you'll learn about how to get the items you've sold to the winning bidders. You'll see how to best pack items for shipping. You'll find out about your shipping options and how to handle the costs involved. You'll also see how fulfillment companies can relieve you of shipping responsibilities. And you'll learn how to make claims if your shipments fail to arrive or get there in damaged condition.

Buyer's Burden

It's customary on eBay for the buyer to bear the cost of your packing and shipping the item. These are commonly referred to as shipping and handling charges, or S&H for short.

Auction Alert _____

Handling charges are often a major point of dissatisfaction with buyers—something you need to be sensitive to. While you need to cover your costs to wrap and ship items, the buyer can feel ripped off on this cost, especially for low-cost items. To help you fix your S&H charges, look at what your competitors are getting—you can see these costs in their listings. Don't use handling charges as a profit center—collect only what it costs you. Under eBay's seller-rating system, you can be judged by your buyers on your S&H charges. eBay can also end your auction if you are reported by another eBay member as charging "excessive shipping," although they do not define that term.

What do the shipping and handling charges include?

- **Handling charges.** This usually is a fee you set to cover the cost of labor and materials to pack the item and, if necessary, get it to the shipper. There's no set rate for handling charges—you must determine what it actually costs you to complete this task. Obviously, the item you're packing has an impact on your costs. Shipping a music CD is a no-brainer, while packing a precious Limoges vase (which should be double-boxed to avoid breakage) is costly and time-consuming.

- **Postage.** By whatever means you send the item—post office or private carrier, such as DHL, FedEx, or UPS—charges are based on the size and weight of the item and how quickly you want it to arrive. Overnight delivery of large, heavy items is very costly.

- **Insurance.** This isn't always used, but when sending valuables that can't be replaced, insurance may be desirable. Insurance can usually be handled through the shipper you use. If you are not offering an insurance option, make this clear in your listing; if you require insurance, state the cost. You may wish to make insurance optional but caution buyers that, without insurance, you have no responsibility for lost or damaged items (unless you agree to self-insure so that you become responsible for loss). If a buyer waives insurance coverage, be sure to keep a copy of this (it will be included on the eBay Checkout page).

Power Point

Shipping costs and insurance rates don't always correlate. The post office may have low postage rates and high insurance costs for an item, while FedEx may cost more for shipping but be lower in insurance. When insurance is part of S&H, always check both shipping costs and insurance rates. But no matter which carrier you use, you can cut insurance costs by using a third-party insurer (see Chapter 15). And always give yourself a little cushion for error (for example, charge $10 S&H if you figure the cost to be $9.10).

Clarifying the Price Plus Shipping

When you post your items for sale, your listing should include a detailed explanation of your shipping policy. There's a Shipping and Payment Details section in the listing in which you can include any specifics you want.

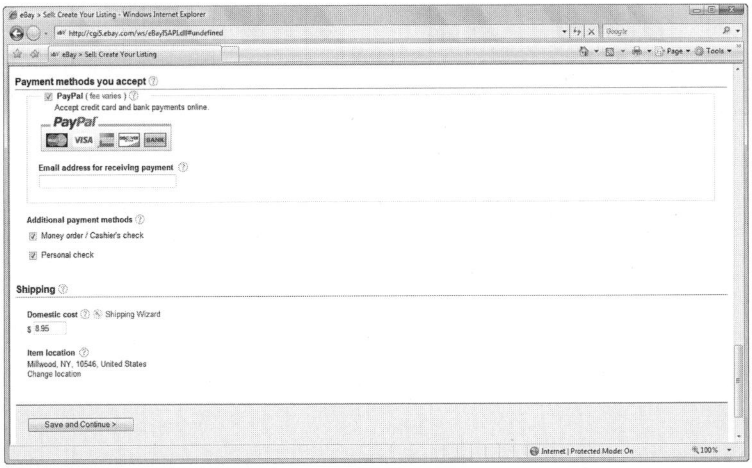

Figure 9.1

Your shipping and payment details.

You should specify that the buyer bears the cost and what the cost will be. Where possible, provide exact shipping amounts, using eBay's shipping calculator or a shipping wizard (shipping calculators are discussed later in this chapter). Depending on what you sell, you may want to charge a flat rate (for example, $1.50 for every DVD shipped), as long as this amount is not excessive.

Here are some ways to handle the listing description for S&H charges:

◆ **Include the total amount for S&H.** For example, the cost may be $9.50 for shipping within the United States. Specify the way in which you ship, such as via the U.S. Postal Service Priority Mail, First Class, etc. Include information on insurance—whether it's mandatory, optional, or not available.

♦ **Suggest that a bidder contact you for details if they want special shipping.** If, for example, a buyer wants overnight delivery rather than standard delivery quoted in the auction, state that you'll price this shipping accordingly.

When you charge sales tax on an item, you may have to include shipping and handling costs when figuring the tax. Different states have different sales tax rules about S&H (see Chapter 16 for more details).

When a buyer purchases multiple items, you can discount the shipping charges because you'll be sending items together. You can set your listing to automatically include Combined Shipping Discounts.

Negotiating with the Buyer

The cost you charge to the buyer may be partially up to him or her. The Sell Your Item form gives you three slots for different shipping services for Domestic and three for International. Use the three slots to provide a slow (inexpensive) option, a middle-cost method, and an express or overnight option at the high end.

If the item is more than a nominal amount, you should usually insist on insurance—it's a protection to both you and the buyer. If you sell something valuable and the buyer doesn't want insurance, this may be a tip-off that the buyer may be trying to scam you in some way. Who wouldn't want to insure a valuable item that could be damaged in shipping (and be willing to pay the insurance cost to do so)?

Power Point _____

When contacting a winning bidder after the close of the auction, be sure to reiterate the buyer's shipping preference that was selected on the eBay Checkout page. Sometimes, he or she will decide to make changes.

If the item is low cost (say, under $10), you may want to self-insure in order to save the buyer insurance costs. By self-insuring, you are bearing the risk of loss or damage—you agree to reimburse the buyer if the item never arrives or if its condition is damaged.

Packing Things Yourself or Using Assistance

Unless you're sending something you can slip into an envelope and aren't concerned about folding or bending, you need to think about packing. This vital step in the selling process ensures that your item will reach the winning bidder in the condition you've advertised. This, in turn, will help to secure positive feedback for you.

You can wrap your items yourself or use professional assistance. Obviously, the choice depends on what you are packing, your skill level in packing, and other factors.

Whether you do it yourself or use professional help, be sure to include with each package a copy of the eBay Checkout page showing the item name, total price paid, etc. Also take the opportunity to thank the buyer for the sale with a personal note, a token gift, or other marketing device (see Chapter 10 for details).

An Educated eBay Seller

Why pay for packing supplies when you can get them for free? To order free supplies, go to:

◆ USPS, at www.usps.com/shop/welcome.htm. You can also obtain free co-branded supplies, including boxes and packing tape, explained later.

◆ UPS, at www.ups.com/content/us/en/resources/prepare/supplies for those with a UPS account.

◆ FedEx, at www.fedex.com (click on Order Supplies under Manage My Account). You must be registered with FedEx to obtain supplies online.

When you are in your buyer mode, save the packing materials, such as bubble wrap and peanuts, on items that come in so you can reuse them when packing the items you sell.

Boxes, Bubble Wrap, and More

Some items are easy to pack. You can even use free shipping supplies from the carrier.

Other items may require specialized care. You may need unusual box sizes, crates, or other materials to accommodate your items. Or you may want to jazz things up with colored bows and tinsel wrapping paper. You can buy these supplies online through eBay sellers (in the search box, just enter the type of supplies you need). For example, one company specializing in shipping supplies, including colored bubble wrap and colored packing tape, is Fast-Pack.com (www.Fast-Pack.com).

You can also purchase supplies at office supply stores, such as Staples (www.staples.com), Office Max (www.officemax.com), and Office Depot (www.officedepot.com)— at their neighborhood stores or online. There are also specialized discount sellers, such as eSupplyStore.com (www.esupplystore.com), for finding shipping supplies.

High-volume sellers may even want to invest in a machine, such as the Mini Pak'R™ from FP International (www.flintl.com) that can produce six different air cushions that are bubblewrap-like packing material. The machine is costly, but this packing material can save money in the long run.

Packing Solutions

It may not be easy for you to properly pack an item for shipping. It may require the help of a professional. For example, say you're in Connecticut and want to ship a motorcycle you've sold to someone in California. You can't just put it in a box with some bubble wrap. You need a professional shipper who can properly crate the bike so that it arrives undamaged.

There are thousands of neighborhood packing experts across the country:

- FedEx Kinkos (www.fedex.com/us/officeprint/packship)

- Pakmail (www.pakmail.com)

- PostNet (www.postnet.com)

- The UPS Store (www.theupsstore.com)

Shipping Calculators

In the old days, to figure what it cost to ship a package, you had to carry it to the post office to find out. Now you can determine the cost from your computer using one of the following online shipping calculators:

- eBay shipping calculator (http://pages.ebay.com/services/buyandsell/shipping.html, and click on Shipping Calculator).

- UPS shipping calculator (http://wwwapps.ups.com/servlet/QCCServlet). This calculator can also provide you with the time it expects the delivery to take.

- U.S. Postal Service shipping calculator (www.usps.com/tools/calculatepostage/welcome.htm?from=home&page=0061calculatepostage).

Post Office Options

You never have to trek to the post office ever again. Now, without leaving home, you can ship your packages through U.S. mail. Using the eBay Shipping Center, you can print shipping labels and pay for postage. The cost is charged directly to your PayPal account. Then you can arrange to have your packages picked up by the postal service (or drop them off without waiting in lines). It's a great time saver for busy eBay sellers, and it's easy to do—all the instructions are provided by eBay.

Figure 9.2

Print shipping labels at your desk.

USPS.com

The post office has a number of online services to make shipping your items easier. In addition to its online postage calculator, you can print postage (and charge it to your credit card), find the four-digit zip code extensions, track packages you've sent, and more.

If you want your packages picked up at your home for shipment, a feature that's increasingly attractive with the high cost of gasoline, you can arrange this online. Simply request a carrier pickup, and your packages will be collected the next postal delivery day for free. To request a carrier pickup, go to http://carrierpickup.usps.com/cgi-bin/WebObjects/CarrierPickup.woa.

Or you can schedule a pickup on demand (go to http://pickup.usps.com/pickup). You can get pickup as quickly as two hours notice. There's a flat charge of $14.25, regardless of the number of packages you have (none can weigh more than 70 pounds) or how you are sending them.

Your Post Office Mailing Alternatives

The post office has a number of different mailing options—some will get your items there sooner rather than later.

- **First class.** Items over 13 ounces are treated as Priority Mail and are subject to its weight and size limitations.

- **Priority.** For items that can fit into a flat rate Priority envelope, the cost is only $4.60 ($8.95 for a flat rate box). The maximum weight for Priority shipping is 70 pounds; the maximum size of a parcel is 108 inches (combined length and distance around the thickest part of the box).

- **Express Mail.** Insurance up to $100 is available at no additional cost; additional insurance is available up to $5,000 (the rates are in the following table).

Power Point

Get $25 worth of postage and a digital scale for free. Print postage online through Stamps.com (www.stamps.com); there's a four-week trial period. Cost: $14.99 per month (cancel anytime), plus postage.

- **Parcel Post.** If slightly slower delivery (by a matter of days) is acceptable, save money shipping packages up to 70 pounds. Rates are based on weight, distance, and shape (for example, there is a surcharge on tubes, rolls, and large packages).

- **Media Mail.** Like Parcel Post, this is a low-cost mailing alternative for books, tapes, videos, and similar recorded materials up to 70 pounds.

The following table lists insurance rates for post office mailings.

Insurance Rates for Post Office Mailings*

Amount of Insurance Coverage			Fee (in Addition to Postage)
$0.01	to	$50.00	$1.65
$50.01	to	$100.00	$2.50
$100.01	to	$200.00	$2.45
$200.01	to	$300.00	$4.60
$300.01	to	$400.00	$5.50
$400.01	to	$500.00	$6.40
$500.01	to	$600.00	$7.30
$601.01	to	$5,000.00	$7.30, plus $.90 for each $100 or fraction thereof over $600 in desired coverage, up to $5,000.

Different rates apply to registered mail; coverage is available up to $25,000.

Power Point _____

If you do not send your item insured or use a shipping method that requires the buyer's signature upon delivery, be sure to send items with Delivery Confirmation so you'll know your item has been delivered to the buyer. (You can use this feature when printing labels with postage through the eBay Shipping Center.) Factor in the cost of this track-and-confirm tool, which is free for Priority Mail or 18¢ for First Class (if you print your postage online). If you take your parcels to the post office to ship, you pay 65¢ for Priority Mail or 75¢ for first-class packages. For greater safety, use signature confirmation, which is $1.75 if you print your postage, or $2.10 if you go to a retail post office location.

More Mailing Options

The post office may be the first mailing resource that comes to mind, but many other carriers can ship your items—some at less cost. In deciding whether to use a post office alternative, consider …

- **Cost.** The charge for shipping is easy to compare.

- **Insurance.** The post office may be less costly when it comes to postage but may charge more for insuring your item.

- **Convenience to you.** Your time is a factor in selecting your mailing alternative. For example, if you have a UPS Store on your street, it may be easiest for you to ship via UPS, even if it costs a few pennies more (the cost is usually borne by the buyer).

- **Shipping location.** You can only use these private delivery services if you are mailing to a street address. You cannot use them if you are sending items to a post office box.

UPS

Formerly called the United Parcel Service, UPS is a private carrier that delivers both domestically and internationally. UPS purchased Mail Boxes Etc., so you can now send packages through UPS at both UPS and The UPS Store locations.

Like the USPS, UPS has teamed with PayPal to provide integrated shipping tools. You can create a UPS shipping label online through your PayPal account. The process for printing the UPS label is the same as the one you use for a post office label, explained earlier in this chapter.

You can schedule a pickup from your home. If you do not have an automatic daily pickup account, you may be charged for this service. Go to www.ups.com/content/us/en/resources/get/pickup.html and click Schedule a Pickup Online.

Power Point _____

UPS offers special discounts (up to 31 percent) to eBay sellers who use PayPal label printing. If interested, go to http://pages.ebay.com/ups/home.html and sign up for the UPS Special Pricing Program.

FedEx

The original overnight carrier provides a full range of shipping solutions. It merged with Kinko's, so you can find FedEx services at FedEx Kinko's Office Print Centers (www.fedex.com/us/officeprint/main/index.html). You can use FedEx to ship overnight or opt for slower, less costly shipping alternatives.

The first $100 of declared value is insured by FedEx as part of the shipping price. Insurance is available on values up to $25,000 (the cost of which increases with each $100 of value). However, FedEx will not insure certain items (over the $100 included in the shipping fee): art works, antiques, glassware, jewelry, fur, and musical instruments more than 20 years old.

FedEx has 44,000 drop-off locations worldwide that you can use if your packages are ready for shipping. If you use FedEx extensively to send your eBay items to winning bidders (your monthly FedEx shipping charges average at least $60), you can pay a flat rate of $8 per week to schedule regular pickups from your location.

Other Carriers

The big three—USPS, UPS, and FedEx—aren't the only shipping companies you can use to get your items delivered in a timely and safe manner. Other options include these:

- ◆ **DHL** (www.dhl.com). A small business center that provides resources and help, such as a full-featured web shipping system and online billing to you (you set up a DHL account, and shipments are billed to you electronically).

- **DSI** (www.dsiinsurance.com). This full-service shipping company boasts the lowest insurance rates (promising savings of up to 90 percent on shipping insurance). Check under Auction Sellers & Buyers in the Industry Solutions section to see how you can save on insurance.

- **Yellow** (www.myyellow.com). A smaller carrier that can ship anywhere and provide specialized carrier services. For example, if you're shipping temperature-sensitive goods, Yellow can provide a solution for you.

When you need to ship items that require special care or service, such as a motorcycle or dining room table, you may want to use a trucking service. You can find a reliable service at a low price by using uShip.com (www.uship.com), where members can list the items they need to ship and receive bids from feedback-rated service providers, including moving companies, freight carriers, and independent drivers.

Skip Shipping Things Yourself

If you use a drop shipper (as explained in Chapter 6), you never have the goods in hand, so you don't have the responsibility for mailing them to the winning bidder. This is all taken care of by the drop shipper.

But you may have your own items that you prefer someone else to warehouse and send out for you if you are doing a high-volume business. This avoids the time and hassle of packing and shipping items yourself. To do this, you need to use a fulfillment company.

You have to determine whether your level of sales activities is high enough to make using a fulfillment company worthwhile. The downside to using a fulfillment company is cost—it's not a cheap service to you. But in deciding whether this alternative is the way to go, consider that using a fulfillment company means you don't have to spend money on storage or labor on packing and shipping. These cost savings offset the charges of the fulfillment company, to some extent.

eBay does not have its own fulfillment company. Fulfillment by Amazon (www.amazonservices.com/fulfillment/) now allows independent sellers, including eBay sellers, to have their items stored, packed, and shipped by Amazon.

Claims for Undelivered or Damaged Items

Despite your best efforts to pack and send your items to winning bidders, things happen. A FedEx plane crashes (remember Tom Hanks in *Castaway*?), or a piece of glassware you've double-boxed and bubble-wrapped arrives smashed nonetheless. How do you recover your money?

Each carrier has its own rules and procedures for getting your money back. For example, say your Express Mail package from the post office never arrives. You must submit a claim no earlier than 7 days but no later than 90 days from the date of mailing—the post office can provide you with a claims form. But when an item arrives damaged, claims should be submitted immediately (there is no 30-day waiting period or other time limit). Be prepared to present your proof of mailing (for example, the Express Mail slip), along with proof of the package's value. Your insurance slip from the post office is not proof of value; you need to show what the item sold for (for example, the eBay checkout page will do).

What can you recover? Just being reimbursed for postage won't make you whole. You want to recoup the value of the item that's been lost or damaged.

If you have insurance on the shipment, your recovery is limited to the declared value of the item you've insured.

Who makes the claim—you or the buyer? Usually you must make the claim, but you may need the buyer's cooperation. For example, say that piece of glassware that you sent through the post office arrived shattered. The buyer must bring the item, along with the original box and other shipping materials (for example, bubble wrap and popcorn) to his or her local post office. It will then be reviewed by a postal inspector.

The Least You Need to Know

- Make sure the buyer understands the shipping arrangement—including cost and method of shipping—to avoid any negative feedback.

- Wrap items properly to avoid breakage of delicate items, and take advantage of free shipping supplies.

- Use online services to simplify your shipping chores, including using online shipping calculators and scheduling personal pickups from carriers.

- Decide which shipping method works best for your item, taking into account the speed of delivery, the cost of insurance, and other factors.

Chapter 10

Marketing Miracles

In This Chapter

- ◆ Devising a marketing strategy to increase sales
- ◆ Using your website to boost your eBay sales
- ◆ *Advertising* your company and your eBay selling activities
- ◆ Driving traffic to your eBay listings
- ◆ Managing your customers to generate repeat business

According to cosmetics mogul Esteé Lauder, "If you don't sell, it's not the product that's wrong—it's you." Items don't sell themselves; there's just too much competition today on eBay. You have to go the extra mile to develop relationships with customers so they'll bid on your items repeatedly. You can't be a passive seller, no matter how great a listing you create. You have to do more, reaching out to existing and new customers through your own website and a slew of promotional activities. Most important, you have to create a plan of attack so you won't waste your time and money on non-productive marketing activities.

In this chapter, you'll learn how to develop your marketing plan so you can continue to grow your business. You'll see how your own separate website can be used to stimulate your eBay sales. And you'll find out about lots of no- and low-cost marketing ideas to drive business your way.

Creating a Marketing Plan

Like a business plan that's used to outline the course of a company for the next several years, a *marketing* plan maps out your strategies for *promoting* your business.

def•i•ni•tion

Many people use the words *marketing, advertising,* and *promotion* interchangeably, but they're distinct activities (though, admittedly, the lines are often blurred). **Marketing** is an umbrella term that covers all activities used to enhance your business visibility and generate sales. **Advertising** means informing the public of the features and benefits of your products. **Promotion** is a way of stimulating an immediate sale, such as offering a discount coupon.

The marketing plan should address these key issues:

- **Your current standing.** Identify your target market and what you are doing to attract buyers and generate sales.

- **Your competitors.** Identify who you are up against and what they're doing to market themselves.

- **Your marketing objectives.** Set numbers on how much you want to grow your sales within a set period (such as increase sales by 10 percent over the next six months) or expand your customer base (such as adding customers from new demographics, for example, selling to men when only women have previously purchased your items).

- **Your marketing strategies.** Spell out what you plan to do to achieve the goals you've set, including your advertising and promotional activities. These are discussed later in this chapter.

- **Your budget.** Determine how much money you plan to devote to implement your marketing strategies.

There's no set format for writing up your marketing plan—you can put it on the back of a cocktail napkin, if it serves your purpose, although it's much better if you keep the plan on your computer so you can update it periodically. Just make sure you cover all the elements that will help you take action.

You can use specialized software for writing a marketing plan, such as MarketingPlan Pro from Palo Alto Software (www.paloalto.com, cost: $179.95). You can get free guidance in creating your marketing plan by going to the Small Business Administration (SBA) at www.sba.gov/smallbusinessplanner/manage/marketandprice/ SERV_MARKETINGPLANS.html.

Writing your plan is only one step in your marketing process. You must follow through on the goals you've set and revisit your projections to see if your efforts are paying off. If not, you may need to revise your plans and come up with new ways to increase your sales. For example, be sure to track your sales figures so you can analyze them—determining which items sell best, what sales promotions are working, and what you need to do to improve sales.

A Separate but Equal Website

If you can handle every aspect of your sales on eBay, why do you need your own website? Simply put, with your own website, you can …

- **Establish credibility.** Having your own website shows buyers that you're not a fly-by-night seller but, rather, you're around to stay. There's a place where buyers can reach you.

- **Create a brand.** The buzzword of the decade, branding, means creating a business image for yourself, like Coca-Cola and Nike. You don't have to be a corporate giant like these companies to establish a business identity that relates to the items you sell. A business name and a logo displayed on your own website are an important way to brand yourself.

- **Drive traffic to your eBay auctions and store.** The greater your presence is on the Internet, the more likely it is that buyers will go to your listings on eBay, to view them and to bid on them. You can drive traffic directly to your eBay listings through your personal website by providing links to them.

Power Point

Earn a Store Referral Fee Credit for driving buyers from non-eBay sites to your eBay store. The credit is 75 percent of the Final Value Fees on purchases from your eBay store resulting from your marketing efforts.

- **Build your business.** You may have more to sell than what you list on eBay. You can use eBay to drive traffic to your website so buyers can view your complete catalog of merchandise. Some sellers use their websites for their high-end items and use eBay for bargains or sale items.

Setting Up Your Own Site

Setting up and maintaining a website can be an expensive undertaking. Unless you are a computer whiz, you may pay thousands of dollars to create a professional-looking website. Then you must pay monthly hosting fees for your site. And you'll want to continually update the material and information displayed there, incurring additional fees for computer assistance if you can't do it on your own.

The first step in creating your own website is selecting a name for it (called a domain name) and registering the name. You can't use a name that's already in use. To find out whether a domain name is taken, go to InterNIC (www.internic.net and click on the "Whois" link) and do a search for the name you want.

Auction Alert

If you don't yet have a name for your website, understand in choosing one that you can't incorporate *eBay* into the one you select. eBay won't give you permission to do so under any circumstances. If you violate this rule, you can be in violation of eBay trademark protection and be subject to penalties.

Take the time you need to find a name that will help to promote your business. It should be easy to remember and easy to spell. It shouldn't be too long (requiring extensive typing).

The name should also be representative of the type of merchandise you sell so that it is memorable. For example, Mountain Sprouts (www.mountainsprouts.com) is an online seller of children's outdoor sporting apparel ("Fun-ctional mountainwear"), and the name says it all.

To build your website, find a host (a company to store your site so people can access it) and get your site listed in search engines—of course, that's a subject for another book. (For more details on building a site of your own, check out *The Complete Idiot's Guide to Creating a Web Page & Blog, Sixth Edition,* by Paul McFedries.)

Tying Your Website to eBay

Obviously, at your website you want to capitalize on your association with eBay to drive traffic to your items for sale there. Having your own site is estimated to increase your eBay sales by 30 to 40 percent! eBay has very strict rules on what you can and cannot do on your own site with respect to eBay.

You can …

- **Mention your sales on eBay.** For example, you can say "Check out my sales on eBay."

◆ **Link your site to eBay.** Go to http://pages.ebay.com/services/buyandsell/ link-buttons.html to find instructions on how to set up a link. It's easy to do. You have a choice of two link icons: one says Go to eBay and the other My Listings on eBay. You can also link from your eBay About Me pages and/or your eBay Store to your own website, but you can't offer any non-eBay merchandise on these eBay pages.

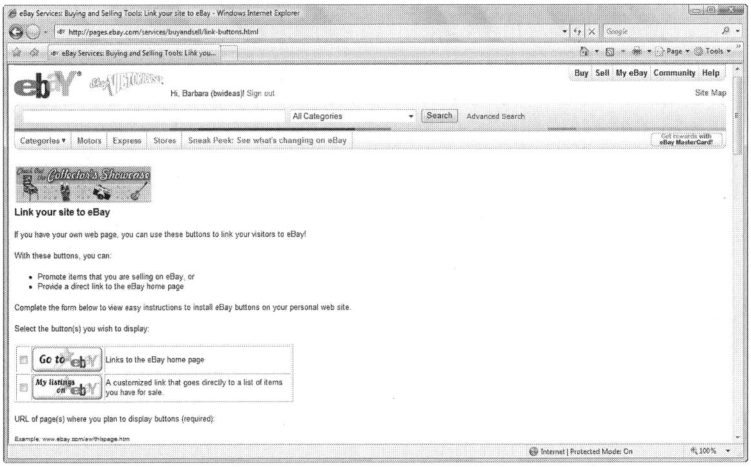

Figure 10.1

You can link your site to the eBay site.

You cannot …

◆ **Use the eBay logo without a written license agreement.** This permission isn't something normally granted to a mom-and-pop website.

◆ **Imply that you are endorsed by or associated with eBay.** If you are unsure whether your website copy may create a false impression that would put you in violation of eBay rules, you can e-mail eBay for its comments. You can join the eBay affiliate program, which entitles you to display an eBay banner and have a chance to earn money. This program is explained later in this chapter.

Generating Website Traffic

Just because you build a site does not necessarily mean that the customers will come to it. You must drive traffic to your site. In addition to capitalizing on your eBay connection, you need to make sure that you can reach consumers who are in an active shopping mode—they are on the web looking for something, and you want them to find you.

◆ **Make your site recognizable to search engines.** If you don't show up on the top few pages, you probably won't be seen at all—few viewers look beyond these pages. Search engine optimization (SEO) is the way to gain favorable placement on Google and other search engines. One of the ways to do this is with keywords—phrases and terms that relate to your items. These words must be included in the text on your web pages (preferably, the home page). You must also include information in the header section of your page (inside a meta content tag in the HTML header section, which is invisible to the browser but will be found by search engine spiders). This means that pages must have content, not merely pictures. You can find keywords at www.terapeak.com and www.wordtracker.com (each costs a monthly subscription fee).

◆ **Pay for placement on search engines.** You can't be ensured of a high listing unless you have the bucks.

Power Point

When you're ready to take your business to the next level, you can spend money to have your listings included in Internet search engines, such as Google and Yahoo!. You pay so that your keywords are included in these search engines; if someone is looking for something that includes your keyword, your listing will pop up (on Google, for example, keyword listings appear on the right column of the page).

◆ **Link up with others.** The more you're on the web, the more likely that search engines will find you and place you higher on their lists. You can increase your web visibility by linking up with other businesses that are not in direct competition with you. Contact any site you want to be listed on, and request a reciprocal link—you usually must agree to list that site on yours. Or you can join a webring, which is a group of websites linked to one another to form a ring so that a visitor goes from one site to the other until the ring is completed.

◆ **Enlist affiliates to sell for you.** Once you've grown to a size that commands respect, you can create an affiliate program in which other people will sell your items for you. As with the eBay affiliate program (discussed in Chapter 18), you must agree to pay commissions or fees to your affiliates. You can use online resources, such as ClickXChange.com (www.clickxchange.com), to develop your affiliate program.

Advertising

Advertising is a subject unto itself. Madison Avenue spends billions of dollars getting consumers to buy products of all kinds. You, of course, don't have billions of dollars to pay professional advertisers to promote your wares. You have to do it yourself. Fortunately, there are many no-cost and low-cost ways to let the public know you exist and drive traffic to your auction listings and store. Here are two ideas:

◆ **Stick your name and logo on everything.** Include it on your shipping labels, stationery, business cards, and every other item that leaves your desk.

◆ **Give away low-cost items with every purchase.** We once received a pen (imprinted with the seller's name and store address) when we received a shipment of a jacket we purchased.

One of the key questions always asked about advertising is how much to spend on this marketing activity. There's no fixed answer. Many people refer to a rule of thumb of 5 percent of revenues, but this is only a generalization—you must decide how much you can afford to spend. But whatever number you arrive at, make sure it is reasonable for the size of your business. Be sure to stick to your budgeted amount and review it constantly to see if you're getting your money's worth.

About Me Pages

eBay lets you create a promotional page in which you describe yourself and your business. It doesn't cost you anything and serves as free marketing. Display an About Me icon on your listings so that interested bidders can read more about you.

For example, you may want people to know where in the country you're located, how long you've been in business, and what items you specialize in. Many sellers also use the About Me page to describe their policies (such as whether they accept returns), shipping and handling details (such as whether deliveries are restricted to the United States), and payment methods.

To create your About Me page, go to the eBay site map and click the About Me link (on the right under Connect), or go directly to http://pages.ebay.com/community/aboutme.html. You can choose the step-by-step method or use your own HTML code. Enter your page content (the amount of content is limited to the page), and then review and submit it. You can add pictures as well as links to other websites (the only eBay-approved way of putting a link to your own website). You can edit your About Me page at any time by following these same steps.

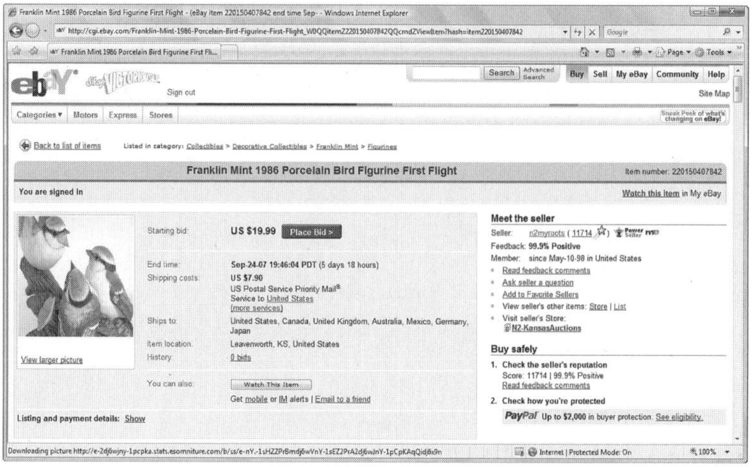

Figure 10.2

Include an About Me icon on your listing pages.

Free eBay Advertising

You can take advantage of the eBay format to advertise your company for free. When you list an item for auction, include information about your business, including the URL of your separate website. Just keep your copy within eBay guidelines—eBay is happy to have you promote your eBay store but not your outside selling activities.

If you have your own logo, a key element in branding your business, you can include it in your eBay listings, with these important restrictions: the size should be 310×90 pixels and must be in one of the following formats: .jpg, .bmp, .gif, or .png. Be sure to add your logo to the eBay Checkout pages and invoice e-mails as well.

Leverage your sales off of promotional days on eBay. These are days when eBay features certain types of items—such as guitars and clothing during the last week of June and the first week of July, and sports memorabilia and jerseys during the second and third weeks of September. Use these days to list items that are the same types as featured items. You'll find a calendar of upcoming events at http://pages.ebay.com/sellercentral/calendar.html.

Paid Advertising

When you can afford it, you may want to venture into advertising media to increase the public's awareness of your business. The methods you use and the amount of advertising you do are a function of your budget. If you have the money and your items are worth the investment, you might consider …

♦ **Print advertising.** When purchasing advertisement space in newspapers and magazines, always include your website and note that you have items listed for sale on eBay.

♦ **Web advertising.** You can pay to become a sponsored link on Google and other search engines so that your website and some information are displayed on the right side of the screen.

Creative No- and Low-Cost Marketing Ideas

Marketing is all about getting the word out there so people will look. Promotional activities you use to drive traffic to your eBay listings are a key way to attract bidders and buyers and to obtain sales.

Your promotional efforts are not a one-time thing. You must continually market your business. You may start out small-time, doing no- and low-cost things to get yourself noticed. But as your business expands and your budget permits, you may want to devote more resources to promotional activities.

For example, use discount coupons to bring repeat business. When you ship items to winning bidders, reward them with coupons that can be redeemed on future sales you conduct. Be sure to put an expiration date on their use (for example, good for 30 days), to encourage rapid repeat business. Make special offers, such as discounts on shipping for multiple purchases or for repeat customers. Include your business card with every package you ship, so customers can contact you directly when they're looking for a particular item and think you may be a good source for them.

eBay Chat Rooms, Discussion Boards, and Blogs

You can interact with the eBay community to discuss your questions and concerns, share experiences, and learn from other participants. eBay makes it possible to join *chat rooms* and *discussion boards* to find other people with interests and concerns similar to yours. You get to know others in the eBay community, and, more important, they get to know you and, perhaps, your area of expertise.

There are general chat rooms and category-specific chat rooms ranging from topics such as advertising to trading cards. Over time, you can get to know other participants and may develop new customers (or even friends) in the process.

def•i•ni•tion

Chat rooms are online places where you can converse through typed messages in real time. As with instant messaging, your typed chat is displayed almost instantaneously, and someone can reply directly to you for everyone else to see. **Discussion boards** are places to post questions and answers.

As with chat rooms, there are general discussion boards and category-specific discussion boards ranging from topics such as animals to vintage clothing. For example, you can learn about the latest selling tips, tools, and resources to increase your sales activities through Seller Central, a discussion board for eBay sellers (http://forums. ebay.com/db2/forum.jsp?forum=143).

Even though you're registered on eBay, you must register separately to join this discussion board. If you've never participated in a discussion board, there's a tutorial to help you learn the ropes.

Today blogs (short for web logs) are the rage for venting opinions, say about a particular eBay experience, sharing your passions, such as your love for a baseball cards, and indirectly marketing wares. A blog can help to establish you as an expert in your category, which will lead to greater sales.

eBay enables you to easily start to blog on its site. Just go to http://blogs.ebay.com and click View Your Blog to begin.

Mailings

Reach out and touch someone—a customer or a potential customer. You can do this to inform them of upcoming sales, special promotions, or other details. For example, if you are opening an eBay store, you'll want to inform the public of this event. Do it with a mailing—either snail mail or e-mail.

You can rent a mailing list, usually for a charge. There are many ways to find lists: through list brokers (listed in your local telephone directory or online), directly from online sites, or even through your public library. The cost may be free (for example, if you use a list from the library) or costly if you buy an extensive, well-tested list. Better yet, create your own list by collecting e-mail addresses from those who bid on your items, ask questions about your auctions, or otherwise communicate with you. It takes time to build your list but this method has the advantage of ensuring the people on the list are interested in the type of items you sell.

Auction Alert _____

When e-mailing multiple parties at the same time, avoid breaking antispam rules created by the CAN-SPAM Act of 2003. For example, you must have an honest subject line and provide an opt-out option for recipients to be deleted from your mailing list. Include in your list only those who have agreed to receive messages from you, such as customers or potential ones. If you don't, you not only risk penalty, but your messages may be deleted or blocked by antispam software. To learn about antispam rules, go to www.ftc.gov/bcp/conline/edcams/spam/business.htm.

You can also include flyers, coupons, or other promotional materials when you send items to winning bidders.

Gift Certificates

Everyone enjoys a freebie now and then. You can stimulate customers to buy by giving away your own coupons for merchandise discounts or free shipping, for example, as rewards for past purchases.

You can also use an eBay gift certificate to reward existing customers or bring in new customers. The gift certificates can be used by a buyer for any item purchased on eBay for which PayPal is an accepted method of payment. (You must use PayPal to purchase the gift certificate.)

You must buy each gift certificate individually (because you are required to enter the recipient's e-mail address for verification purposes). The amount of the certificate can range from $5 to $500, at your option. You can include a gift card with each certificate. The gift certificate can be sent to the recipient by e-mail or you can print it out and deliver it yourself.

Remember that giving away a gift certificate is a real expense and something you don't want to do routinely. It may make sense to reward loyal buyers on high-end items or for a special sale.

Gift certificates may be a good holiday gift for special customers as well as your vendors. Gift certificates can encourage your customers to continue to shop with you during this season. And you can use them to thank vendors for their association with you.

Auction Alert _____

Just because you give away a gift certificate doesn't require the recipient to use it with you—he or she can redeem it on any eBay purchase that accepts PayPal.

As mentioned earlier, you don't have to use eBay gift certificates; you can create your own and point out to customers that they are redeemable only on your sales. Look at the eBay gift certificate to get an idea of the information you might want to include on your personalized gift certificate.

Alternatively, you can use MyStoreRewards (www.mystorerewards.com), a program that encourages shoppers to repeatedly buy from you. After you join the program, your buyers accumulate credit on each purchase and so have good reason to buy again from you. Over 250,000 auctions have used this service thus far. Cost: $7.95 per month, plus 1 penny for each e-mail invitation and reminder you send to customers and 10 cents for each rebate reward issued.

Publicize Your Expertise

A great marketing tool is writing an eBay review about a product experience or a guide about an area in which you have special knowledge, such as an area of collectibles (there are more than 13,000 guides on collectibles). For example, there's a guide on the care and cleaning of UGG boots. Guess what! Along side the guide is a listing of the writer's UGG boots for sale. Guide readers can rate the usefulness of the guide and guide writers can enter the inner circle of the Top 25, 100, 1,000, or 5,000 Reviewers, which gives you another icon to add to all your listings.

For more information about reviews and guides, go to http://reviews.ebay.com.

Using the eBay PowerSeller Status

Becoming an eBay PowerSeller isn't only recognition of the sales level you've achieved. It is a status that you can use to leverage more business. Customers gain confidence in buying from PowerSellers because they are assured that the sellers are for real and will deliver on their promises.

Display the PowerSeller icon next to your seller's user ID to alert viewers to your status. This is not done automatically; it is a preference you must set with your listings (go to My eBay; Preferences; Logos and Branding).

Requirements for becoming a PowerSeller are discussed in Chapter 17.

Keeping Tabs on Your Customers

Customers are a precious commodity—it's a marketing axiom that it costs more to bring in a new one than to retain an existing one. You want to build up a database of your customers so you can easily contact them when you want—to let them know about a new sale or promotional activity.

You can create your own database using Microsoft Excel or any other spreadsheet software. Customize your information so you record what particular customers have purchased. This enables you to approach them with similar items for sale.

Alternatively, you can use various tools to build your database (see Chapter 20).

Soliciting Positive Feedback

One of the main ways in which customers can have confidence in dealing with perfect strangers on eBay is to rely on feedback from past customers. The level of feedback has almost risen to cult status—the more feedback ratings you've achieved, the higher your status is. This status is denoted by colors and stars.

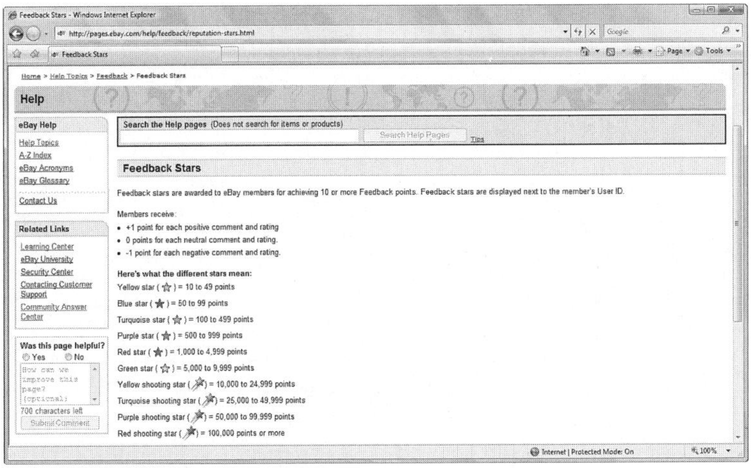

Figure 10.3

On eBay, you can receive star ratings.

Here are two suggestions for managing your feedback rating:

- **Solicit feedback.** Ask a customer for positive feedback, and agree to give a similar rating to the customer. Do this in your post-auction communication. If the customer hasn't posted anything, send a reminder.

Power Point

Use the eBay Selling Manager to automate the feedback you leave for your customers. This is a great time saver for you. You can store up to 10 positive feedback comments (go to http://pages.ebay.com/help/sell/leave-feedback-for-buyer.html).

- ◆ **Contest undeserved negative feedback.** If you receive negative feedback that you believe is undeserved, take steps to have it removed. Follow the eBay Feedback Removal Policy at http://pages.ebay.com/help/policies/feedback-abuse-withdrawal.html. You may be able to remove the negative remarks by mutual consent. If not, proceed to a dispute-resolution service by Square Trade (www.squaretrade.com), a company that eBay has certified for this purpose (there's a fee for this service).

Building Up Goodwill

Your name and reputation are key to standing out in the eBay crowd. But recognize that it takes time and effort to build up goodwill. Don't expect that your first listing will put you in the winner's circle—it may be years before you command the kind of goodwill achieved by long-time eBay sellers.

The Least You Need to Know

- ◆ You need to devise a marketing plan that can be used as a roadmap for your advertising and promotional activities.

- ◆ You can benefit from having your own separate website, using it to drive customers to your eBay auctions and store.

- ◆ Advertise your business on everything you do—attach your name and logo to shipping labels, business cards, and your personal website.

- ◆ Use no-cost and low-cost strategies, such as participating in eBay chat rooms and discussion boards, to drive traffic your way.

- ◆ Take good care of your customers so they'll think highly of you, leaving you positive feedback and buying from you again.

Chapter 11

International Sales

In This Chapter

- ◆ Deciding whether to deal with foreign customers
- ◆ Taking payments from customers abroad
- ◆ Becoming accustomed to Customs
- ◆ Shipping your items overseas
- ◆ Avoiding international scams and fraud

Selling on the Internet gives you the opportunity to reach customers at just about any point on the globe. But trading outside of the United States entails special issues you won't face with domestic customers: the type of currency you'll use, how you'll ship, and, most important, how you can avoid fraud.

In this chapter, you'll read about the pros and cons of selling to international customers. You'll gain an understanding of Customs requirements. You'll find out what methods of payment are preferable from non-American customers and how to ship abroad. Finally, you'll learn how to spot frauds and avoid them.

Overseas Customers

While any one of the approximately 143 million registered eBay users beyond the United States can view your auctions and eBay store listings, you don't have to agree to sell to overseas customers. You may want to limit sales to domestic customers to avoid headaches. (Remember that Canada is a foreign country.)

Auction Alert _____

If you decide to accept bids from foreign buyers, make sure you list measurements in metrics and clearly state your shipping and payment policies. Also, if you receive an unusually large number of customers from a particular country, it won't hurt to learn about them so you can make your listings even more user-friendly to foreigners.

You can try to restrict potential buyers from outside the United States from bidding by posting a disclaimer:

ATTENTION INTERNATIONAL BIDDERS: This auction is for buyers in the United States only. If you are an international bidder, including a person from Canada, and want to bid, contact us _prior_ to bidding to obtain individual permission. This may be granted after you accept the shipping costs quoted to you.

You can also check an international buyer's feedback; if it is good, you can waive your bidding restriction.

You can opt to block international customers from bidding by creating a Buyer Requirements Bidding List. To do this, use the Additional Information section of the Sell Your Item form and check the selection "Block Buyers Who:" for countries to which you do not ship. But before you block out anyone, consider that you are excluding a huge number of potential customers, who may be willing and able to buy your items.

What about when you want to buy rather than sell overseas? You need to learn the rules of the road and, most of all, steer clear of any sellers who seem dubious. Check their feedback before bidding. eBay has antifraud software designed to weed out unscrupulous international sellers, but it isn't fail-safe.

Currency

With today's international e-commerce, five currencies are in widespread use: U.S. dollar ($), Canadian dollar ($ CD), pound sterling (£), yen (¥), and euro (€).

Make it clear on your listings that you accept payment _only_ in U.S. dollars, if you want to do so. However, you can accept any of 16 currencies when using PayPal, an option that can make you more customer friendly. Find these currencies at www.paypal.com/cgi-bin/webscr?cmd=_display-xborder-fees-outside&countries=.

Getting Paid Through PayPal or Otherwise

When selling to a customer who is outside the United States, the payment method becomes even more important than for domestic transactions.

You can agree to accept PayPal, which now is available in 190 countries and regions. There are about 153 million account members.

PayPal does not provide any protection for sales outside the United States, Canada, and the UK; international sales other than Canada and the UK are specifically excluded from the PayPal Seller Protection Policy. However, PayPal offers two tips to minimize possible fraud:

♦ Never ship to a U.S. user at a non-U.S. address. You may be shipping to a non-U.S. user who is merely claiming to be a U.S. user. Check the buyer's account type in the payment's transaction details to be sure.

♦ Ship only to the address on the transaction details page, called a Confirmed Address. An address is a Confirmed Address if the buyer's credit card billing address is the same as his or her shipping address.

Auction Alert

You may not want to accept any type of payment other than bank checks for overseas purchases. The reason: you have no protection against chargebacks. When using PayPal, a foreign buyer can tell PayPal she didn't get the goods, and your account will be charged back; the same is true with credit cards.

Customs

When you send something to another country, your item must clear Customs here (the country of export) as well as the place you're sending it to (the country of import). To do so, your item must be accompanied by the appropriate documentation—Customs forms describing the contents of the package and sometimes other documents.

An overseas buyer may ask you to state on the Customs document that the $1,000 silver punchbowl he purchased only cost $25 or is a gift from you (his supposed uncle), so he can avoid paying duty in his country. *Never, never,* agree to falsify a

U.S. Customs form. First of all, it's illegal to do so. But also, if the item fails to arrive, you have no protection for the full value of the lost item. It's wise to include a statement in your listings that you will not underreport the value of items for Customs, and then follow through on this pledge.

Documents for Exporting Goods

When you ship internationally through the U.S. Postal Service or most major carriers, the export document process is seamless; you merely complete a single form (usually PS Form 2976-A, explained later in this chapter) and the carrier does the rest. But when you ship certain items or are shipping to certain countries, you may have to complete a package of forms. Here are some basic types of export forms you may need to use (depending on the country to which you are shipping):

Power Point

It's always a good idea to include a copy of any Customs and shipping documents *inside* the package. This will ensure that the item can pass Customs if forms attached on the outside fall off.

- **Shipper's export declaration.** This document is used to compile export statistics.

- **Certificate of origin.** This document shows the Customs authorities at the country of import where the item came from. Your shipper certifies this information based on the information you provide. It is necessary because some countries restrict certain imports. In some countries, this document isn't required.

- **Your invoice.** Your invoice should detail your sales transaction—a description of the item and its cost. Again, it is sometimes required by the country of import.

- **NAFTA certificate of origin.** This document is used when sending items of no more than $1,000 to either Mexico or Canada. Under the North American Free Trade Agreement (NAFTA), preferential treatment is given to items sent within the United States, Canada, and Mexico. You can complete the form in English, even when sending to Mexico.

- **Country-specific documents.** The country you're mailing to may have its own requirements, so ask your carrier.

AES*Direct* (www.aesdirect.gov) is the automated export system sponsored by the U.S. Census Bureau. This Internet-based system enables you to file the shipper's export document electronically instead of using a paper form. You can learn how to use this electronic system by taking an online tutorial.

What's the Custom of Customs?

The rules in each country can differ, depending on the item you're shipping. For example, *documents* are treated differently than nondocuments. In some countries, blank CD-ROMs are classified as nondocuments.

All countries require you to declare the value of the item you're shipping (value for this purpose is the amount of the winning bid). Many buyers on eBay request that you falsify documents to state that the item is a gift of no value or fudge the actual value of the item so that they save on import duties. Again, never do this. All countries agree that only an actual gift should be marked as a gift, and undervaluing or mismarking an item is illegal.

def•i•ni•tion

An item that is typed, written, or printed and has no commercial value is called a **document**. But different countries have broader or narrower definitions of what constitutes a document.

When items are returned to you, the buyer may be entitled to a refund of any duties or import taxes that have been paid. Ask the buyer what forms or information are required from you to enable him or her to obtain that refund (also called a duty drawback).

A Few Forms, No Headaches

Documentation from the USPS is easy (the form you use depends on whether you want insurance for the item):

- **Customs CN 22 (PS Form 2976), Sender's Declaration.** This is a simple form on which you list the name and address for you and the buyer, describe the contents, and list its value. You must certify that the item is not prohibited by postal regulations. This is often called the "short form." Some countries require the "long form" (below) in all cases (https://webapps.usps.com/customsforms/helppickaform.htm).

- **Customs Declaration and Dispatch Note (PS Form 2976-A).** This is a duplicate form containing the same information as on the CN 22. This form is used when insuring the item. It is often referred to as the "long form."

You can complete and print your documents online instead of completing paper forms. Go to www.usps.com/global/customsforms.

Other shippers, such as FedEx or UPS, will provide you with forms to be completed for international shipping.

Using Customs Brokers

If you are doing a high-volume business abroad, you may want to use an agent to handle the Customs work on your behalf. A Customs broker can be an individual or a company, but it must be licensed by the U.S. Department of the Treasury to act in this capacity.

Here's what a Customs broker can do: prepare and file Customs documents; arrange for payment of duties, where necessary; take steps to release the items held in Customs; and represent you in any Customs matters. A good Customs broker should also advise you on shipping methods and routes.

> **Power Point**
>
> If you want to use a Customs broker, consider one who is a member of the National Customs Brokers and Forwarders Association of America, Inc. (www.ncbfaa.org), or the International Federation of Customs Brokers Associations (www.ifcba.org). To see whether a company is a member, you can do an online search of its directory.

Many Customs brokers work with eBay sellers to provide solutions for cross-border selling. For example, A&A Contract Brokers Ltd. (www.aacb.com) provides Customs broker services as well as warehousing and distribution for your items in Canada (which can reduce your shipping costs and eliminate the need for Customs forms). The company hosted an eBay workshop covering the mystery of Customs in 2004 that you can still read at http://forums.ebay.com/db2/thread.jspa?forumID=93&threadID=400092188.

Watch Out for Fraud

You may encounter misrepresentations and other fraud when dealing with international customers. This is especially so in certain countries, the most frequently noted country of which is Nigeria.

An Educated eBay Seller

If you have experienced fraud, you can try to prevent it from happening to someone else. You can alert certain international consumer-protection agencies by going to eConsumer (www.econsumer.gov) and filing a complaint; more than 2 dozen governments share this information. Other places to contact include Interpol (www.interpol.com).

A tip-off to potential fraud is having a buyer in one country direct shipment to another. Carol sold scarves to a buyer in the Congo who requested that the items be shipped to Spain. The goods were charged to a credit card; after she shipped, the buyer requested a chargeback from the credit card company. Carol was out the scarves and the money.

Always Insure

When sending items worth more than a few dollars, it makes sense to insure them. Unfortunately, there is a lot of theft overseas—in post offices and private delivery companies (more in some countries and less in others). A buyer who has paid for an item and fails to receive it through no fault of yours is upset nonetheless and may not be a return customer—insurance can at least let you refund the money without suffering an economic loss.

If you don't insure, then at least use some shipping method or tool to ensure that the item arrived, such as delivery confirmation or tracking the package. For example, PayPal requires you to use a signature confirmation on all packages over $250 to be eligible for its Seller Protection Policy.

Use Escrow Services

When you are dealing in higher-priced items—either buying or selling them overseas—consider using an escrow service for protection. As a seller, your item won't be delivered to the buyer until payment has been received; as a buyer, the payment won't be disbursed to the seller until shipment is complete.

Numerous escrow services can be used internationally—only use an eBay-approved service. eBay has approved certain escrow services when dealing in specific markets, although you are not restricted to these markets when using the following services:

- ◆ **Australia (eBay.com.au users)—EscrowAustralia (www.escrowaustralia. com.au).** Here you deal in the Australian dollar (AU$) and track items via international trade partners with local knowledge and experience. You must register to use this service (registration is free). Cost: AU$9.90 and up. There is a calculator on this site to compute the buyer and seller amounts.

- ◆ **Italy and Spain (eBay.com.it and eBay.com.es users)—Escrow! (www. escrow-europa.com).** Fees are based in euros (an international currency converter on the site can help you see the fees in U.S. dollars). Cost: for items up to

$5,000 or €5.000, or £3,500, the fee is 3.8 percent when charged to a credit card (which must be in euros), or 2 percent when paid with a bank transfer (minimum cost is 8 euros for credit cards and 4 euros for bank transfers); lower rates apply to higher-priced transactions.

◆ **Germany (eBay.com.de)—iloxx Safe Trade (www.iloxx.de).** Go to Google first to obtain a translation of the site if your German isn't adequate. Fees are based in euros. Cost: minimum €4,50.

◆ **France, Netherlands, Belgium, Denmark, Sweden, and Norway (eBay.com.fr, eBay.com.nl, eBay.com.be, eBay.com.dk, eBay.com.se, and eBay.com.no)—Triple Deal (www.tripledeal.com).** Currently, this escrow service operates in 10 countries and projects worldwide operations soon. Cost: items less than €250 have a fee of €4,50; other fees apply to higher-priced items (determined on a per-transaction basis, so if you sell several items to the same buyer in one transaction, the fee is determined accordingly).

Shipping

Unless you use drop shippers or fulfillment companies, the burden is on you to wrap your items and ship them to the winning bidder. Although you don't bear this cost—you bill the buyer for any shipping, handling, and insurance costs—you still want to minimize costs wherever possible to keep buyers happy.

The shipping method you use depends in part on the type of items you're sending and the country of destination. For example, if you are sending a very large package, you may not be able to use the USPS because of its size limitations. But it has been our experience that, when mailing to Italy, the USPS is the safest method (there are too many stories of thefts involving other carriers), provided you're within the package size accepted at the post office. Of course, in some other countries, private carriers may be preferred over the USPS.

Power Point

No matter which method you use to ship items abroad, keep in mind that delivery depends in part on how fast the items clear Customs in the foreign country. You have no control over this—items can be held up in Customs for months! You can only ship promptly; actual delivery depends on the buyer's Customs experience. It's helpful to inform foreign buyers about the date you shipped items and provide them with any tracking information so they can see where the hang ups are and you can avoid negative feedback.

USPS

You can use the United States Postal Service to send items abroad using standard or expedited services. The type of service you select affects your ability to track the package, how quickly it will arrive, and what you'll be charged (the amount of which is usually borne by the buyer). Insurance limits vary by country of destination.

In May 2007, the Post Office simplified your international shipping and mailing choices:

♦ **Priority Mail International** (which is essentially Parcel Post, but a bit faster). This enables you to send packages just about anywhere, with delivery on average from 6 to 10 days (depending on where you are and where the item is going). Cost: Starts at $16 for Canada and $16.50 for Mexico (flat rate boxes for up to 20lbs are available for $23); prices are higher for other countries (such as $37 for flat rate to the UK or minimum $20 for by-weight).

♦ **Global Express Guaranteed (GXG).** This can be used to send items to more than 200 countries for arrival within 1 to 3 days, with tracking available. Cost: starts at $28.50 to Canada, $28.75 to Mexico, and $37 to the UK

♦ **Express Mail International.** This can be used when mailing to more than 190 countries for arrival in 3 to 5 days, with tracking available to major destinations. Cost: starts at $22 for Canada and Mexico; $25 for other countries.

If you want to see the complete rate table for international mailings, you can view USPS Publication 51 at http://pe.usps.gov/text/pub51/welcome.htm.

UPS, FedEx, and DHL

You can use private carriers in the United States to ship your items overseas. Look for the following when selecting your carrier:

♦ **Destination.** Make sure the carrier will deliver to the location you want. Each has its own restrictions. For example, FedEx in India will only ship to limited locations, which may be miles from where the buyer is located. Ask your buyer for guidance in this regard; if he or she has previously purchased goods from the United States, the buyer will have already worked out a shipping solution.

♦ **Package size.** Check the carrier's size and content restrictions.

♦ **Shipping alternatives.** Check the delivery time for the different shipping options each carrier offers. Some may be a few days; others can take weeks to certain locations.

♦ **Cost.** Check the cost for postage and insurance. Also determine whether there are additional fees charged by the carrier to act as your customer's broker. While the post office doesn't do this, private carriers may have added costs, which are charged to the sender.

Be aware that if the buyer fails to pay Customs charges, the shipper can recoup the funds from you.

The Least You Need to Know

♦ Selling to customers outside of the United States can entail added headaches but can be worth the effort.

♦ Decide carefully on the method of payment you'll accept from people outside the United States.

♦ Make sure you understand the Customs forms required or work with a knowledgeable Customs broker who can help you.

♦ Use escrow services and insurance to minimize any problems from fraud.

Part 4

So Now Your eBay Business Is Growing!

Running an eBay business is much like running any other small business. In addition to the fun part of selling, you have to attend to the drier details of running a business. Maybe it doesn't sound like fun, but you don't have a choice.

Some fundamentals in running a business involve keeping track of revenue and expenses and paying taxes. Even if you work with an accountant to handle these matters, you have plenty of responsibilities yourself and must know what they are to stay out of trouble. And it may be time for your business to grow up and incorporate or become a limited liability company. Doing this as well as following other laws is important to avoid problems.

This part of the book focuses on things you need to know to run an eBay business, including keeping books and records, paying taxes, preparing for the unexpected with insurance and disaster plans, and making sure you follow the law. You'll also learn how to look for potential fraud so you can avoid it.

Keeping Books, Records, and Inventory

In This Chapter

- ◆ What you should know to set up your systems
- ◆ The importance of tracking your inventory
- ◆ Why you should save receipts and which ones to save
- ◆ The importance of watching your financial numbers

The fun part of your eBay business is undoubtedly finding your items, selling them, and, most important, getting paid. But you can't ignore the mundane chores you also have to do when you run a business, which includes keeping track of your activities. You need to maintain good records of what you buy and sell, and the expenses you ring up in doing these things.

In this chapter, you'll see why it's important to be thorough in tracking your sales and expenses. Then you'll learn how to set up your records and track your inventory. You'll also find out how long you should keep your paperwork and why watching your financial numbers helps you remain profitable.

Why Bother with Paperwork?

You may be casual about keeping track of your household finances—putting receipts in a shoebox or tossing them. At tax time, you wade through your canceled checks and scraps of paper to come up with the numbers for your income tax return. But you can't use this approach for your business; you *must* keep formal books and records.

As bothersome as this sounds, there are good reasons for doing so:

◆ First, these records will help you know how your business is doing—are you making a profit or are you in the hole?

◆ Second, the tax law requires you to keep records! You don't have any choice in the matter. You'll find more about taxes in Chapter 16.

◆ Third, records are essential if you want to borrow money from the bank or credit union for your business. Applications for loans ask for reams of numbers about your business, and the only way to supply this information is by turning to the records you've kept.

Tracking Your Progress

It's not enough to say you're doing as well as you can. You want to know if the way in which you're doing it is working for you. Are your ads drawing sales? Are the items you're selling bringing in bids? Are the winning bids sufficient to give you a reasonable profit? Are you paying the least you can for insurance? Do you have enough income to pay your bills as they fall due? You can't know the answer to these questions unless you can turn to your records.

For example, do you know what gross profit or profit margins are and what yours are? You may be selling like crazy and bringing in revenue but not really making a penny, and you may not even realize it. Let's take things one step at a time.

◆ **Gross profit** is the starting point for determining profitability. Gross profit is figured by subtracting the cost of the inventory you've sold from the revenue you reaped on your sales.

◆ **Gross profit margin** is a percentage showing your business efficiency (how profitable you really are). Gross profit margin is figured by dividing your gross profit by your total revenues. The higher the percentage is, the better off you are.

Understanding Your Tax Responsibilities

Even if you could justify in your mind why you don't need any formal bookkeeping for your business, the tax law overrules you. It says you must keep not just any records, but *good* records of your income, expenses, assets, and liabilities.

These records enable you to properly report on your tax return all of the income you receive in your business, as well as claim all of the write-offs to which you are entitled. Remember that time you drove from your home in New Jersey to Adamstown, Pennsylvania, to explore (and hopefully get things at a steal from) the antique shops on a glorious fall weekend? If you didn't keep track of what it cost you for this trip, forget about trying to remember six months later when you're preparing your return.

You must produce records if the IRS asks for them. This can happen if you're unlucky enough to be audited and the IRS questions a certain deduction you've claimed or income you supposedly failed to report. Technically, the tax law requires that your business records be available at all times for inspection by the IRS. You must retain them for a minimum of three years (the usual time in which the IRS can examine a return), but it's useful to retain some records even longer than required. For example, if you buy equipment for your business, you'll need to save the paperwork for the full time you use the equipment, and then for at least three years thereafter.

An Educated eBay Seller

Find detailed guidance on record keeping from Uncle Sam. Download IRS Publication 583, "Starting a Business and Keeping Records," from www.irs.gov. Take a free online tutorial in basic bookkeeping from the Small Business Administration (SBA) at www.onlinewbc.gov/docs/finance/bkpg_basic1.html#how.

Financial Reporting Reasons

Maybe you think you'll never need or want a bank loan. But as your business grows or you are ready to take it to the next level, you can use additional capital to buy more inventory so you can make more money on your sales. In order to get the money you need, from a bank or even a private individual, you'll have to show the following financial statements:

def•i•ni•tion _____

The **income statement** for listing revenue and expenses within a set period also goes by several other names, including profit-and-loss (P&L) statement, earnings statement, and statement of operations.

♦ A **balance sheet** listing your assets, liabilities, and what you've already invested in the business (your equity) at a set point (such as the end of each year). You'll probably have to provide separate balance sheets for your business and personal holdings.

♦ An *income statement* showing the income and expenses of your business during a set period (usually at the end of each quarter of the year or at the end of the year).

Setting Up Your System

You can't water your garden unless you put in an irrigation system. And you can't build your business if you don't have a system for keeping track of your sales and expenses.

There's no single system you should or must use. I'll give you some suggestions, but you can use whatever method enables you to stay on top of your numbers and properly report your transactions. Your bookkeeping system should include the following:

♦ **Chart of accounts.** This is a list of accounts or categories that you will track in the general ledger. Examples of accounts include rent, utilities, advertising, insurance, and Internet fees.

♦ **General ledger.** This is the main record of your business's income and expenses, assets and liabilities, and owner's equity (your investment in the business).

♦ **Accounts receivable statement.** This is the total amount owed to you from sales that remain uncollected.

♦ **Inventory listing.** This is made of the items you hold for sale to customers.

In general, you want a system that's easy to use and will make your life as simple as it can for a business owner. The simplest way to keep track of your sales is to list your totals for each day. This way, you can total sales for each month and then get a grand total for the year. This is your system for keeping a record of your income; I'll explain the way to put your system to work in just a moment.

When it comes to keeping track of expenses, things can get a little more complex. As I already told you, set up headings (or "accounts") for each type of expense you usually have, whether they occur monthly or annually or at some other time frequency. Then record, day by day, any expenses you have under each of your headings.

You can get as detailed or fancy as you want. For example, under the account titled Utilities, you can create subaccounts for electricity, gas, and other utility costs.

 Auction Alert

> If you have more than one business, you must keep separate books and records for each one. For example, if your main business is consulting and your sideline is eBay, keep two separate sets of books—one for the consulting business and the other for your eBay business.

Paper Journals

Remember Bob Cratchit in Charles Dickens's *A Christmas Carol*, bent over his desk late into the evening every night? He was keeping the books for Ebenezer Scrooge. The principles of record keeping haven't changed much since then. The aim is to write down everything you do each day for business—record every sale you complete and everything you spend.

Let's say that, for the most part, you pay everything that you buy for your business by check and, for some unfathomable reason, you don't want to use software. Then it makes sense to use a check disbursement journal to record your expenses. The following table provides a sample of how you can set up and use this type of journal. Any expense for which there is no heading is listed under the general account with a special notation explaining the type of expense.

Check Disbursement Journal

Day	Paid to	Check Number	Phone	Car	Supplies	General Account	
2	Ma Bell	68	$86.74				
2	Assured Ins.	69				Business policy	$359.00
4	Hi Gas	70		$119.20			
6	Office Co.	71			$84.44		
7	USPS	72				Postage	$102.07

You can find journals for your bookkeeping in any office-supply store (or online at eBay). Look for them in the section on account books. You'll find them called account books, journals, columnar books, and record books. One journal can last you for years.

Or you can simply buy a pad of columnar paper. This is special paper with 2 to 36 columns that you can use to report your expenses.

Software to Simplify Your Life

Remember the paperless society we were all promised with the advent of the personal computer in the 1970s? You need only look in the wastebasket by the side of your desk to know that this has turned out to be a myth. But there are certainly some things you can now do—and do very well—without paper. Keeping your business records on your computer is one of them.

You can use a software program or an online solution specially designed for business record keeping. You're on the computer a good part of the day anyway with your eBay activities, so why not devote a few minutes more each day to track your income and expenses?

Off-the-shelf accounting products will do everything you need them to do and more. The product you choose depends in part on the amount of business you do. A simple solution will work for modest businesses. Once you grow and need to integrate many activities beyond eBay, you may want to use a more sophisticated accounting product. In any case, it's usually a better idea to use an online product—not only do you create great records, but you're also assured that they are protected in case of a disaster. If you use software, then you should back up data to protect it from catastrophe.

For those just starting out, the easiest accounting solutions include:

◆ KeepMore from SageFire (www.keepmore.net) is an easy-to-use online product (you don't need to know anything about accounting to use it). Best of all: if you authorize eBay to share your transaction information, then all your sales will be entered automatically; you don't have to do a thing. Cost: $19.95 per month.

◆ Office Accounting Express from Microsoft (http://office.microsoft.com/en-us/accountingexpress/FX101729681033.aspx) is another easy-to-use product to track expenses and all eBay activities. Cost: free.

◆ Peachtree First Accounting (www.peachtree.com) provides basic accounting tools. Cost: $69.99.

◆ Simple Start Online from Intuit (www.quickbooks.com/simplestart) helps you track money in and money out. Cost: $9.95 a month. The software version is free, or $99, depending on the version you select. This product also works with eBay Accounting Assistant to export eBay data into your books (explained later in this chapter).

For more extensive accounting solutions, such as expanded payroll functions that may be necessary when you have employees, there are many other choices, including:

◆ Office Accounting from Microsoft (http://office.microsoft.com/en-us/accounting/default.aspx). This product enables you to save money on credit card processing and contains eBay and PayPal tools. Cost: varies.

◆ Peachtree Pro Accounting (www.peachtree.com). This software includes all accounting essentials. Cost: $169.99. ePeachtree online accounting services start at $150 per year.

◆ QuickBooks Pro from Intuit (www.quickbooks.com). Use this product for all accounting functions, including tracking inventory and accepting credit card payments. Cost: online at $19.95 a month; software at $199.95 for Windows or Mac. Export your eBay data to QuickBooks using Accounting Assistant (http://pages.ebay.com/accountingassistant). Cost: free, but must be subscriber to eBay Stores, Blackthorne, or Selling Manager (basic or pro versions).

In selecting a software program, make sure that the information you log can be input into tax software. This will make your tax return preparation a snap—press a button, and the sales and expense figures leap from your accounting software into your tax return!

If you work with an accountant, be sure that your accounting data can be accessed by him or her. For example, with Simple Start Online you can give your accountant access to your files so you don't even have to send them. If you have desktop record-keeping software you can transfer your data electronically to your accountant for fast (and probably less costly) service.

If you don't want to invest in an accounting solution, you can create your own record keeper using spreadsheet software such as Microsoft Excel. Remember that it's not the program you use, but the diligence with which you use it that ensures good record keeping.

The Accounting Method to Your Madness

Unless you're familiar with accounting, you probably don't know that there are different ways to log in your income and expenses. But there are, and you need to know which way to keep your records. These ways are called accounting methods, and you must use one consistently, year in and year out, in keeping your books. There are two main methods—one is simple, and the other is a little more complex. The simple method is called the cash method; the other one is the accrual method. Each of these is defined in the following subsections.

Which one should you use? Unfortunately, you probably should be using the one that's a little more complicated, in order to meet tax rules. For most small businesses, the method you use doesn't really affect what's reported for tax purposes—they each even out in the end.

Cash Basis

The *cash method* doesn't mean you must deal in cash only. It's the name of an accounting method that dictates when to log income and expenses.

The cash method is easy to use, and, whether you know it or not, you're already using it for your personal tax return. You know that when you get a dividend check, you're going to report the income on your personal tax return in the year you received it (even if you don't cash it until next year); when you pay the real estate taxes on your home, you're going to deduct them in the year you mailed the check. That's how you use the cash method.

def•i•ni•tion

The **cash method** means reporting income when you receive it and expenses when you pay them.

Unfortunately, you probably can't use the cash method if you maintain inventory for your business. You must use the accrual method, so keep reading.

Accrual Basis

According to the IRS, you must use the *accrual method* of accounting if your business involves inventory. Casual sellers on eBay don't have to track their sales using this accounting method, but you do if eBay is your business. (Some small businesses with inventory are permitted to use the cash method, but those in retail or wholesale cannot—only those with customer-made goods may use the cash method.)

If you're leasing the computer you use to operate your eBay business, you know that the lease payment check is due on the first of every month (or whatever day the lease agreement specifies). Because this expense is fixed and you know exactly when it's owed, you can enter it in your books on the day it is due if you are on the accrual method. Let's assume that the due date is the first of every month. The fact that you don't mail the check until the third of the month and Dell doesn't cash it until the fifteenth doesn't change a thing.

def•i•ni•tion

The **accrual method** means reporting income when you earn the right to receive it (even if you actually get it in the next year) and expenses when you're obligated to pay them (even if you actually pay them in the next year).

The same is true for logging your sales. After you've sold an item and told the buyer exactly what's owed to you (the winning bid plus postage and handling), you can accrue the income. You may get payment the same day through PayPal or a credit card charge, but you may have to wait a week or more for a check. Still, under the accrual method, the income has been earned and you must report it when the item is sold.

What happens if that check never arrives and you've already logged in the income? Cancel the sale on your books and move on. Or leave the sale on your books and, for tax purposes, claim a bad debt deduction to offset the income you report. If you're not sure what to do, talk with an accountant.

Tracking Inventory

To run your business, you need to know what you have on hand to sell and when you need to buy more inventory to replace the items you've sold or are about to sell. It doesn't matter whether each item is unique, such as a custom-made puppet, or whether there are multiples of manufactured wares, such as a dozen copies of the same comic book or watch.

Figuring Inventory

The items you have on hand to sell in your eBay business are part of your inventory. In technical language, inventory means merchandise you hold for sale to customers in the normal course of your business. Inventory includes not only the items you have, but also any supplies that will become part of the item. For example, if you're selling refurbished computers, spare parts are included in your inventory.

Power Point

Take a physical count of your inventory on a regular basis, and do so at least annually. This will enable you to verify that you've been keeping an accurate count for your bookkeeping. It can also help you detect theft that, unfortunately, may occur if you have employees or other visitors to the place in which you store your inventory.

If you make your inventory, it includes all the raw materials and supplies you use that become part of your merchandise. For instance, if you're selling handmade sweaters, the wool or cotton skeins you use to make them are a part of your inventory.

We're going to get a little more technical here, so hang on. When it comes to reporting your income for the year, you don't report each item separately. Instead, everything is lumped together under the umbrella of inventory. In order to know how much income to report, you need to know what your inventory was at the start of the year (opening inventory), what you bought during the year and added to inventory, and the inventory remaining at the end of the year (closing inventory). Armed with these three categories, you can arrive at one key number: your cost of goods sold. This number enables you to figure what you made on your sales for the year. The following example illustrates how this works.

Inventory Example:

Your receipts from sales for the year total $48,655. Is this your profit from sales? No. Your profit is only $18,088. Your profit is the difference between what you take in and your cost of goods sold, which you determine as follows:

Opening inventory	$4,825
Purchases	+$29,644
Total	$34,469
Closing inventory	−$3,902
Cost of goods sold	$30,567
Total (gross) receipts	$48,655
Cost of goods sold	−$30,567
Your profit from sales	$18,088

Don't worry—you don't necessarily have to go through these lengthy computations yourself. A tax software program or your accountant will run the numbers at tax time for you, based on the figures in the books you've maintained throughout the year.

FIFO or LIFO?

Say you sell perfumes on eBay. You may buy one lot of Shalimar in February and a second lot of the same perfume in June. You paid $5 per unit in February and $6 per unit in June. When you report your inventory, what cost do you base it on? The answer depends on whether you use FIFO or LIFO, which are each methods for identifying the cost of your inventory.

FIFO stands for first in, first out and is an inventory-identification method that assumes you sell the first items you purchased (or made). For example, you would sell all of the units in the $5 lot of Shalimar before you go on to sell units from the $6 lot.

LIFO stands for last in, first out and is an inventory-identification method that assumes the opposite of FIFO. With LIFO, you assume that you sell the last items you purchased before you sell those first items you purchased. In this example, I assume that you sell the $6 units before tapping into the $5 units.

Which is better for you—FIFO or LIFO? The one you select will affect your cost of goods sold, which, in turn, will affect your profit for the year. The preferable method depends on the trend in prices. When prices are rising, using LIFO will result in a larger cost of goods sold so that closing inventory will be higher and your reportable profits (and the taxes you owe on them) will be lower. But when prices fall, the opposite result occurs—you'll wind up paying more taxes with LIFO than if you'd used FIFO.

If you use one method this year, you can change to another method (with IRS permission), but there may be a tax cost involved. The bottom line is to start off with a method you can live with for years to come.

Auction Alert

Although understanding LIFO may sound simple, in operation, the rules for using LIFO are very complex. For example, you may be required to group items and rely on price indexes. As long as you keep good records, your accountant can help you identify the cost of your inventory.

Valuing Your Inventory

Thought we were finished discussing inventory? Think again! FIFO and LIFO help you identify the items you're treating as sold for the year. But then you must value them. Again, you have choices: cost, lower of cost or market, and retail.

- **Cost,** which is what you paid for them, is the method we used to explain FIFO and LIFO. Cost takes into account the invoice price minus any discounts you received and any transportation costs you paid. This is the easiest valuation method to use and probably the one you should start out with (you can make a switch later).

- The **lower of cost or market method** for valuing inventory compares the market value of each item on hand on the inventory date with its cost and uses the lower of these two amounts. You can't use this method if you're using LIFO to identify your inventory.

- The **retail method** takes into account markups (and, if using LIFO, markdowns), which are expressed as a percentage of the total retail selling price. This sounds complicated because it is; unless you're an accountant, you may need to use one to help you in this regard.

Which valuation method should you use? Again, your tax professional can help you make a choice. Putting your choice into operation is automatic—you supply the data, and your accounting software does the rest.

Saving Your Receipts

Unless you have unlimited space, those boxes, file cabinets, and envelopes filled with credit card slips, canceled checks, and scraps of paper can easily clutter up your home or office. Still, certain receipts are worth keeping. The key is knowing what to save and for how long to save it.

You want to be able to make use of those scraps when you need to track your inventory and to meet your tax obligations. You don't need to save two receipts for the same purpose—if you keep a canceled check for an item you've purchased, you don't also need to save the sales slip for the same item.

Inventory-Related Receipts

Found a dress from the 1960s in your attic to sell on eBay? Maybe you'll strike it rich and collect more than you dreamed of. But how much of what you receive on this sale is income? The answer depends on whether you have receipts. You report only your net take, which is the amount over and above what it cost you. It's up to you to prove this, and you need receipts to do it.

Buying items isn't the only way to acquire them. You may be lucky enough to inherit something of value that you want to sell on eBay. In order to avoid treating all of the selling price as your income, you need to know your *basis* in the item. Basis is a tax term—if you buy something, cost is your basis. If you inherit it, basis usually is the value of the item when the person who left

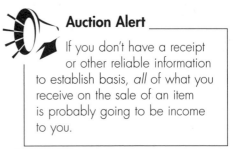

Auction Alert

If you don't have a receipt or other reliable information to establish basis, *all* of what you receive on the sale of an item is probably going to be income to you.

it to you died (what that person paid for it is irrelevant). Ask the executor or personal representative of that person's estate about the value. Get it in writing, and keep this information with your records.

If someone made a gift of an item to you, your basis usually is what that person paid for it. Ask your generous benefactor what he or she paid for the item. Again, get it in writing and keep this information with your records.

Save inventory receipts at least for as long as you hold the items as merchandise, plus the time required for tax receipts (which we explain shortly). This way, you'll be able to show how much you paid for items so you won't over report income on your tax return.

Power Point

Use your inventory receipts to build up a database of suppliers and potential buyers. When you have the time, mine your receipts for this information and enter it on a database you set up for this purpose. In this way, you'll easily find old suppliers you want to reach and potential customers to sell to.

Tax-Related Receipts

Two kinds of paperwork are involved for taxes: your books and receipts. *Receipts* is a generic term that includes such items as these:

- ◆ Bank deposit slips
- ◆ Canceled checks
- ◆ Credit card charge slips
- ◆ Invoices for items you've sold and things you've bought
- ◆ Sales receipts from purchases you made in cash

Auction Alert

If the IRS thinks you omitted more than 25 percent of your income from your tax return, it has six years in which to audit you. If you fail to file a return, there's no limit to the time that the IRS has to go after you.

These receipts provide all the information you need to enter the numbers in your books. Got an invoice showing you billed a customer for the camera you sold? Enter this in your books.

Receipts are also the supporting documents for the positions you take on your tax return. If you claim a deduction for supplies you buy, you want to have a credit card slip or sales receipt showing that you bought them.

How long must you hold on to your receipts for tax purposes? The simple answer is at least three years, which is the usual time in which the IRS has to question your return and ask to see your receipts for deductions you've claimed. When you're safe from audit, the only reason to hang on to your receipts is an inability to throw things out.

The more complex answer to how long you must hold on to your receipts is for as long as you need to. For example, if you bought something that's still sitting in your inventory, hold on to the invoice or other paper showing what you paid for it until you sell it (and then for at least three years after that).

If paperwork relates to employees you have, there's a different period for holding on to your paperwork. You're required to keep paperwork for employees for at least four years. For example, keep time slips of employees for at least this period. If you have independent contractors, retain any Form 1099-MISC that you have issued to them for at least four years as well. The good news is that retaining these records will not only help you for tax purposes, but it also may come in handy if you get into hassles with your state labor department (for example, an employee files an unemployment or disability claim).

Power Point

Make sure you label your CDs so you can easily retrieve the receipts, if you need them. Best idea: use one CD for each year so that all receipts for the tax year are in the same place.

Although receipts may go after a while, keep your books indefinitely—they don't take up much room (not even if you store them on your computer), and you never know ….

Storage Ideas

Low-tech or high-tech, there's a storage system for you for your receipts. Use whichever one serves you best.

The easiest way to keep receipts in some sort of order is to use a 12-month accordion file. Put receipts for each month in their proper slot as you collect them. Another alternative is to use envelopes for each month of the year in which to save your vital papers.

If space is precious, don't squander it on housing your receipts. Instead, use a scanner to load up receipts and canceled checks and burn them on a CD that takes up virtually no room.

Key Financial Numbers to Watch

There's an old joke about someone in business who lost a dime on every widget he sold. Someone asked him how he expected to make up the shortfall, and he answered, "with volume." Don't let this happen to you, losing money because you don't know how much you need to earn in order to be profitable. Knowing your numbers enables you to cut expenses when necessary, increase prices when possible, and understand what tacking on added expenses will mean to your bottom line.

- **Break-even point.** This is the point at which your total cost (your administrative costs as well as the cost of your merchandise) equals your total sales revenue. In other words, it's the amount of sales you need to make in order to cover your expenses (keeping in mind that, as your sales increase, your expenses do, too, because of the cost of merchandise and other sales-related costs). At this point, you've neither made nor lost money.

- **Gross profit margin.** This is essentially the portion of money from every sale left over for you after covering the cost of the items (essentially, your markup on each item). You want a high gross profit margin—it means more money for you. Figure your gross profit margin by dividing your gross profit by your sales.

  For example, say you sell in your eBay stores only T-shirts, all priced at $20, that cost you $5 each. In 2007, you sell 1,000 units, or $20,000, so your gross profit on these sales is $15,000. Your gross profit margin is 75 percent ($15,000 ÷ $20,000).

- **Operating profit margin.** This figure takes into account income from operations—it ignores interest and taxes you pay. Figure your operating profit margin by dividing your income from operations by your sales.

  For example, say it costs you $5 in business expenses (your salary, monthly telephone bills, Internet access, and so on) for every T-shirt you sell, so your income from operations is only $10,000. In 2007, if you sell the same 1,000 units as just mentioned, your operating profit margin is 50 percent ($10,000 ÷ $20,000).

Power Point

The higher the percentage is for your net profit margin, the better you're doing. There's no set percentage you can look to in deciding whether you're doing well—it depends on what type of items you sell. Typically, jewelry has higher markups than electronics, so profit margins on jewelry are greater.

◆ **Net profit margin.** This is your actual profit after factoring in all the expenses it took to earn the income from sales. A net profit margin factors in the cost of merchandise, operating expenses, interest, and taxes, and any other business cost you can think of. Figure your net profit margin by dividing your net profit (what you have left after paying all your expenses of making the sales) by your sales.

For example, say your taxes and interest reduce your net profit to $5,000. Your net profit margin is 25 percent ($5,000 ÷ $20,000).

The Least You Need to Know

◆ Record keeping is a must-do chore—it's required by the tax law, and it's necessary for tracking your financial health.

◆ Keeping tabs on inventory is necessary but can be complicated.

◆ Store receipts for inventory items and tax-deductible expenses for as long as you need them.

◆ Keep an eye on your financial numbers, to make sure that your expenses are kept in toe so you can remain profitable.

Chapter 13

Keeping It Legal

In This Chapter

- ◆ Getting a business license and sales tax number
- ◆ Getting other IDs for your business
- ◆ Using trademarks
- ◆ Following eBay policies
- ◆ Incorporating your business

When it comes to operating your business in compliance with the law, there's bad news and good news. The bad news is that there's a lot to know and a lot to do. The good news is that many of the things you must do get done only once.

In this chapter, you'll learn about licenses you need for your business to keep things on the up and up. You'll see how to obtain protection for your business name. You'll also find out about eBay policies to follow to keep things legal. Finally, you'll learn about how to formalize your business setup to obtain certain protection under the law.

Your Business License

The government is always sticking its nose in your business. You can't get married without a license from your state through your city or town. And you shouldn't run a business without getting a license for your operation. While the police won't knock at your door for operating without one, getting a license is for your protection.

The registration process is called a DBA ("doing business as"). It simply informs your locality of the name of your business and that you are the owner.

What's involved in registration? Let's answer a good reporter's questions—who, what, where, when, why, and how.

Why and When Do You Get a Business License?

Some localities require businesses to register, so getting a license is necessary to comply with the law. But even if you're not required to register, it makes good business sense to do so. It protects your business name by preventing anyone else in your area from using it. For instance, your own name may be Maria Sanchez, but your business name may be Maria's Handiworks, Amazin' Auctions, or anything else you can dream up.

 Auction Alert _____

Registering your business locally does not protect your business name beyond your area. Before selecting a name for your business, do your own Internet search to see what pops up. Try Hoovers (www.hoovers.com) to search for a company name. You may want additional name protection through trademarking (explained later in this chapter).

Who Needs a License?

Not every business is required to register. You need a license if you are a ….

- **Sole proprietorship.** This type of business means you're the only owner and you haven't taken any other formal or legal steps to create a special business entity.

- **Partnership.** This type of business is formed when two or more people come together with the intention of making a profit. Again, they don't have to take any formal steps to become a partnership (although having a written partnership agreement is highly advisable to anticipate resolutions to problems that could arise among partners).

You do not need to register if you've taken steps to create a formal business entity, such as incorporating your business or forming a limited liability company under your state's laws. These types of business organizations are already registered with your state, as you'll see in a moment.

Just because you sell online into states other than your own does not require you to register in those states. You usually need a physical presence in a state before you are considered to be in business there. So unless you have an office or a warehouse or you hire a sales force in another state, you don't have to worry about multiple registrations.

Where Do You Get a License?

Check to see if you are required to have one by contacting your city or town hall or county offices. You can let your fingers do the walking, through your telephone directory or the Internet, to find the right contact information.

You may have to appear in person, along with identification (a driver's license or passport), and swear before a notary that the information you've provided is true. If you have partners, all of you would have to go together. In some places, you may be able to file by mail.

> **Auction Alert**
>
> Some states, such as Tennessee, had tried to impose a requirement that eBay sellers obtain auctioneer licenses. Today, states have backed off from this, but be alert to possible changes in the future.

How Do You Get One and What Does It Cost?

You can obtain the DBA form from your town or county clerk's office. The form may also be available online, saving you the aggravation of getting through to an automated phone menu.

You don't need an attorney to complete the form—just fill in the blanks and sign on the dotted line. You may need to get it notarized.

The cost is usually modest. For example, in one of my locations, the cost is a one-time fee of $35.

Your Sales Tax Number

Most states and the District of Columbia, excluding Alaska, Delaware, Montana, New Hampshire, and Oregon, have a sales tax. (Hawaii does not have a sales tax either, but it imposes a general excise tax on all business activities, such as 4 percent on retail sales.) As you probably know, sales tax is imposed on the buyer but collected by the seller.

Even though you sell online, you may have to collect sales tax and remit it to your state. In order to comply, you need a sales tax number used to identify your business so that your state knows the payment is from you.

The same number is also called a resale number because you use it to avoid paying sales tax on items you buy to resell to others. It's your passport into the world of tax-free buying for your business inventory.

The Sales Tax Rules

When must you collect sales tax? When can you avoid paying it on goods you buy? Just because you sell online doesn't automatically exempt you from collecting sales tax.

The rules on collecting sales tax on items you sell online aren't completely black and white. Here's what we know for sure. If you sell to anyone in your state, you must collect your state's sales tax on the item. It doesn't matter that the sale was conducted online. Of course, there are more than 8,500 different sales tax jurisdictions when you count each city, town, and county, and each place has its own rules on which items and services are or are not subject to its sales tax.

 Auction Alert

The Internet Tax Nondiscrimination Act (formerly the Internet Tax Freedom Act), which expired on November 1, 2007, but is expected to be extended or made permanent, bars states from taxing Internet access fees (such as AOL charges). Contrary to many news stories, it does *not* excuse sales tax collection on online sales. If your state has a sales tax, you must collect it on sales made to people within your state. However, you are not obligated to collect sales tax on sales to buyers out of your state.

But what about sales to out-of-state buyers? Here's where things get a little grayer. To be obligated to collect sales tax on those buyers, you need what's called a *nexus* with that state, which is a physical collection there. If you don't have an office or a sales force outside your own state, you probably don't have to collect sales tax in other states. However, Congress is considering new law to require Internet sellers to collect sales tax in every state they sell to, even if there's no physical presence.

An Educated eBay Seller

Ask your state tax, finance, or revenue department (each state has its own name for the money agency) for a merchant's guide to sales tax. This guide describes your sales tax obligation and lists the items that may be exempt from your sales tax, as well as the amount of the tax you must collect. Remember, the amount varies with the location of the buyer within your state because of local sales tax rates, but you may be able to apply a simplified rate for all in-state buyers.

Don't pay any sales tax on items you buy for resale. You're exempt from this tax as long as you have a sales tax number (also called a resale number). But exemption isn't automatic, so speak up. If you want to claim exemption from paying sales tax on merchandise you buy for resale, inform the seller. You may be asked to complete an exemption form that the seller supplies to you. You must include your resale number on the form. Some sellers ask for this information with every sale; others keep your resale number on file so you have to complete a form only once.

The Sales Tax Procedures

Understanding the sales tax rules may be difficult, but getting your sales tax number is easy. Contact your state revenue, tax, or finance department and request a sales tax package. This package provides you with the information you need to …

◆ Obtain your sales tax number.

◆ Know how much sales tax to charge on your sales.

◆ Learn when and how to remit your tax collections to the state.

Getting IDs

Thought you had covered all your bases with licenses and registration? Think again—there's more. Home building contractors, plumbers, electricians, accountants, attorneys, and doctors all know they need special government-issued licenses to operate their businesses. eBay sellers may also need additional government IDs. If you have employees—even a spouse or someone else related to you—you need more numbers from the government. From the federal government, you need an employer identification number (EIN). From your state, you need a number for unemployment insurance purposes.

An Educated eBay Seller

Obtain your employer identification number instantaneously from the IRS by applying online at http://sa.www4.irs.gov/sa_vign/newFormSS4.do. A blank Form SS-4, "Application for Employer Identification Number," will pop up. Just complete it and click Next. If you're a sole proprietor, the legal name you enter on the form is your own name; the trade name is your DBA. There's no cost for getting your EIN.

Your Tax Identification Number

Your Social Security number may not be enough identification for you. In some cases, you also need an EIN. This is technically called an employer identification number, even if you don't have any employees.

You must obtain an EIN if …

♦ Your business is a partnership, a corporation, or a limited liability company. If you already have an EIN from your sole proprietorship and then you take in partners or incorporate your business, you'll need a new EIN (you can't continue to use the old one).

♦ You have any employees.

♦ You set up a qualified retirement plan.

Power Point _____

If you are an independent contractor working for others, you may want to use an EIN instead of your social security number. This is a preventative measure against identity theft. You can use it, but make sure you use the EIN on all tax returns so the IRS knows it's you (for example, it can match the income reported on Form 1099-MISC issued to you by the person you worked for with the amount of income you report on your return).

You may also need an EIN to set up a business bank account; the bank may require this information before you can open the account.

If you move to a new location or change the name of your sole proprietorship, you don't need a new EIN and can continue to use the same EIN you've been using.

Your State Unemployment Insurance Number

If you have any employees (including yourself, if you work for your corporation), you must obtain an unemployment insurance number from your state's department of labor. This is true even if you're the only employee of your corporation.

Your state's unemployment insurance number is separate from your EIN number. It's important to use the separate number on all forms and correspondence with your state unemployment insurance division or department.

For details on applying for your number, ask for an employer's guide from your state's department of labor or unemployment insurance division.

Making Your Mark

Just because you filed a DBA with your county doesn't mean your name is protected outside your area. That little ™, ℠, or ® you often see at the end of a company name is a designation for a mark, which is a word, a phrase, a symbol, a design, or a combination of any of these things that distinguishes you from someone else.

Technically, you create a trademark either by simply using it or by registering it with the U.S. Patent and Trademark Office (USPTO) at www.uspto.gov. You don't need to register a trademark in order to use it and the ™ symbol, but certainly registration gives you greater protection. Use of a trademark by you can be usurped by registration by another, showing that he, she, or it used the mark first.

A registration mark can be created and used only by actually registering it with the USPTO. There's no shortcut here.

Auction Alert _____

Even though you sell worldwide, your mark may be a domestic thing. Generally, you can't ensure international protection for your trademark unless you've first registered it in the United States. And then you probably need to register on a country-by-country basis to be protected in each country. For small businesses, it's not worth the cost (even though new laws make multicountry registration easier and less costly than before).

What's in a Name?

What's a name worth? Ask Coca-Cola, McDonald's, or eBay, all of which have registered their names. As you grow your business, you want to be identified with it. You want customers to remember who you are—not just individually, but as a business.

Sure, protection for your mark can be costly. There are government registration costs (in the hundreds of dollars), and there are attorney's fees for the process (which can run hundreds or even thousands of dollars). You can do it alone, but we don't advise it—you're in business to sell, not to learn everything there is to know about mark registration.

Where to Find Assistance

Before you do anything, you can study up on what registration is all about. You'll find heaps of understandable information from the USPTO at www.uspto.gov.

If you decide to register your mark, we highly advise that you work with a knowledgeable attorney. Remember that registration and the related legal fees are a one-time investment, so make sure you do it right. To find an attorney, call your local bar association and ask for referrals to attorneys who specialize in intellectual property, or go to Martindale's website at www.martindale.com (search by area of law under Intellectual Property to find an attorney in your locality).

Understanding the eBay Policies

eBay is largely governed by community values, the key of which is the belief that people are basically good. Toward this end, eBay encourages open and honest communication to ensure a fair playing field for buyers and sellers.

But unlike Blanche DuBois in *Streetcar Named Desire*, eBay doesn't rely solely on the kindness of strangers to police its sales activities. It has a slew of policies and rules that you should live (and conduct your business) by. You'll find a complete listing of eBay rules and policies at http://pages.ebay.com/help/policies.

But we'd like to help you get started by explaining some key subjects.

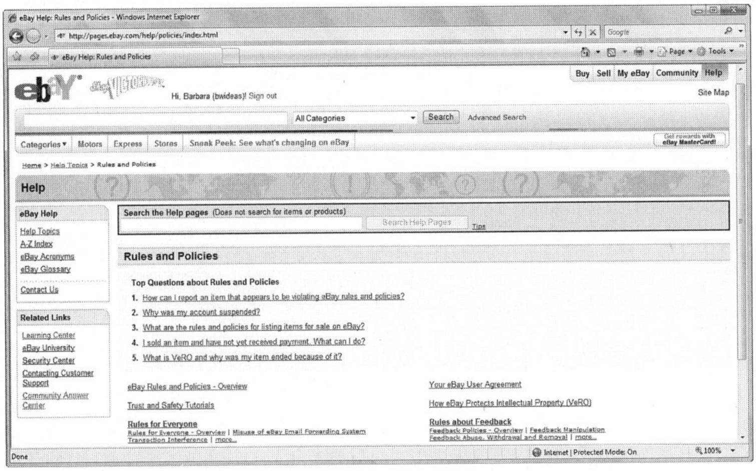

Figure 13.1

Play by the eBay rules.

Understanding the Rules for Listing and Selling

Take the time to familiarize yourself with eBay rules for listing and selling items. This can save you time and trouble later. For example, it can save you the bother of listing an item that will only be yanked by eBay because it is prohibited. (For more details on what you can and cannot sell on eBay, see Chapter 4.)

Understand your recourse if you encounter a nonpaying bidder or buyer (NPB), someone who wins your auction and then seemingly disappears. How can you recover eBay fees? What other punitive steps can you take against the nonpaying bidder? These matters are covered in Chapter 8.

Know in advance what happens to an auction in a program when the eBay system goes down. This event, called a *hard outage*, may result in credits for eBay fees and the extension of auction deadlines, depending on the length of the outage.

Learn how to work with eBay to remove negative feedback that you believe is undeserved; removal isn't automatic, and you need to take steps to make things happen. eBay is not legally responsible for third-party comments posted on its site, but it will remove feedback under certain circumstances, such as when the feedback is vulgar or obscene. You and the other party can mutually agree to have it removed.

Auction Alert

You can't list for sale any item that's prohibited—you'll find a complete list of these things in Chapter 4. You may also be barred from selling certain questionable items that can be listed only by certain people who have met certain requirements.

Alternatively, if you can show that the feedback was abusive, eBay will remove it. For steps on how to proceed with removal, go to http://pages.ebay.com/help/policies/feedback-abuse-withdrawal.html.

Using the eBay Name

Just because you sell on eBay doesn't entitle you to claim any particular association with the company. For example, if you have your own website, you can't use the eBay logo without prior written permission (which usually isn't granted without a licensing agreement).

You can use the word *eBay* on your website or otherwise in a descriptive manner. For example, you can say to your viewers that your items are listed for sale on eBay. You can't imply that your company is sponsored by eBay or endorsed by it.

Power Point

If you have achieved PowerSeller status, you are allowed to use the PowerSeller icon on your personal website, business card, and other marketing items. This does not violate eBay policy, and you do not need prior written consent to do so. For more about PowerSellers, see Chapter 17.

Deciding Whether to Incorporate or Form an LLC

Starting out, you may be in business for yourself and operate somewhat informally as a sole proprietor. There's nothing wrong with this. But at some point, this method of operation may no longer serve your needs.

You have two choices: you can incorporate your business, which creates a separate business entity—the corporation. You can also form a limited liability company, which is a relatively new type of business form that's allowed in every state. You can opt for either one whether you're the only owner or you have co-owners.

Before we explain *why* you might want one type of entity or another, make sure you understand the dictionary terms we'll be using. Owners of a corporation are called shareholders or stockholders. A corporation is governed by its bylaws and the laws of the state in which it is formed. The people who see that the business follows the bylaws (or change them, when necessary) are called directors; those who see to the day-to-day operations are called officers (a president, a secretary, and a treasurer). The same people can act as directors and officers.

For limited liability companies, or LLCs, as they're known, the terminology is completely different. Owners are called members. The company is governed by articles of organization. The people who run LLCs can be managers, specially selected individuals, or they can be the members themselves—you'll probably run your LLC if you use this business format.

What Flavor of Business Do You Like?

Some people like to vacation at the beach, while others prefer the mountains. Is one better than the other? No, they're just different choices you make. The same is true for the structure you adopt for your business.

There are two key reasons to ramp up your business to another level. First, you gain personal liability protection. This means that if the business is sued, your home and other personal assets can't be claimed by creditors. One eBay seller of reconditioned chain saws set up an LLC before listing his first one—you can certainly see why he thought he needed personal liability protection. Sure, you may carry insurance to protect you and the business, but in today's litigious society, you can't be too careful.

Second, you obtain a veneer of professionalism when you put on the mantle of a separate business entity. You look more official because you *are* more official. For marketing purposes, a formal entity implies stability—you'll be around tomorrow if a customer has issues. Banks are more willing to lend you money because they know they're dealing with a person who has made an investment in and commitment to the business. And it's easier to bring in new partners and share ownership of the business.

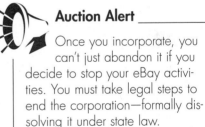

Auction Alert

Once you incorporate, you can't just abandon it if you decide to stop your eBay activities. You must take legal steps to end the corporation—formally dissolving it under state law.

Forming either of these entities is a big step. Before you take it, think about the following:

◆ **Organizational costs.** Creating a business entity requires a one-time filing fee. You may also incur legal fees for a lawyer to handle the setup for you. The choice of entity does not make too much difference in the costs you'll pay—for example, state fees for incorporating and forming an LLC are about the same.

◆ **Cost of operations.** Because these entities are separate from you, there's more formality to operating them. There are separate tax returns at the federal and state levels, which entails extra costs for compliance.

♦ **Tax costs.** It's difficult to generalize about whether setting up one of these entities will cost you more in taxes than if you left things alone. We'll get to this question later in this chapter.

Taxes Do Matter

Should you incorporate or form an LLC? This is a highly controversial question among attorneys today, and there's no consensus on the better choice.

Both offer you personal liability protection. Both entail formal steps and costs to create under state law. Both have ongoing reporting, such as separate tax returns. Both offer unlimited life for the company—even if you die, the business goes on.

An Educated eBay Seller

What's the *S* all about? The name comes from the subtitle in the Internal Revenue Code. In 2003 (the last year for which statistics were available), there were 3.3 million S corporations and 33.8 percent were owned by a single individual.

But tax-wise, the choices couldn't be more complex. If you incorporate, there are two ways to go: be taxed as a regular or C corporation, or elect to be taxed more akin to a partnership by choosing S corporation status after being set up like any other corporation under state law.

A C corporation is a separate taxpayer, while owners of an S corporation report their share of the company's income, deductions, and credits on their personal returns. (States may permit S status or tax corporations that have elected this treatment for federal tax purposes as regular corporations for state income tax purposes.)

Limited liability companies, like S corporations, are pass-through entities in which owners report their share of LLC items on their personal returns. The following table compares some of the basic tax rules for each type of entity.

Tax Rules for Corporations and LLCs

	C Corporation	S Corporation	Multi-owner LLC	Single-owner LLC
Federal	Form 1120	Form 1120S; Schedule K-1 for each shareholder	Form 1065; tax return Schedule K-1 for each shareholder	Schedule C of Form 1040

	C Corporation	S Corporation	Multi-owner LLC	Single-owner LLC
Who pays tax on income	C corp.	Shareholders report their share of tax items on their personal returns	Members report their share of tax items on their personal returns	Member pays tax with personal return
Return due date	March 15	March 15	April 15	April 15
Extended due date	September 15	September 15	October 15	October 15

For Do-It-Yourselfers

Moving beyond your simple sole proprietorship is a big step. You can certainly take the bull by the horns and create your business entity. Use reliable online do-it-yourself sites, such as …

- BizFilings (www.bizfilings.com)

- MyCorporation (www.mycorporation.com)

- Legal Zoom (www.legalzoom.com)

> **An Educated eBay Seller**
>
> Perhaps you've seen ads about incorporating in Delaware or Nevada, or heard that Fortune 500 companies formed their corporations in these states. Don't bother doing so yourself (unless you live in Delaware or Nevada). For small companies, there's no advantage to setting up your framework out of state. You'll still have to register to do business within your state—that's added paperwork and cost you don't have to incur.

You're going to do things only once, and you want to do them right. The cost of assistance may be only a few hundred well-spent dollars to obtain peace of mind that you didn't overlook anything or make a mistake.

◆ Talk over your decision with your accountant, to get his or her perspective on your decision.

◆ Let your lawyer handle the setup or at least review your decision on entity selection if you're going to handle the setup yourself.

Find out from your advisors what you need to do every year, if anything, to keep your status legal. For example, for LLCs, you may need to place a public notice in the newspapers announcing their formation, and you may have to pay your state ongoing fees to remain valid.

The Least You Need to Know

◆ Obtain all licenses and ID numbers needed for your business.

◆ Protect your mark by registering it with the federal government and policing its use.

◆ Learn about eBay policies and procedures that can help you.

◆ Protect yourself by incorporating or forming an LLC.

Chapter 14

Protecting Your eBay Business from Fraud

In This Chapter

- ◆ Spotting possible fraud so you can avoid it
- ◆ Using feedback to limit your dealings to good bidders
- ◆ Blocking unwanted bidders
- ◆ Avoiding business identity theft
- ◆ Avoiding hijackers

With 244 million registered users on eBay and many hundreds of millions of non-eBay people with e-mail, you're bound to come up against scams and frauds. The only way to make sure you don't become a victim is to follow the Boy Scout motto and "Be prepared." Learning about the types of scams and frauds you may encounter can arm you with enough ammo to shoot holes in the cons and avoid problems.

In this chapter, you will learn to recognize the types of frauds, both small and large, that you may be exposed to when selling (and buying) on eBay. You'll also find out what you can do to protect yourself and your customers and maintain your good business image.

Minimize Headaches from Small-Time Fraud

You can't avoid it today—there's always going to be someone out there trying to separate you from your money. The way to protect yourself is get wise to what's going on and take whatever steps are available to minimize the damage.

Learn to recognize possible fraud so you won't be suckered in. Take advantage of eBay protections, such as *feedback* on bidders (discussed in more detail later in this chapter).

Unfortunately, there are some bad sellers, too, and they give reputable sellers a bad name. A ring of stamp dealers sold thousands of altered postage stamps through eBay and, despite an MSNBC exposé, it took nine years for eBay to join Stamp Collectors Against Dodgy Sellers (SCADS) in trying to bring them to justice.

Bad Buyers

Sellers often get a bad rap, with buyers claiming that goods are misrepresented, sellers use shills (friendly bidders working for sellers) to artificially drive up prices, and buyers don't receive what they've won because things aren't shipped. But buyers can be equally bad. They can cost you time and money. Here's how:

- **Bid shielding.** The flip side to shilling is shielding, in which a bidder gets a pal to artificially drive up the price as a way to discourage other legitimate bidders. At the last minute, the shielder (the pal) cancels his or her high bid so that the bidder has no competition to win the auction at the last minute at a low bid.

- **Bid siphoning.** With this type of scam, con artists lure bidders off eBay to sell what is purported to be the same item, but at a lower price. (These scamsters may contact bidders directly through e-mail or the Contact eBay Member link on eBay.) Of course, bidders lose any eBay protection, such as partial reimbursement for losses resulting from nondelivery or misrepresentation, by responding to e-mail offers.

♦ **Nonpayment.** The flip side to nondelivery of merchandise is nonpayment by the buyer who receives the merchandise. The buyer may, for example, revoke payment so that you don't get to keep your money, but you're already out the merchandise.

Protection for sellers against bad buyers is to know who you're dealing with. For this, you need to check the feedback score on the potential buyer.

The eBay Feedback System

How can you trust people who buy from you? How can people trust you as a seller? One way is to look at the feedback score, a rating system established by eBay to let the bidding public know about buyers and sellers. The feedback rating system is simple: you get a +1 point for each positive comment, a 0 for each neutral comment, and a –1 for each negative comment.

A buyer of your auction can enter a positive, neutral, or negative rating. You can do the same for people who buy from you. Then eBay displays the total of all feedbacks and calculates a feedback score. In unsatisfactory transactions, consider contacting the other party to see if you can resolve the issue before you leave feedback. You typically have 90 days after a transaction to record your feedback.

Auction Alert

Don't agree to sell to anyone who has a large number of negative feedbacks; they're there for a reason. You don't want the headaches that may be involved in completing a sale with this person—just move on to someone else.

Here's how the score is figured: subtract the number of negative feedbacks from the positive ones. This gives you the feedback score (the number you see in parentheses after your user ID). This is calculated based on "unique users" which means only one comment per user counts. So if one buyer leaves you three positive feedback comments (based on three purchases), it only counts as +1 for your feedback score. For example, say you have 2,854 total positive feedback comments, 2,420 of them were from unique users, and you have 2 negative comments. Your feedback score is 2,418:

2,420 unique positive feedbacks – 2 negative feedbacks = 2418 feedback score.

Now, to get the percentage (called the feedback rating) you need to look at the total positive feedbacks received (it's on the feedback profile page). This is not the feedback score. Subtract the number of negative feedbacks from the total positive feedbacks.

Now, divide this number by the total number of positive feedbacks and multiply by 100. This gives you a percentage. Let's go back to our example. You have 2,854 total positive feedbacks and 2 negative ones. Your feedback rating is 99.9 percent:

2,854 total positive feedbacks − 2 negative feedbacks = 2,852

2,852 ÷ 2,854 = 0.9992

0.9992 × 100 = 99.9% (the feedback rating)

Usually, a high feedback score and rating is a good sign that the person is trustworthy, but not always. Check your trading partner's Feedback Profile to read comments and look for negative remarks.

Colored stars are awarded to eBay members for receiving a feedback score of 10 or more and feedback stars are displayed next to the member's user ID. The following table shows what each color star means.

The eBay Color Star System

Color	Points
Yellow star	10–49 points
Blue star	50–99 points
Turquoise star	100–499 points
Purple star	500–999 points
Red star	1,000–4,999 points
Green star	5,000–9,999 points
Yellow shooting star	10,000–24,999 points
Turquoise shooting star	25,000–49,999 points
Purple shooting star	50,000–99,999 points
Red shooting star	100,000 points and higher

You can respond to any feedback you receive. You should certainly do so if you receive negative comments that you think are unjustified.

You aren't required to check feedback on your bidders, but you'd be foolish not to. Unless you personally know who is bidding on your items (as you may grow to do over time), feedback is the only way to identify the good and bad buyers. Find a buyer's feedback by clicking on the Feedback Score (in parentheses after his user ID) on your auction page or by entering his or her eBay user ID on the Forum Feedback: Find Member page.

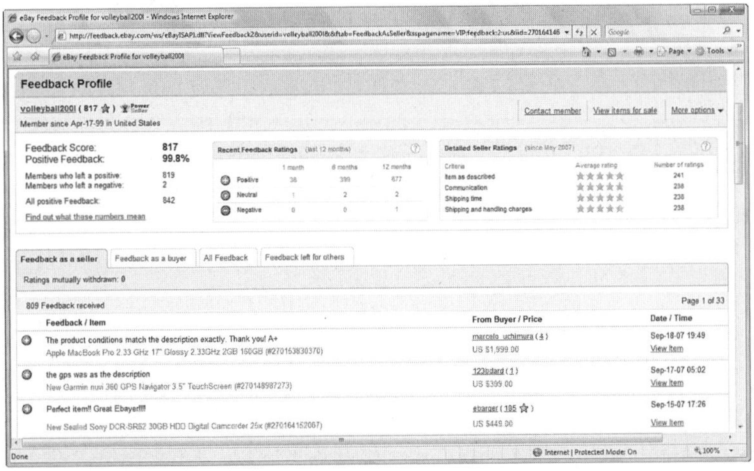

Figure 14.1

Always check a buyer's feed-back score.

How do you read the score? The absolute number is only a starting point. You need to look further to really get a handle on a bidder's score. After all, when a person does hundreds or even thousands of trades, there's bound to be some negative remarks—warranted or unwarranted. For example, if you leave a negative comment about a buyer who did not pay you on time, the buyer may leave a negative comment about you as retaliation. Look at the totality of the feedback—thousands of positive remarks are all the assurance you need of a good (versus a bad) buyer.

There's a second feedback system on eBay, called Detailed Seller Ratings, which was introduced in 2007. It allows buyers to rate sellers on a scale of 1 to 5 stars on four areas: (1) item as described, (2) communication, (3) shipping time, and (4) shipping and handling charges. Whether buyers will take the time to add this feedback rating remains to be seen.

Scams Focused on eBay Sellers

There seems to be no limit to the eBay scams you may encounter. They often pop up as e-mail offers and appear to be legitimate—they use all the right terminology and usually include an unauthorized use of the eBay logo. But they're as fake as a $3 bill. Here's a collection of some scams we've come across.

- **Fake job postings.** For example, you might come across a job posting for a part-time sales representative in the United States for an overseas employer. The rep is hired to sell goods that are never delivered to the buyer, while the scamster loots the rep's PayPal account.

- **Pyramid schemes.** Pyramid schemes (also called matrix schemes) are presented as buyers' clubs, offering items such as cheap iPods, but they are only the old "last one in is a rotten egg" scheme. You're advised not to bid on items, but instead to just send money to the scamster, so steer clear of these when buying up merchandise.

- **International scams.** For example, you might become the target for an international business scam, directed at sellers with great feedback; in this scam, someone may request your help. A supposed company located in Rumania, Indonesia, or some other far-off place, is overstocked and needs your help in selling items off. You sell on your site, take your cut of the sale, and send the balance of what you collect to a foreign bank account. The foreign company, however, never ships the goods (the company never really existed in the first place), and your eBay rating is destroyed. Even worse, you could be investigated for mail fraud or theft and face costly legal hassles.

> **An Educated eBay Seller**
>
> You can learn about security measures afforded from eBay. This includes scam alerts as well as resources and tips for selling safely. For details, go to pages. eBay.com/securitycenter/index. html. Tools and other fraud protection measures are explained later in this chapter.

- **Fake escrow services.** Real-looking websites entice sellers into working with them to complete sales. The problem that sellers soon discover: they'll never see their money. The escrow service tells a seller that payment has been received, so it's okay to ship. But the escrow service never remits payment to the seller.

- **Account takeover.** Scammers target sellers with high feedback scores by sending fake (but real looking) e-mails purportedly from eBay and PayPal. The purpose is to convince you to click on a link so the scammer can gain access to your account.

Blocking Unwanted Bidders

When you start out, you welcome one and all to your auctions and storefront. But as your business grows and you experience a wide range of bidders and buyers—some of whom are honest and cooperative, and others who are not—you may want to limit participation in your sales.

You may not want someone bidding on your sales who has lots of negative feedback. You can include language in your listing to require that anyone with 5 or 10 negative feedbacks contact you *before* bidding. You can assess each case on an individual basis, barring one individual whom you think is not trustworthy but permitting another who may have made some honest mistakes in the past to now become your customer.

If you had a nonpaying bidder—someone who won an auction but failed to pay for the item—you can bar this person from bidding on your future auctions. Or if you want only your existing customers to participate in your sales, you can restrict those who can bid on your listings. You can find tools both on eBay and elsewhere to restrict participation in your auctions and eBay store.

> **Power Point** _____
>
> You can cancel bids from people who fail to meet your listing requirements. For example, if you require that someone with five negative feedbacks contact you before bidding and the person bids anyway, you can block the bidder in the Sell Your Item form (under Bidder Requirements) or delete his or her bid.

- ◆ **eBay Blocked Bidder/Buyer List**
  (http://pages.eBay.com/services/
  buyandsell/biddermanagement.html)
  enables you to set up a list of bidders who can no longer bid on or purchase your listings—just enter their user IDs. You can add or delete bidders at any time (you don't have to give eBay a reason for doing so). You can block up to 1,000 user IDs.

- ◆ **eBay Preapproved Bidder/Buyer List** (http://offer.ebay.com/ws/eBayISAPI. dll?BuyerBlockPreferences) enables you to create an exclusive list of bidders or buyers whom you want to participate in your sales—only those on the list can buy from you unless they contact you so that they can be placed on your list.

Before you block out any bidder or buyer, consider the potential downside. You are cutting off customers who may have the interest and the money to buy now (even if there had been a problem in the past). This issue may not be significant to you because there are plenty of fish in the sea (potential customers).

Look Out for Big-Time Fraud

Being stiffed by one bidder who promises to pay but doesn't is certainly a costly inconvenience, but it isn't devastating. You can recover; you can resell the item to someone who will pay. Or, if you've shipped without receiving payment, you can deduct the loss on your tax return.

But there are bigger concerns out there today. The information on your computer can be destroyed. Or you can lose it all—your business, your good name—if you're not careful.

Fake e-mail with attachments can contain viruses or worms that eat up your computer hard drive. E-mail that you open with HTML content embedded can alert the sender that your e-mail address exists, exposing you to continued contact. Some of the e-mails may be sent using the words *eBay* or *PayPal* in the sender or message line. Ways to protect your computer system are discussed in Chapter 16. Each year thousands of businesses have their identities stolen as well. Someone charges merchandise to your account or uses your business's identifying information (such as your IRS employer identification number) to set up bogus accounts used to buy merchandise, ruining your business credit. Another problem: businesses' customer databases are breached so identity thieves can steal customers' identities, leaving businesses vulnerable to customer lawsuits about lack of security.

An Educated eBay Seller

Here are six proven ways to prevent business ID theft (adapted from the Better Business Bureau Online [www.bbbonline.org/IDtheft/business.asp]): (1) Shred all documents containing your business bank account and credit card numbers, (2) guard your blank checks with your life (and personally review your bank statement every month), (3) install firewalls and other security protection software on your computer to make it difficult for hackers to gain access to your system and keep security measures up to date, (4) know who your employees are (conduct background checks before hiring them), and limit their access to your sensitive business information—use screening before hiring, guard computer passwords, and change them frequently, (5) don't use social security numbers for employee or customer identification and never give out their personal information to a government agency, credit bureau, or other party unless you verify who you're dealing with, and (6) encrypt all data on your computer and remote access devices.

Business Identity Theft

Business identity theft, like personal identity theft, can be devastating. You can lose not only all your money, but also your company's good name. You may be able to recover your money, but it may be nearly impossible to restore your good name. The *only* protection is not to lose your business identity in the first place. This means keeping your business information out of the hands of identity thieves. Learn the tricks of their trade to avoid becoming a victim.

Gone *phishing?* Identity thieves use a variety of devices and ploys to obtain your sensitive business information, such as your business bank account. They come to you as *spoof e-mails*.

Once identity thieves have your information, they can use it to gain access to your account or, even worse, obtain credit based on your company's credit history to rack up debts that you are responsible for (until you can prove identity theft). For the latest updates on phishing so you can avoid these scams, go to www.antiphishing.org.

def•i•ni•tion

Identity thieves troll for sensitive business information by **phishing**, which is sending out bogus e-mails to which you respond and include such information. These descriptive e-mails are called **spoof e-mails.**

You can install the eBay toolbar, which includes Account Guard. This feature will warn you when you are on a spoof website. There is an Account Guard button that changes color to red if you are on a potential spoof website. If you are on a verified eBay or PayPal website, the color is green. If you attempt to enter your eBay or PayPal password into any nonverified eBay or PayPal site, you will see a warning box pop up before information is sent to the site. Also, Internet Explorer 7 has a phishing filter that will automatically warn you if it thinks there is a risk of the site being a spoof.

Auction Alert

Never respond to any inquiry allegedly from eBay or PayPal asking for account verification. Don't be duped by the somewhat official-looking URL that may include *eBay* or *PayPal* somewhere in its string of letters and numbers. Ignore the "Dear eBay Member" or "Dear PayPal User" correspondence. Real e-mail from eBay always has a line at the top that says "eBay sent this message to John D. Smith, (allaboutfishing)" (except with your name and User ID) and if it's account related, the e-mail will be in your My Messages inbox . Hang up on phone callers offering a prize from eBay. It's just a phishing scam by identity thieves to obtain your personal information, including your credit card or bank account number. If you have doubts about the authenticity of an eBay or PayPal e-mail, you can simply go directly to the respective site (don't use a link in the e-mail) and perform the activity requested in the e-mail (this way, you aren't giving personal information to a possibly bogus inquiry).

Account Takeovers on eBay

Hijacking—taking over your account information—can and does happen on eBay. Someone steals your account information (or attempts to) so that you can't log into eBay anymore. What should you do about account takeovers?

Power Point

Look on eBay for any active bids or listings in your name that may be unauthorized. For example, a hijacker may have used your account information to bid on an item (the hijacker hopes to receive delivery based on your good feedback rating), leaving you holding the bag (no goods but still responsible for payment, unless you can convince the seller of the hijacking).

♦ If you've been hijacked on eBay, take action immediately. Don't ignore the problem—it won't go away.

♦ If you can't log onto eBay, you'll have to contact eBay for assistance through Live Help (the link is on the home page).

♦ If you can log on but you suspect that you've been violated in some way, immediately change the password on your e-mail account. Then request a new eBay password and change the secret question and answer on your eBay account. Just as when registering as a first-time seller, you'll have to verify your new contact information. Also, make sure that none of your other account details (address, phone number, preferences, etc.) have been changed.

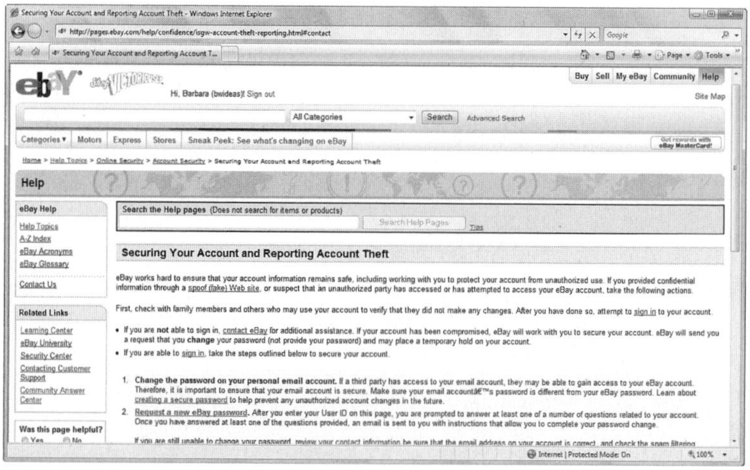

Figure 14.2

eBay can help you keep your account safe.

A new way to protect your account from being hijacked is to use the PayPal Security Key. This is a device that generates a six-digit code at the push of a button—you can keep it on your key chain. You add the code when you sign in on your eBay account (the code changes each time you sign in). Cost: one-time fee of $5.

Account Hacks

In this situation, someone gains access to your sensitive business information—your URL, customer base, and more—and exploits this information illegally.

For example, one eBay seller says that her PayPal account was debited for $300 for a camera she never purchased. She immediately tracked down the seller of the camera and learned that someone had used her eBay information to buy the camera and have it shipped to Hong Kong. The bogus buyer also charged it to her PayPal account. The seller was quick to comprehend the situation and let her off the hook (he recovered his money through PayPal). But it took her months of back-and-forth debate to square her account with PayPal.

Account hacking may be totally separate from your eBay activities, but it can severely undermine your ability to do business on eBay. A good hacker can learn about your sourcing information, your customers, and other information you consider private.

There's no totally foolproof way to prevent hacking. The best you can do to prevent account hacks from gaining access to your information is to work with computer experts to insulate you as much as possible. The more difficult you make it to gain access, the safer you will be. You can take these actions:

Power Point

Be careful when you respond to e-mail of any kind. It may be only a ploy to hijack your e-mail to use in spamming. Ignore any e-mails that sound bogus—they probably are. If they don't make sense, don't try to make sense of them; just erase them.

- **Install a firewall.** A firewall will put a barrier between you and the hacker.

- **Protect your computer.** If you want to block someone from getting on your computer—a child or an employee—use a password to limit access to your computer system to only those with this password information. Change the password frequently (at least monthly).

- **Use a different password for your eBay and PayPal accounts.** That way if a hacker gets into one of your accounts, he doesn't automatically have access to the other.

◆ **Recognize an unsolicited request for personal information.** For example, use care in responding to an "Ask Seller a Question" form. A simplistic question such as "Got anything else for sale?" is usually a tip-off that the question is only a ploy to obtain your e-mail address for spamming purposes (you respond, and the sender then has your address). Before answering, check to see if the sender has any feedback, as a way to verify whether the person is for real. Alternatively, the seller can respond using My Messages and block the buyer from seeing his e-mail address.

Use eBay Resources for Redress

eBay may be able to come to your aid in time of need. Given the right circumstances, there may be help available to correct a problem. Here are some eBay resources to consider:

◆ Relief from nonpaying bidders (NPBs)

◆ Redress for unfounded negative feedback

◆ VeRO program for protecting intellectual property

Relief from NPBs

If someone wins your auction but never pays up, you're stuck with a nonpaying bidder, or NPB, for short. You have two options. First, you can decide to offer the item to the second-highest bidder (for his highest bid). You'll get less for your item but avoid the chore of relisting it for sale. Contact that bidder to see if he or she will buy the item for the underbid amount using the Second Chance offer (discussed in Chapter 7).

But if you don't want to go this route (there was no underbid, or it was too low for you) or it doesn't work out (the underbidder doesn't accept the Second Chance Offer), you can get *some* redress from eBay. You can file an Unpaid Item dispute with eBay (you must wait 7 days after the listing closes; you have up to 45 days to file). eBay contacts the buyer; if there is no response within 7 days, the seller may close the dispute and file for the Final Value Fee Credit (and the buyer gets an Unpaid Item Strike, which is like a negative feedback report on his eBay record). If the buyer responds but still fails to complete the transaction, you'll still get the Final Value Fee Credit (but the buyer avoids an Unpaid Item Strike). You can relist the item—you pay a second listing fee but receive a credit for this amount if the item sells the second time around. Be sure to relist using the link in My eBay or on the ended auction page to be eligible for the credit.

The seller must close the dispute to claim the Final Value Fee credit and relist for free. Follow the steps in the Unpaid Item process. Go to http://pages.ebay.com/help/tp/unpaid-item-process.html.

What You Can Do About Unfounded Negative Feedback

It's a free country, with free speech. But what happens when someone exercises his or her Constitutional rights and maligns you undeservedly? This frequently happens when a seller leaves negative feedback about a buyer, who then retaliates by saying something bad about the seller, even though it's untrue.

eBay has a strict policy on removing negative feedback. You can't do anything about someone's poor opinion of you if it's true. eBay will not remove feedback because it's inaccurate or unfounded. However, you can work with a buyer to file a Mutual Withdrawal from Feedback (the comment will remain but it will not adversely affect your feedback score and rating). Of course, anything said about you that's defamatory, consider obtaining a court order against the buyer and then show the order to eBay so the defamatory statement can be removed.

Follow the eBay Feedback Abuse, Withdrawals, and Removal policies at http://pages.ebay.com/help/policies/feedback-abuse-withdrawal.html.

The VeRO Program

Do you suspect your images are showing up on someone else's listing? Does someone else's listing sound awfully familiar to you (in fact, just what you've written yourself)? VeRO, which stands for verified rights owner, is the eBay program designed to help you protect your intellectual property. It can notify violators, take down listings from violators, suspend eBay accounts, cancel PowerSeller status, and help you find repeat offenders.

Power Point _____

As a preventative measure, watermark your photos so they won't be used by other sellers. For example, Auctiva (www.auctiva.com) has a free feature to automatically add a watermark to all your photos.

To use the program, you have to report any suspected violation of your rights to eBay, using its Notice of Claimed Infringement form that you can print out from http://pages.ebay.com/help/community/NOCI1.pdf. Fill it out and fax it to eBay for action to proceed.

To learn more about VeRO, go to pages.ebay.com/help/tp/vero-rights-owner.html.

Be an Antifraud Deputy

You can help stem the tide of fraud by alerting the authorities about any ongoing fraud activities. Yes, this takes time, but it may save you from being a victim later.

Tell eBay about frauds you encounter that involve eBay. For example, if you receive a phishing e-mail that purports to come from eBay (when you know it's bogus), report it to eBay at spoof@eBay.com. Tell PayPal about any phishing e-mail that purports to come from PayPal (but you know does not because the company would never ask for your personal information) at spoof@paypal.com.

Power Point _____

If you fall victim to a scam—you don't get what you pay for or the sales come-on is deceptive—report this to the Federal Trade Commission at http://rn.ftc.gov/pls/dod/wsolcq$.startup?Z_ORG_CODE=PU01. This may not help you, but you can take comfort in knowing that you may have prevented someone else from being another victim.

The Least You Need to Know

- Educate yourself about possible scams and frauds so you can steer clear of them.

- Use the eBay feedback ratings as your first line of defense against bad bidders.

- Protect yourself from business identity theft by carefully guarding your business's sensitive or confidential information.

- If you've been hijacked on eBay, take action immediately to limit your liability.

- Help to make the Internet a safer marketplace by reporting any actual or suspected scams to the proper government authorities.

Chapter 15

Preparing for Catastrophe

In This Chapter

- ◆ Learning about your insurance needs
- ◆ Upgrading your existing coverage
- ◆ Shopping for extra coverage
- ◆ Protecting your shipments
- ◆ Developing a disaster plan

As the old saying goes, plan for the worst and hope for the best. After all, things happen that you have no control over—power outages, destructive storms, accidents, thefts, and on and on. Or you can become ill or injured and be unable to run your eBay activities. Any unexpected event can undermine your business and cost you hundreds or even thousands of dollars in losses. Just picture your inventory sitting in your basement when a flood sweeps into your area.

In this chapter, you'll learn about the kinds of coverage you should be thinking about for your own protection. You'll see why you may not have the existing coverage you think you do. And you'll learn about developing an emergency plan to help your business survive any type of disaster. Finally, you'll find out about various types of coverage that you may want to consider in addition to those already discussed.

What Type of Coverage Do You Need?

You may know all you need to know about car insurance, but what about business coverage? This is a whole new ballgame, and you should learn the rules.

You want to insure against five main areas of exposure:

- **Property loss.** In this situation, your computer, inventory, or other business items are damaged, destroyed, or stolen.

- **Liability.** In this case, someone (other than you or an employee) who is on your premises for business purposes is injured there. Although the probability of any liability arising is small because you ship all your goods to distant customers, you still want protection in case you have any onsite visitors.

- **Data reconstruction.** This is the cost of replacing information on your computer that has been lost or damaged in a catastrophe.

- **Business disruption.** Business interruption coverage pays your business bills if a disaster closes you down. Personal disability coverage helps you pay your personal bills if you become unable to work.

- **Employee-related coverage.** The law mandates that you carry certain types of insurance for employee protection, such as workers' compensation, unemployment insurance, and sometimes short-term disability coverage. You may opt to carry other employee-related coverage, such as health care.

For more information about insurance for small and home-based businesses, visit Insure U at www.insureuonline.org/smallbusiness.

Power Point _____

It's advisable to work with a knowledgeable insurance agent who can assess your needs and review your existing coverage to determine what additional insurance you may require. Don't have an agent? Ask around for a referral or contact major small business carriers, such as The Hartford (www.thehartford.com) and Travelers Insurance (www.travelers.com), for a listing of their agents.

Proper Property Insurance

Property insurance, also called casualty insurance, gives you coverage for damage, destruction, or theft of your property. A tree falls on your home office, smashing through the roof, damaging part of your home, and destroying your computer there. Or a thief walks off with your computer in the middle of the night. Are you covered for these losses?

Don't assume that your homeowner's policy (if you own your home) or your tenant's insurance (if you rent your home) will protect you. Read the fine print. You may have only partial coverage or none at all. Your policy may have limits or exclusions (items not covered) that mean you, not the insurance company, will bear the loss.

For instance, your homeowner's policy may limit coverage for a computer to $2,500, even though your system costs $4,000. Or your policy may not cover *any* business-related items, including your computer, your digital camera, and your entire inventory.

> **Power Point**
>
> Check whether your policy covers business property you take off the premises. For example, if you take a laptop to Starbucks, your satellite office, and it's stolen, are you protected? You may have to upgrade a policy to cover this contingency.

If You're Sued ...

What happens when the woman selling you an attic-full of old designer dresses who stopped by to drop them off falls on your icy driveway, is injured, and sues you? Don't think this can't happen to you (alright, you don't get ice-related injuries if you live in Hawaii, but other things can happen).

Liability insurance provides compensation to people (other than you) who get hurt on your property. Make sure you have all the protection you need. Again, read the fine print in your homeowner's or renter's policy to see if you're covered. There may be *no* coverage for any customer, supplier, or other business visitor to your premises.

Liability coverage requires the insurance company to defend you—provide a lawyer—and pay any resulting award up to the limits of your policy. This coverage is a must in today's litigious society.

Data Reconstruction

If you've ever had a hard drive crash, as we did, you know how devastating it can be to your business. Essentially, you're out of business until you can get your computer up and running again.

Power Point _____

If you work on more than one system at a time—for example, your desktop and laptop—be sure to keep all systems up to date on data. If one system goes down, you can shift to the other without losing a beat.

It may not be difficult to restart your system, but information can be lost. That customer list you so painstakingly built up has vanished; your sales figures are gone. There are ways to retrieve or reconstruct the data you had saved. But this takes the assistance of a computer expert and costs money.

Don't assume that your homeowner's (or renter's) policy will cover this cost. In all likelihood, it will not cover a single penny of it. You need special insurance coverage for data reconstruction.

Business or Personal Disruption

Events happen that can temporarily put you out of commission. Power outages, storm damage, or who-knows-what in today's post-9/11 era can keep you from operating your business. Still, there are bills to pay. For instance, you may have employees' salaries, insurance premiums, utility bills, and other expenses that need to be paid.

The solution: carry business interruption insurance. This coverage will help you pay the bills until you're back in business. The coverage may even pay for rent and other costs of a temporary location.

Outside events are one thing. When something happens to you, personally, then what? An accident or physical or mental illness or condition can sideline you from running your eBay business. How will you pay your bills? The best solution: personal disability coverage.

For example, Guardian disability insurance (www.disabilityquotes.com/occupations/homebasedbusiness.cfm) will write a policy for someone in a home-based business for at least three years, who works a minimum of 30 hours each week, and earns at least $35,000 a year.

Protecting Your Employees

If you work alone as a self-employed individual or use independent contractors for assistance, skip this section because you don't have any employees to be concerned about. But if you've hired workers to help you in your eBay business, pay attention to what insurance the law requires you to carry. If you've incorporated your business, you should also pay attention because you are an employee of your corporation.

- **Worker's compensation coverage.** This benefits employees injured on the job. Don't think that sitting at a computer is injury-proof—your employee can fall on the stairs getting to the laptop. This coverage is state-mandated to protect employees.

- **Unemployment coverage.** This insurance protects workers you lay off or fire. It is required on a state and federal level and is paid as a tax to Uncle Sam and to your state revenue, tax, or finance departments.

- **Disability insurance.** As with worker's compensation, this benefits workers who can't work because of an injury or illness that isn't caused by the job. Some states require employers to provide short-term disability coverage (you may opt to pay for long-term disability insurance).

 Auction Alert

If you're self-employed, you can't obtain workers' compensation and unemployment coverage even if you are willing to pay the costs—this protection is only for employees, which you're not. But you can purchase personal disability coverage to pay you if you become physically or mentally incapacitated and can't work (explained later in this chapter).

For information about the types of state-mandated insurance you must carry for your employees, contact your state labor department. The state, however, doesn't sell you worker's compensation or disability insurance; you buy what you need through private insurance companies.

We Got You Covered

You may not need all types of insurance covered here; however, you can change your existing homeowner's policy to include your business needs or buy a separate business policy, if necessary.

Although there's no law that you need to have this insurance to start your business, you'd be foolish to do so without it. Get your insurance in place so that you're covered when you begin your eBay activities.

Modifying Your Homeowner's Policy

If you already have coverage on your home, you may be able to upgrade it so that your business is covered. Obviously, this is the simplest way to be protected. You may be able to put a *rider* on your homeowner's policy to cover the full cost of a potential computer loss.

def•i•ni•tion _____

A **rider** is an addition to your existing policy to cover a specific item or event. You can use a rider for both property and liability coverage. An endorsement on a policy is a correction or change (a rider can be an endorsement).

Generally, the cost of modifying your existing coverage is less than you'd pay for a separate business policy. For example, if you have only occasional business visitors, a rider to cover any liability for injury may be under $50 a year.

Unfortunately, you may not be able to take this easy, low-cost step. Some homeowner's policies can't be changed to include business coverage of any kind. In this case, you need to change insurance companies or look for a separate business policy.

Comprehensive Policies

For a few hundred dollars a year, you can protect your office equipment, furniture, and inventory, as well as provide liability protection. The policy may also include the cost of data reconstruction if there's any damage to your computer records. Some policies may include coverage for lost income that results when you're forced to shut down because of fire or some other disaster.

This type of policy, called a business owner's policy (BOP), is sold to small businesses by a number of major insurance companies. In the past, it was difficult to buy a BOP for home-based businesses, but today this policy is readily available—just make sure the company knows where you're based.

An Educated eBay Seller

BOPs for small businesses, including those operating from home, are available from the following insurance companies. Premium costs vary by company, according to the amount of coverage you take, and your location. Shop around:

- Safeco Insurance Company (www.safeco.com)
- The Hartford (www.thehartford.com)
- Travelers Insurance (www.travelers.com)
- Zurich North America (www.zurichna.com)

How to Buy Insurance You Need

You can buy whatever type of insurance you need in two ways: directly from the insurance company or through an insurance agent (someone who sells insurance for one insurance company) or an insurance broker (someone who sells products for more than one insurance company). How should you buy insurance?

It depends on what insurance you're shopping for, how much you know about the coverage you're buying, and the choices you have. Some insurance companies sell only through agents or brokers, but a call to them can provide you with a referral to someone who can help you.

You're probably bombarded by e-mail with insurance offers galore. Some may be legitimate companies; others may be scams to avoid.

Here are a couple of pointers to keep in mind when buying insurance so you get the coverage you need at the lowest price:

◆ **Be sure to cover all your bases.** The policy should protect you to the extent you require—for your property as well as your liability exposure. For example, when it comes to property losses, the policy may pay you only what your items are worth today in view of their age, not what it will cost you to replace them. You may be able to buy "replacement value" coverage so that if the computer you now have is stolen, you can be covered for what you have to pay to replace it.

◆ **Check on deductibles.** The higher the deductibles (the portion of costs you must bear before the insurance company takes over), the lower your premiums will be. You can reduce your annual insurance costs by raising your deductibles.

Insurance on Items You Ship

The good news is that the cost of insurance on items you sell and ship is usually borne by the buyer. You bill the buyer for the price of the item, plus shipping, which includes insurance.

Of course, the flip side is that when you're the buyer in acquiring your merchandise, you're going to be the one who pays for insurance. But as you'll see shortly, this may or may not be an added cost to you.

Shifting Costs to the Buyer

There's no eBay rule determining whether the buyer or the seller pays for insurance. But it has become customary on eBay that the buyer usually pays this expense.

Auction Alert

You can insure a package only up to the value of its contents (typically what you sell an item for). The coverage for any loss (what the U.S. Postal Service will pay on a claim when a package is lost or the contents are ruined) is the depreciated value of the contents.

Insurance on items you ship can be purchased on a per-package basis from the shipper. Whether you ship an item with the United States Postal Service, UPS, or another carrier, you can obtain insurance coverage—costs vary with the shipper you use. The cost for insurance depends not only on the shipper you use, but also on the value of what you're insuring—the more expensive the item is, the more costly the insurance is. You can insure items whether you send them using package services (first class, Priority Mail, or Parcel Post) or Express Mail.

For example, when shipping a package by U.S. Mail, you can insure it for up to $5,000. The insurance cost for a $100 package is $2.05; for a $1,000 package it's $10.90, and for a $5,000 package, it's $46.90. The following table lists the insurance fees through the post office. A package that you want to insure for more than $5,000 has to be sent registered mail; you can insure its value for up to $25,000 (insurance fees for registered mail are higher than for other means of shipping).

If you're printing and paying for shipping labels from your computer, the insurance limit for parcels is $500. If you want higher coverage, you'll have to visit the post office.

Insurance Fees

Insurance Coverage Desired			Fee (in Addition to Postage)
$0.01	to	$50.00	$1.65
$50.01	to	$100.00	$2.50
$100.01	to	$200.00	$2.45
$200.01	to	$300.00	$4.60
$300.01	to	$400.00	$5.50
$400.01	to	$500.00	$6.40
$500.01	to	$600.00	$7.30
$601.01	to	$5,000.00	$7.30, plus $.90 for each $100 or fraction thereof over $600 in desired coverage, up to $5,000.

Different rates apply to registered mail; coverage is available up to $25,000.

If you're doing a lot of bulk shipping, you may be eligible for reduced insurance costs through the post office; you can opt to pass along these savings to the buyer.

Alternatively, you can use a third-party insurer to cut insurance costs. For example, with U-PIC (www.u-pic.com), a division of UPS, you can obtain insurance that's good for any shipper you use—USPS, UPS, DHL, or FedEx. Insurance savings can run 60 to 80 percent, savings you can pass along to customers. You simply register at the site to become approved for coverage. Once you get the go ahead, you can then complete online forms for each shipment you insure.

Covering Insurance When You Buy Merchandise

Take off your seller's hat and put on your buyer's hat. Now *you* must bear the cost of insurance in most cases. How you do this can vary.

You can pay per package, as you would charge a buyer who wins your auction. Alternatively, your property loss coverage may be all that you need for protection. Check the terms of your property loss or BOP policy to see whether it covers items shipped to you. If so, don't pay for the same coverage twice—tell the seller you decline any insurance coverage being offered to you because you're already protected.

Contingency Plans

Insurance is great, but money alone won't protect your business operations when disaster befalls it. It's important to anticipate what impact an unexpected event could have on your eBay activities and then devise a plan to follow in case of emergency. This process may also help you rethink your insurance coverage and add to what you already have.

Some actions you can take are common-sense, no-cost steps. For example, if your basement is prone to filling up with water during heavy storms, don't ever, ever store inventory there. Other actions may cost you now but save you money later.

 Power Point

Attack dogs aren't for everyone. Instead, protect your business assets from theft by installing a burglar alarm. The portion of the monthly monitoring cost related to your business is tax deductible.

Develop a Disaster Recovery Plan

When hurricanes hit the Gulf region in 2005 and the blackout in the summer of 2003 struck a good part of the eastern United States, eBay sellers in those parts of the country were paralyzed for hours, even days or weeks; they couldn't check their listings and were deprived of bids from buyers in these areas. (eBay, based in California, and with some servers in Utah, continued to operate.) This experience should be a lesson to us all—expect the unexpected and learn to deal with it.

Think through and write down a plan of attack—things you can do before there are any problems and how you will handle those that arise.

Even if you never devise a comprehensive disaster plan, here are some simple no- or low-cost measures to protect your business in case of emergency:

- **Have a back-up power source for your computer.** This is a device that you attach to your computer and plug into a wall socket. It's called an Uninterruptible Power Supply, or UPS for short, and looks like a large power strip. The UPS allows you to complete anything you're doing if an outage strikes. You can then shut down your system properly and avoid computer problems. One of the leading companies providing home and office back-up power source solutions, including back-up power sources and surge protection, is APC (www.apc.com).

Power Point

Back-up options abound, from burning files onto CD-ROMs, backing up to a second hard drive, and using automated back-up to an Internet site. Our advice: keep back-ups offsite (for example, store back-up CDs in your sister's home) or sign up for automated back-up and never think about it again.

- **Use a surge protector for your computer.** This is a device that protects your machine from electric company spikes in service and from lightning. Back-up UPS equipment usually includes surge protection.

- **Back up your computer files.** It won't help to create a great database of customers and suppliers if it's lost when your hard drive becomes corrupt or is stolen.

- **Use wireless Internet access.** You may be safe from blackouts if you connect to your auctions through wireless technology (provided you have adequate battery power to keep you running). Connect your laptop to the Internet through high-speed general pack radio service (GPRS) so that you're always "on." To be connected, your computer must permit wireless connections and you must pay for Internet access. T-Mobile wireless Internet (www.t-mobile.com), for example, costs just $19.95 per month for unlimited nationwide use, a small price to pay for your business to be always connected.

◆ **Find alternative suppliers.** You may be disaster-free, but your vendor may experience a crisis preventing shipments to you. The vendor may be located in a different place and experience a natural disaster or simply go out of business suddenly. Create ties with other suppliers so you're not dependent on a single source.

◆ **Clone yourself.** No, you can't do this yet, but you can find someone—a spouse, friend, or business partner—to take over things if accident or illness befalls you. It may be especially useful to find someone in another part of the country you can turn to for assistance if the only thing keeping you from eBay is a power outage in your area. You may be able to develop a reciprocity agreement—you'll help someone if they agree to help you in case of disaster. Be sure you trust the person with your user ID and password information to access your account. And make sure you're clear about whether any compensation for this assistance is owed.

An Educated eBay Seller

Want to learn more about how to be prepared for a disaster? Find additional information through the Insurance Information Institute (www.iii.org). You can download two free booklets, *Open for Business: A Disaster Planning Toolkit for the Small Business Owner* and *Getting Back to Business: A Guide for the Small Business Owner Following Disaster*, from the Institute for Business and Home Safety, at www.ibhs.org/business_protection. The American Red Cross has a free *Business and Industry Guide for Preparing for the Unthinkable*, available at www.redcross.org/services/disaster/0,1082,0_606_,00.html.

Learn About eBay Disaster Plans

eBay had a power outage in 2001 that shut down operations for more than 24 hours. The result: an irate eBay community and better back-up plans for eBay. Since then, things have run flawlessly. But just in case, here's what you should know if problems develop at the source—eBay.

If eBay experiences a blackout or any technical difficulties, it will send out announcements. It will then extend all of the auctions for the period it was down. For example, if eBay experiences a five-hour blackout, the auctions will be extended automatically for five hours.

Fill in Insurance Gaps

Think you have all the insurance you need to run your business and protect yourself? This may or may not be so. Let's run down some other types of coverage you may want to consider in running your eBay business. Your decision obviously depends on your individual circumstances and your need for additional protection. Costs may be steep for various types of coverage—shop around for the best deals.

> **Power Point** _____
>
> Without health coverage, one major illness can wipe you out financially. If you run an eBay business, check for options through your local Chamber of Commerce (check for local chambers through www.uschamber.com/chambers/directory/default) or other business associations or organizations to which you may (or could) belong, such as the National Federation of Independent Business (NFIB, www.nfib.com); you'll probably pay less for coverage through these groups than you would for coverage you buy on your own. Shop around (check local listings of insurance carriers or ask your insurance agent). PowerSellers may be able to purchase medical policies through eBay (see Chapter 17).

♦ **Accident and health insurance.** Unless you have medical coverage elsewhere.

♦ **Cyberliability coverage.** If you maintain a website in conjunction with your eBay activities, this coverage protects you from copyright and trademark infringements as well as actions arising from misinformation. It's a relatively new type of coverage and may be hard to find, but it is worth considering by the right type of business.

♦ **Flood insurance.** Your homeowner's or renter's policy may not protect you from water damage resulting from flooding. To learn more about this type of insurance, go to www.floodsmart.gov.

Don't feel overwhelmed by the range of coverage explained here. It may be a good idea to sit down with a knowledgeable insurance agent and discuss your business so you can decide how best to protect yourself.

The Least You Need to Know

♦ Carry protection against property damage or loss and liability.

♦ Check out your existing coverage to see if it's adequate or needs to be upgraded or changed.

♦ Look into a comprehensive business owner's policy.

♦ Properly (and cheaply) insure shipments.

♦ Create a disaster plan.

Chapter 16

Cutting in Uncle Sam: Taxes

In This Chapter

- ◆ Determining your tax status
- ◆ Facing up to your tax obligations
- ◆ Taking a home office deduction
- ◆ Claiming various tax deductions

There's no magic number you must exceed before you're required to report your income. Don't believe anyone who tells you that you have to report income only once it's a meaningful number. Technically, *all* income must be reported, whether you have a good year or a bad year, or your income equaled your expenses for the year. But tax rules are tricky when it comes to deductions for expenses you incur in generating your eBay income. Here's where some knowledge can be a great help in nailing down deductions.

In this chapter, you'll learn about how the IRS views you so that you can position yourself to maximize your deductions. You'll find out about the extent of your tax obligations, which includes not only income tax, but also sales tax and other taxes. You'll see how to figure your home office deduction. Finally, you'll learn about the various types of write-offs to which you may be entitled.

Business or Hobby?

When you sell something on eBay, Uncle Sam may view you as wearing one of three hats: that of a casual seller (someone with only an occasional sale), a hobbyist (someone in it for fun, whether making or losing money), or a real business owner (someone in it to make a profit). The hat you wear determines how you report your income and expenses for tax purposes.

There are no dollar amounts that the government uses to decide what hat you're wearing. The tests are rather cloudy, but you need to put the right hat on if you want to be able to take deductions on your return.

You're probably a casual seller if you list an item or two only periodically, perhaps that dusty vase you found in your attic or the never-used hockey skates in your garage. You haven't really started a business if this is your level of activity for now. The tax law gives you good news and bad news.

The good news is that your gain on the sale (the difference between what you receive from the buyer and your tax basis—usually what you paid for the item) can be treated as a long-term capital gain. There is a special tax rate for this gain: 28 percent if you are in a tax bracket that is equal to or higher than this rate (for example, the 28 percent, 33 percent, and 35 percent tax brackets).

The bad news is that you cannot take any losses on the sale of these items. If you paid $200 for hockey skates and you sell them for $45, you can't write off your $155 loss. It's a nondeductible personal loss.

Hobby Activity

Whenever you do something that involves a good amount of personal pleasure or recreation, such as dog breeding or stamp collecting, you may not be able to write off all of the expenses you incur in the activity. You may be treated as only a hobbyist. If so, the tax law limits what you can deduct.

eBay may be your passion, but it isn't necessarily your business, says the IRS, if you don't have a real expectation of making a profit. This problem won't be raised if you're making money on eBay; it becomes an issue only when you have *losses*. That's when your profit motive may be called into play.

def•i•ni•tion

Losses has a very specific meaning for tax purposes: it is the amount of your expenses in excess of the income you derive from your eBay activities. For example, if you add up all of your costs, including your Internet access fees, your home office deduction, and other eBay-related expenses we'll talk about in more detail in this chapter, and these costs are more than the money you make on eBay, you are in a loss position.

Let's assume that you can't prove a profit motive and are only a hobbyist. If so, here is how you treat your income and expenses:

◆ Report all of your income. This is ordinary income. It is taxed at the same tax rate as salary, interest income, IRA distributions, pensions, and other ordinary income items.

◆ Deduct expenses only to the limit of your income (for example, if you made $1,000, you can deduct only $1,000 of expenses).

Auction Alert

Deductions by hobbyists can be claimed only as miscellaneous itemized deductions. This means you get no write-off if you claim the standard deduction. If you do itemize, the first 2 percent of your adjusted gross income is nondeductible; only expenses in excess of this 2 percent floor are deductible to the extent of your hobby income. And, if you're subject to the alternative minimum tax, a shadow tax system designed to ensure that even those people with a lot of write-offs pay *some* income tax, you can't deduct your hobby expenses.

Let's say that you have losses and you want to prove your eBay business isn't just a hobby. What can you do? Here's how the problem can play out in the real world. Just having a loss one year isn't a problem; it's not uncommon to have a loss during the start-up years of any business when you're putting money in to get things rolling.

However, after several years, the IRS may say you've had your chance to establish yourself. Now it's time to show you aren't a mere hobbyist in for the fun of it. You must show you are running your eBay business with a reasonable expectation of making a profit. There's no formula for proving what's in your head. The following factors come into play; there's no set number of factors you must meet to prove your profit motive—the more, the better.

♦ **You have a business plan showing how you expect to make a profit.** You can create your business plan using commercial software (for example, Business Plan Pro, eBay edition, at www.paloalto.com) or follow the outline at the Small Business Administration website (www.sba.gov/starting_business/planning/writingplan.html).

♦ **You carry on your business in a businesslike fashion.** This means keeping good books and records of your sales and expenses, and having a separate business bank account and a separate business credit card.

♦ **You put in a lot of time and effort.** Being a part-timer or only moonlighting at your eBay business doesn't mean you lack a profit motive, but it's more convincing to run the business full-time.

♦ **You depend on your eBay business for your livelihood.** If your spouse is a highly successful trial attorney and you dabble at selling dolls on eBay, the IRS may say it's a hobby for you.

♦ **You use experts and advisors and change methods in an effort to become profitable.** If you're continually learning ways to improve your business and you work with an accountant who tells you how to do things better, you're showing that you don't view this as a hobby.

Power Point

Just getting started in your eBay business and think you'll have losses for some time? You can opt to rely on a presumption that you have a profit motive and keep the IRS off your back for five years. As long as you do, in fact, turn a profit for three of these five years, you automatically are viewed as having a profit motive when the IRS looks at your returns at the end of the five-year period. Opting to use this presumption guarantees that the IRS will examine your return at the end of five years, something that may or may not have occurred without making this election. If you don't make the election and the IRS examines you anyway, you don't need three years of profitability because you can always try to prove a profit motive using the factors just listed.

Mind Your Own Business

Let's assume that you are in your eBay business to make a profit, no ifs, ands, or buts about it. Then how do you report your income and expenses? You may not have to know all the ins and outs of reporting because you rely on a tax professional (like about 80 percent of all small business owners), but you still should understand some basics.

Your income and expenses are reported for federal income tax purposes on IRS Schedule C if you are self-employed. This schedule is part of your Form 1040. You list your income and expenses on the lines provided on the schedule. You also use this schedule to report your income and expenses if you formed a limited liability company (LLC) and you are its only owner.

If you have any other type of business entity, such as a partnership or S corporation, or a limited liability company with two or more members, you report your share of the entity's profit (the difference between its income and expenses) on Schedule E of your Form 1040. How do you know how much of the entity's profits belong to you? The entity must send you a Schedule K-1 to allocate this amount to you.

Auction Alert

Thus far, eBay has not been required to report sellers' activities to the IRS. However, there has been a proposal to require eBay and other online sites to report on Form 1099 annual sales of $5,000 or more (similar reporting is already required in Australia). Whether this becomes a requirement remains to be seen.

Remember all those great record-keeping rules we told you about in Chapter 12? Here's where they come into play. You use your records to help you report the income and expenses of the business.

Let's say you're self-employed and show a loss for the year on your Schedule C, the form you file to report your eBay income and expenses. You can use the loss to offset other income on your return, such as a spouse's salary or interest income.

If you show a profit, even better. You can try to reduce the tax bite on your profit by setting aside some money in a qualified retirement plan—contributions to the plan are tax deductible within set limits. But if you have a profit from your self-employed eBay business, you may owe self-employment tax (explained later in this chapter in the section "Employment Taxes").

Your Responsibilities to the Tax Collector

If you want to do things right so you can sleep at night, there's a lot to know about what taxes you owe and where and when to pay them.

You face an array of tax responsibilities on both a federal and state level, including …

- **Federal and state income taxes.** If you have a corporation, you may owe a fee called a franchise tax (even though your eBay business isn't a franchise).

◆ **Employment tax.** If you have any employees (including yourself, if your business is incorporated), you'll have to pay employment taxes. If you're self-employed, you may owe self-employment tax. These taxes are explained later in this chapter.

◆ **Sales tax.** You collect this on certain auctions.

Income Tax

Whether you make a profit or show a loss, you may have to file a tax return for your business. The type of return you file depends on how you've set up your business, as detailed in the following table.

What Tax Return to File

Your Business Entity	Federal Tax Form
C corporation (regular corporation)	Form 1120
Limited liability company with multiple owners	Form 1065
Limited liability company with one owner	Schedule C filed with Form 1040
Partnership	Form 1065
S corporation	Form 1120S
Self-employed	Schedule C filed with Form 1040

If you're self-employed, you must pay your income tax through estimated tax payments due four times during the year. If you've always worked for someone else, you may not be familiar with this type of payment—your taxes have been withheld from each paycheck. But if you don't pay sufficient estimated taxes, you can be subject to penalties that mount up.

If you still have a paycheck coming in the door (yours or your spouse's), you can avoid the need to make estimated tax payments by increasing your withholding to cover what you would have paid in estimated taxes. You can learn about making estimated taxes in IRS Publication 505, "Tax Withholding and Estimated Tax," which you can download from www.irs.gov.

Power Point _____

How will you have the money to pay your estimated taxes? Start a savings or money market account to build up a fund for this purpose. Put money into it on a regular basis so it will be there when it's time to make your estimated tax payments. For example, whenever you make a sale, put one quarter of what you collect into this tax account.

Employment Taxes

If you have employees (or if you are an employee of your corporation), you are responsible for collecting and paying over to the government employment taxes. These include …

- ◆ **Income tax withholding on wages.** The withholding amount depends on the employee's marital status and number of withholding allowances. If you are in a state with state income taxes, you must withhold for both federal and state taxes.

- ◆ **Employee share of Social Security and Medicare taxes** (called FICA tax). For 2007, the Social Security portion is 6.2 percent on wages up to $97,500; the Medicare portion is 1.45 percent on all wages.

- ◆ **Employer share of Social Security and Medicare taxes.** Whatever you withhold for the employee share is the same amount you must match for your employer share.

- ◆ **Federal unemployment tax** (called FUTA tax). This tax is based on a percentage of payroll, up to a set limit.

- ◆ **State unemployment insurance, which is levied like a tax.** The rate you pay is fixed by your state and may vary by your experience with unemployed workers (there's a basic rate to start, and then the rate adjusts when you are in business and have or do not have unemployed former employees).

Think you've escaped employment taxes because you're self-employed? Not so. Being self-employed means you pay both the employee and employer shares of Social Security and Medicare taxes. Collectively, this is called self-employment tax. The only saving grace: you can deduct one half of your self-employment tax as an adjustment to gross income on your tax return (you don't have to itemize to claim this deduction).

An Educated eBay Seller

Want to learn about your employer responsibilities to collect taxes and pay them to the government? You can find out about your federal obligations by downloading for free from www.irs.gov these IRS publications: Publication 15, "Circular E-Employer's Tax Guide"; Publication 15-A, "Employer's Supplemental Tax Guide"; and Publication 15-B, "Employer's Guide to Fringe Benefits." For state employment tax information, contact your state tax, finance, or revenue department.

Sales Tax

Sales tax is a tax levied at the state and local levels (Uncle Sam has nothing to do with it). There are more than 8,500 sales tax jurisdictions nationwide. The question of whether you must be familiar with all of them and collect sales tax whenever you sell an item on eBay is one of the most common questions around. The answer isn't a simple one, but bear with us.

You must collect sales tax on auctions to buyers within your state if your state has a sales tax (only Alaska, Delaware, Montana, New Hampshire, and Oregon don't have any state sales tax, although some localities within these states do levy sales tax). It doesn't matter that you never meet the buyers face to face.

You aren't required to charge sales tax on sales made to buyers in other states if you don't have any connection to those other states. Just selling through the Internet in those states isn't the type of connection that obligates you to collect sales tax. You probably need a physical presence in a state (such as an office or a sales force, something you don't have with a typical eBay business that you run from your home).

Home Office Deduction

The great thing about starting an eBay business is that you may be able to deduct some of your personal expenses as a business write-off. For example, if you rent your home and use a spare bedroom there to run your eBay business, you may be eligible to deduct a portion of your rent, utilities, and other costs, something you couldn't do if you didn't have your eBay business.

But don't get your hopes up too soon. In order to claim a *home office deduction*, you must cross two big hurdles:

◆ The home office must be your principal place of business for your eBay activities.

◆ You must use the space regularly and exclusively for business.

def•i•ni•tion

A portion of the rent you pay for your home (or mortgage interest, real estate taxes, and depreciation on the home, if you own it), plus utilities, homeowner's insurance, and maintenance costs are lumped together as one grand deduction called a **home office deduction.**

Do You Qualify?

To deduct expenses related to running your business from home, you must show that your home office is the principal place of your eBay activities. Usually, this isn't hard to do as long as you don't have any other location you use for this purpose. For example, if you're a stay-at-home parent using eBay as a means to generate some extra income, then your home certainly is the main place for your eBay activities. Congratulations, you've passed the first hurdle.

If you already have a bricks-and-mortar store, you probably can't claim a home office deduction when you opt to do your eBay activities from home *if* these activities are related to your store. If you have a day job and you run your eBay activities from home, hurray for you—your home office deduction is well deserved.

Now to the second hurdle—using the space regularly and exclusively for business. You must devote the space to your business; you can't use it for business by day and for family fun at night. The den is out if this is the only place for your family to watch TV. The kitchen is also out because where else will you prepare meals and eat them?

You don't have to use an entire room for business; a portion of your family room can do. You don't even need to physically partition the space for business. Just be sure to respect the space as your office for eBay business.

As with all rules, there are exceptions, and the "regular and exclusive use" rule has an important exception. If you use space in your home to store your inventory, it doesn't have to be on an exclusive basis. So if you use a corner of your finished basement for this purpose and your children play here, no problem.

What Can You Deduct?

Proving that you're worthy to claim a home office deduction gives you the opportunity to subtract from your business income a wide array of expenses related to your home, things you're paying for anyway.

Two categories of expenses help to make up your home office deduction: direct expenses and indirect expenses. Direct expenses are costs related solely to the home office, such as painting the spare bedroom you use for business. *All* of your direct expenses go into the home office deduction.

Indirect expenses are costs that relate to the entire home, such as your monthly rent, if you are a tenant. In this case, you must allocate the portion of the rent that relates to the space used for business. Usually, the allocation is made on a square-footage basis, using this formula:

Let's say your home is 2,000 square feet and your home office is a room 10 feet by 20 feet, or 200 square feet. Your home office use is 10 percent of your home (200 square feet divided by 2,000 square feet). Of every indirect cost, 10 percent of it can be included in your home office deduction.

Here is a list of the most common indirect expenses you can have:

- Deductible mortgage interest
- Real estate taxes
- Casualty and theft losses
- Depreciation
- Rent
- Utilities
- Insurance

- General repairs to the home (such as painting the outside of the house)
- Security system
- Snow removal
- Cleaning
- Homeowner's association fees

Deductible Depreciation

Depreciation is a deduction for a portion of the cost of your home claimed over a period fixed by law (for your home office, it works out to about 40 years). Here is how you figure this deduction:

1. Start with your home's basis (how much you paid for it). Don't count the land on which the home sits.

2. Compare basis to its value at the time you start to use a home office. Again, don't count the land on which the home sits.

3. Take the lower of basis or value—this is the amount to be depreciated.

4. Apply the home office percentage representing the portion of the home used for business.

5. Apply the depreciation percentage from the following table to find your depreciation deduction. The percentage you use depends on the month in which you start to use the home office and how many years you've used it as such.

Depreciation Deduction Rates

Year	Jan	Feb	Mar	Apr	May	Jun
1	2.461	2.247	2.033	1.819	1.605	1.391
2–39	2.564	2.564	2.564	2.564	2.564	2.564
40	0.107	0.321	0.535	0.749	0.963	1.177

Year	Jul	Aug	Sep	Oct	Nov	Dec
1	1.177	0.963	0.749	0.535	0.321	0.107
2–39	2.564	2.564	2.564	2.564	2.564	2.564
40	1.391	1.605	1.819	2.033	2.247	2.461

Auction Alert

Think you can claim the full home office deduction? Maybe not. The deduction is limited to the extent of gross income from your home office activity (eBay selling). As long as you make money, go ahead and claim the full write-off. If not, the deduction is limited this year (you get to carry forward the unused portion of the deduction and can claim it if and when you become profitable). Don't feel too confused—the gross income limitation is built into the home office deduction form you must complete, IRS Form 8829.

For example, if you start using your home office for business in March, your depreciation rate for the first year is 2.033% and 2.564% for years 2 through 39. If the basis for your home office is $10,000, then your depreciation deduction for the first year is $203.30 ($10,000 × 2.033%).

What if You're Incorporated?

The home office deduction applies if you are self-employed or are an owner in a partnership or limited liability company. But what if you're incorporated so that you're an employee of your corporation?

As an employee, you can claim the deduction only if you meet both home office deduction hurdles *and* show that you use the office in your home for your employer's (the corporation's) convenience. This probably isn't difficult to do if your business doesn't have any other location. But if it does, you must show that you use your home office because there isn't adequate space at the company's other location or for some reason other than your preference to work from home.

As an employee, your home office deduction can be claimed only as an unreimbursed miscellaneous itemized deduction. If you don't itemize, you don't get any write-off. If you do itemize, your miscellaneous deductions can be claimed only to the extent that they exceed 2 percent of your adjusted gross income.

If your corporation pays you rent for use of the home office, the corporation can deduct the payment. But, by the same token, you must report the rent and can't claim any deduction for expenses related to your home.

Other Write-Offs

Every dollar that you deduct reduces the income on which you pay taxes. You pay taxes only on your net profit, and deductions are subtractions against this figure.

What's a deduction worth to you? It depends entirely on your tax bracket. If you're self-employed and in the 25 percent tax bracket, every dollar you write off is worth 25¢ to you. That's the amount of tax you save by claiming the deduction.

If you have enough deductions, you may wind up in a lower tax bracket. For example, instead of being in the 25 percent, your deductions may drop you into the 15 percent tax bracket.

Just about every penny you spend on business is a write-off. The general rule for determining deductibility is whether an expense is ordinary and necessary for your business. But even if an expense is ordinary and necessary, the tax laws may impose limits to prevent complete deductibility or affect the timing of when to claim a write-off, but think in terms of deductions. Whatever you spend money on in your business can probably be subtracted from your income.

Common Business Deductions:

Accounting fees	Legal fees
Advertising	Merchant authorization fees
Bad debts	PayPal fees
Bank charges	Repairs and maintenance
Car and truck expenses	Subscriptions and dues
Commissions and fees	Supplies
Computers and software	Taxes and licenses
eBay fees for listing and selling items	Travel, meals, and entertainment (including attendance at eBay Live!)
Education expenses (such as the cost of attending eBay University)	Utilities, including monthly cell phone and Blackberry fees
Insurance	Wages
Interest payments	

In some cases, business expenses may be treated as a tax credit instead of a deduction. This type of write-off is worth more than a mere deduction. A tax credit reduces your taxes dollar for dollar. For example, if your eBay business blossoms so that you hire two employees and set up a qualified retirement plan for them and you, you can claim a $500 tax credit for administrative costs in each of the first three years of having the plan. Say your tax bill would have been $4,300. With this tax credit, you pay only $3,800 ($4,300–$500).

> **An Educated eBay Seller**
>
> To learn more about your deduction options and where to claim them, see IRS Publication 334, "Tax Guide for Small Business," at www.irs.gov.

Your Car Expenses

If you hop from flea market to flea market in your SUV, you can deduct the costs of using your car for business. There are two ways to deduct your costs: actual expenses or the IRS standard mileage allowance.

If you use the actual expense method, you must keep track of your expenses:

- Depreciation, if you own the car. Depreciation for cars is *very* complicated (if you want to learn more, see IRS Publication 463 at www.irs.gov).

- Garage rent

- Gas

- Insurance

- Lease payments, if you lease the car

- Licenses

- Oil

- Parking

- Repairs

- Servicing

- Tires

- Tolls

- Towing

Instead of keeping detailed records on these expenses, you can rely on an IRS standard mileage rate—a cents-per-mile rate that's adjusted annually to take inflation (or deflation) into account. For 2007, the rate is 48.5¢ per mile. This rate takes into account *all* of the expenses listed above, except parking and tolls, which you can deduct in addition to claiming the standard mileage rate.

Using the standard mileage rate simplifies your record-keeping life (though you still need to track your mileage, date, and business purpose of each trip). But it may not adequately reflect your actual costs. For example, even though the price of gasoline rose by 46 percent in the first six months of 2007, there was no upward adjustment to the IRS standard mileage rate.

Auction Alert

You can't claim a deduction for your car use without a written or electronic mileage record—you must say under penalty of perjury on your return that you have this record.

However you figure your car expense deduction, you must keep track of the miles you drive for business. This means noting the odometer readings for every business outing and the date and purpose of the trip. Keep this log in writing or by using a PDA. Measure your mileage from your home to your business stops and back again.

Travel and Entertainment Costs

Unless you're locked in your home office behind your computer 24/7, you probably get around town to do some business. Maybe you meet with a vendor from whom you buy inventory. Maybe you go out of town once a year to eBay Live!. The cost of your travel and entertainment (T&E) may be partially or fully deductible.

Here's a rundown of some T&E expenses you may have:

- **Local transportation costs.** If you get around town by subway, bus, or taxi— to get to the bank, visit your accountant, or meet up with a new vendor—you can deduct these costs.

- **Travel to another city.** If you go out of town on business, your transportation costs (such as airfare or train fare), lodging, half of your meals, and all incidental expenses (such as use of the hotel fax machine) are deductible. However, there are limits when you combine business with pleasure on these trips.

Power Point _____

To learn all the ins and outs of T&E expenses, download for free IRS Publication 463, "Travel, Entertainment, Gift, and Car Expenses," from www.irs.gov.

- **Business meals.** Feeding yourself on your turf is your own business, and Uncle Sam won't share the cost with you when you eat alone. But if you wine and dine customers, employees, or vendors, you can write off 50 percent of any meal— breakfast, lunch, dinner, or even high tea. And, as we've covered, you can deduct half your meal costs while you are away from home on business, even when you dine by yourself.

- **Entertainment costs.** If you take a vendor to a ballgame or show, 50 percent of the cost of tickets is deductible. Of course, you must entertain for business and not purely social purposes.

- **Gifts.** You can be as generous as you want with your customers and suppliers. But the government will underwrite your generosity only up to $25 per person per year. A bottle of wine within this dollar limit is fine; front-row seats to a Broadway show at $200 a seat for a supplier to use on a trip to the Big Apple (without you) still is only deductible up to $25!

The following table shows you what T&E expenses you *can't* write off.

Limits on T&E Expenses

Type of Expense	Limit
Club dues (other than chambers of commerce and other business, professional, and civic organizations)	Not deductible
Entertainment	50 percent of cost not deductible
Gifts	Cost over $25
Meals	50 percent of cost not deductible
Travel costs of your spouse	Not deductible (unless your spouse works for you)

Do you attend eBay Live! or an eBay summit? You can deduct your travel expenses for this convention or any eBay summit. Deductible expenses include …

- ◆ **Transportation to and from the convention.** This includes airfare to get to the convention, as well as local transportation costs (for example, taxi fares) to get from your hotel to the convention center.

- ◆ **Lodging.** If you stay extra days beyond the days of the convention to sight see, the room cost of these days isn't deductible. But if you spend extra days meeting with suppliers, the cost of the extra days is deductible.

- ◆ **Meals.** All your food costs are deductible. But there's a 50 percent limit (the other half is not deductible).

- ◆ **Fees.** These include eBay Live! or other convention attendance fees.

Equipment and Supplies

The word *equipment* may conjure up pictures of John Deere tractors or factory drill presses. But it includes just about anything you use to run your business, such as a computer, a desk, and a telephone.

Obviously, you need certain things to run your eBay business. The basics were laid out for you in Chapter 2. What we want to help you think about here is what your decision means taxwise. You have two choices: buy or lease the things you need. If you lease equipment, you can deduct your lease payments that you make each month.

If you buy equipment, you may be able to deduct the cost up front, even if you finance the purchase. A special tax rule, called first-year expensing or a Section 179 deduction, enables you to write off in 2007 up to $125,000 of the cost of equipment in the year you acquire it, instead of having to depreciate the cost over a fixed number of years, typically five years or seven years, depending on the type of equipment you buy. (The dollar limit is adjusted annually for inflation.) Here's what you need to know in order to use this expensing option:

> **An Educated eBay Seller**
>
> The rules for expensing and depreciating business equipment are complicated. To gain a better understanding, read IRS Publication 946, "How to Depreciate Property." You can download this publication for free from www.irs.gov.

- **You must elect to use it.** The deduction isn't automatic. The election is made in Part I of IRS Form 4562, "Depreciation and Amortization."

- **You must be profitable to use it.** If you are having a bad year, don't make the election and simply figure the depreciation allowance for the item. This allowance will be figured into your loss for the year.

- **Check state income tax rules.** Many states have not adopted the expensing option; you'll have to use depreciation for state tax purposes even if you expense the item on your federal tax return.

Supplies you buy for your business are 100 percent deductible. Supplies are a broad category and include packing materials (for example, tape, boxes, bubble wrap, and labels), office supplies (for example, computer paper, paper clips, and cellophane tape), and cleaning supplies (for example, paper towels, spray cleansers, and window cleaners).

Other Deductible Expenses

If you incur it, you can probably deduct it. From your banking fees, PayPal fees, and merchant authorization charges for accepting credit card payments, to copying you do at the local library in researching a rare item you've found, as long as the expense is for your eBay business, it's most likely a tax write-off.

To help you get a general idea of the types of expenses you can deduct, just take a look at the deduction section of your tax return. For example, the portion of Schedule C for self-employed individuals provides special lines for deductible expenses.

Of course, you're not limited to these categories of deductible expenses. You can list other types of deductible items in Part IV of Schedule C. And there's a special line for including your home office deduction.

Figure 16.1

Deduct your expenses.

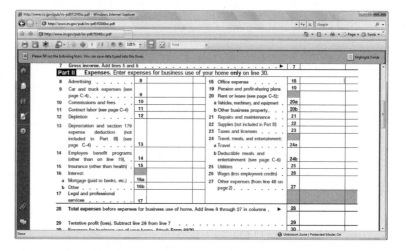

An Educated eBay Seller

Want to learn more about deductible expenses? You'll find a laundry list of items you can write off explained in IRS Publication 535, "Business Expenses." For the self-employed, these expenses are also covered in IRS Publication 334, "Tax Guide for Small Business." You can download these very helpful publications for free from www.irs.gov.

The Least You Need to Know

◆ Your tax status as a casual seller, hobbyist, or business owner determines how you report income and expenses on your return.

◆ Running a business entails income tax, sales tax, and possibly employment tax responsibilities.

◆ If you run your eBay business from home, you can claim a home office deduction.

◆ You can deduct various business expenses, including business use of your car, travel and entertainment costs, and expensing of equipment costs.

Part  Taking Your eBay Business to the Next Level

You've made it. Your business is humming along. Your feedback rating is superior, and you're beaming with confidence. Now's the time to ratchet up your business and take it to the next level.

In this part of the book, you'll learn about what it takes to become a PowerSeller and the rewards it can bring you. You'll become acquainted with other selling venues to take you through multi-channel selling to the next level. You'll discover alternatives for bringing in another pair of hands to help you and what it means for your business. You'll find out about auction-management tools that can make your business run more efficiently so you can conduct more sales. You'll see how to find the money you need for expansion. And you'll find out all the ways you can continue to learn and stay current, as well as connect with the eBay Community, so you can grow your business.

Chapter 17

Power Up to PowerSeller Status

In This Chapter

- ◆ Becoming a PowerSeller
- ◆ Using PowerSeller status as a marketing tool
- ◆ Reaping the benefits of PowerSeller status

If eBay is your full-time or part-time business, you may reach a level of activity that garners you a special status, called PowerSeller. Becoming and retaining this special status opens up a new level of possibility for you on eBay.

In this chapter, you'll learn how to achieve the prized PowerSeller designation. You'll find out how to use this exclusive title to market yourself and realize even greater sales on eBay. You'll also learn about the wide array of benefits that you become entitled to just for being a PowerSeller, including access to eBay customer service and attending special events.

So You Want to Be a PowerSeller

Who doesn't want to become a PowerSeller? Becoming a PowerSeller is quite an achievement. It means your sales activity has reached a critical mass and you gain entry into the wonderful world of PowerSeller.

No one (outside of eBay) knows the real numbers on how many sellers have achieved PowerSeller status. Just accept the fact that it's a select few—some estimate that about 4 percent of sellers have this designation. Only a handful are in the highest tier of PowerSeller—Titanium—as explained later in this chapter.

Power Point _____

Becoming a PowerSeller is a goal to aspire to if you make eBay your full-time business. It may take time—months, if not a year or more—but going for the designation is essential. Run the numbers to see for yourself. After all, achieving the gold level—the third tier—only means you're making sales of $120,000 per year. After you net out your cost of inventory and other expenses, you're far short of making millions! But it's not peanuts either.

Becoming a PowerSeller doesn't mean you'll pay lower eBay listing and other fees—the fees remain the same for *all* eBay sellers. It won't cut your PayPal fees either. Becoming a PowerSeller doesn't mean you can coast. If you fail to maintain a certain level of activity, you'll lose your special designation.

Is there any downside to being a PowerSeller? Other than the hard work you probably put in to become and remain a PowerSeller, there's nothing negative about it. There's no cost or application process. You can pass up on any or all of the benefits that you'll find out about in this chapter.

What It Takes to Become a PowerSeller

To become a PowerSeller, you must meet *all* of the following criteria:

♦ **Active member.** You can't become a PowerSeller on the day you complete your first sale on eBay. You have to be an active member for at least 90 days. Also, your account must be in good financial standing.

♦ **Revenues.** Those little sales can add up to PowerSeller status. You must average a minimum of $1,000 in sales each month for three consecutive months. Sales (final values not including shipping costs) count not only on eBay.com, but also Half.com, eBay Express, and eBay Motors.

- ◆ **Number of sales.** One giant sale won't cut it. You need to average at least four sales a month for three months to qualify for PowerSeller status.

- ◆ **Feedback.** It may take time to meet this requirement—you need an overall feedback score of at least 100, of which at least 98 percent is positive. So if you only have 100 feedback, no more than 2 of them can be negative in order to be 98 percent positive. Feedback for purposes of figuring PowerSeller eligibility is different than the usual way. Ordinarily, only unique feedback (from different people) counts, but for PowerSeller status, *all* feedback (including from repeat buyers) counts.

- ◆ **eBay values.** While you don't have to take a written test or swear on a Bible, you must agree to uphold eBay community values, which includes being honest, timely, and willing to give everyone you deal with respect. You must follow all eBay listing policies as well.

You don't have to apply to become a PowerSeller; it's automatic. eBay monitors your activities and once you meet the criteria, you'll be notified that you're now a member of this exclusive club. Then you simply enroll (follow the instructions that eBay gives you) and you're in. There's no membership fee or enrollment cost to become a PowerSeller.

Power Point

When responding to your invitation to enroll as a Power-Seller, it sometimes happens that you'll receive an e-mail message that you are *not* eligible. Try again. If this fails, contact eBay via powersellerinfo@ebay.com.

Welcome to the club! That's what the package you receive from eBay tells you. The package outlines the perks of your new-found status (explained later in this chapter).

Auction Alert

There are people on sites other than eBay who are selling PowerSeller designations. For a fee they promise you can step into their shoes and operate on eBay as a PowerSeller. While eBay has not yet caught onto this scam, it surely will at some point, and those who have bought their way into PowerSeller status may find they're not only out the money they paid to the scamster who sold it to them; they may also be barred from selling on eBay. And even if not barred, they may lose the status if they fail to maintain PowerSeller requirements.

PowerSeller to the Tenth Power

"PowerSeller" is an umbrella term for sellers who meet certain criteria. But all PowerSellers are not created equal. The following table shows the level of sales needed for each type of PowerSeller designation:

PowerSeller Designations

Tier	Monthly Sales Level
Bronze	$1,000
Silver	$3,000
Gold	$10,000
Platinum	$25,000
Titanium	$150,000

What do these designations mean to you? Plenty! The good news is that buyers don't know the difference—even if you're only a Bronze PowerSeller, you still call yourself a PowerSeller and use the PowerSeller icon on all your eBay transactions.

Seasonal sellers take heart! You too can be a PowerSeller for your season, even though you don't maintain the same level of sales activity throughout the year. If only the summer months or the Christmas season are hot for you, eBay will determine whether you qualify to display the PowerSeller icon for your season.

Figure 17.1

Recognize a PowerSeller by his or her icon

High-volume, low-dollar sellers—you can also be PowerSellers. Even though you don't meet the monthly sales level in dollars, eBay now gives PowerSeller status based on the number of sales. Details of this are not available as the book is going to press, so check on eBay.

There are incentives from eBay that encourage you to rise through the ranks. The higher your status, the greater attention you command from eBay and this can help you grow your business. Priority eSupport (help through e-mail) helps you resolve problems that you can't otherwise deal with through standard Live Help channels open to any eBay user. Access to the toll-free number for Silver PowerSellers and up saves time and aggravation in resolving problems like removal of feedback, reporting a violation, asking why your listing was ended early, and resolving billing issues. A special Trust and Safety phone number is available from 6 A.M. to 6 P.M. PST, with questions handled within 36 hours.

eBay values its Gold, Platinum, and Titanium PowerSellers so much that these sellers are assigned their own account managers to help their eBay businesses run as smoothly as possible (the same account managers usually handle PowerSellers selling the same items, such as electronics, clothing, or music). These PowerSellers can meet their account managers in person at events such as the annual eBay Live! convention. The following table shows the level of support services you qualify for once you attain a tier of PowerSeller status.

PowerSeller Support Services

Tier	Priority eSupport	Toll-Free Phone	Account Manager
Bronze	Yes	No	No
Silver	Yes	Yes	No
Gold	Yes	Yes	Yes
Platinum	Yes	Yes	Yes
Titanium	Yes	Yes	Yes

If your sales activities grow, eBay will notify you when you've been boosted to the next tier. You don't have to take any initiative to see that the higher status is awarded to you. For more information about the PowerSeller program, go to http://pages.ebay.com/services/buyandsell/welcome.html.

Staying a PowerSeller

Becoming a PowerSeller is step one. Now you have to work hard to keep this status. Don't worry—one slow month won't throw you out of the club. eBay monitors your sales activities every month.

You keep your PowerSeller status as long as you continue your 98 percent positive total feedback rating, average at least four sales a month, meet the sales amounts, and continue to comply with eBay policies.

If you fail to meet the criteria, you have a 30-day grace period to bring your activities up to speed. You can contact eBay to put your PowerSeller status "on hold" if you're going on an extended vacation or have other special circumstances, such as a family emergency.

Auction Alert

Violating eBay's shill bidding policy can cost you your PowerSeller status. Shill bidding is a practice that artificially drives up the auction price with the help of a friend or relative and is forbidden on eBay. If a PowerSeller violates this policy or any other eBay policy (such as soliciting off-site sales or misrepresenting an item) more than a certain number of times within 60 days, he forfeits his status: Bronze—4 violations; Silver and Gold—5 violations; Platinum—6 violations; and Titanium—7 violations.

PowerSeller Status as a Marketing Tool

Because selling on eBay requires that buyers trust you, the ability to display your PowerSeller icon can mean more money for you. Some discussion boards question whether the icon translates into more sales, but we think it can't hurt (after all, buyers know you've done a certain level of business to qualify as a PowerSeller, so you probably aren't a fly-by-night seller).

The PowerSeller icon appears next to your user ID on all your ongoing sales and links to your PowerSeller information page. This doesn't happen automatically; it is a preference you set within Selling Preferences in My eBay.

You can also use the PowerSeller icon on:

- About Me page
- Item listings
- Store pages
- Your personal website (apart from eBay)

Figure 17.2

Add the PowerSeller icon wherever you can be found

Being a PowerSeller entitles you to a 30 percent discount on SquareTrade (the usual cost is $9.50 per month). SquareTrade is a seal that you can display on your auctions and other selling sites to assure buyers that you adhere to the highest standards for customer service—SquareTrade won't let anyone use the seal unless they agree to the company's standards. Currently, more than three million listings show the SquareTrade seal.

> **Power Point**
>
> Use eBay-provided templates to add the PowerSeller logo to your business cards and letterhead. This will reinforce your status when you communicate with existing and potential customers.

PowerSeller Perks

Being a PowerSeller has its privileges. It not only helps you in marketing on and off eBay; it also entitles you to some things that non-PowerSellers can't get. And it doesn't hurt your ego to know you've achieved this special status.

Once you become a PowerSeller, you'll receive a certificate of achievement from eBay. While this piece of paper may not seem like much, the benefits that come along with it are significant.

Personal and Business Benefits

If eBay is your business, you probably want certain benefits—the same benefits you'd look for when working for a large corporation.

◆ **Health care.** Currently, Mercer Health & Benefits, a company working with eBay's PowerSellers, can help find medical plans for individuals and small businesses in every state. eBay makes available to PowerSellers a discount prescription and health card—the card is free. The discounts can save you money on prescription drugs, vision care, vitamins and supplements, and hearing aids.

◆ **Unpaid Item Protection (UIP).** In a pilot program begun on August 1, 2007, and set to run for the remainder of 2007, PowerSellers can receive credit for their listing upgrade fees if they file an Unpaid Item Claim (http://pages.ebay. com/services/buyandsell/powerseller/unpaiditem_protection.html). Presumably, if the program proves successful, eBay will extend it.

Reseller Marketplace

One of the largest challenges to selling on eBay is finding items at affordable prices that you can list for sale. Being a PowerSeller gives you access to the Reseller Marketplace. This is a liquidation site where you can buy inventory in discounted lot sizes from manufacturers, liquidators, and wholesalers.

There's no charge for accessing this portal to a wide world of exclusive sourcing for your eBay activities. Just log in using your PowerSeller user ID and password. You don't have to go through the Reseller Marketplace to find things for resale, but it's a great resource if you need it.

PowerSeller Community

PowerSellers are an elite group and enjoy interacting with others in the group. Here are some ways to optimize your status:

◆ **Participate in discussion boards.** There are discussion boards on eBay dedicated to PowerSellers. Learn trading secrets and points from others who've achieved this special status. Discuss with other selling whizzes any problem bidders and other issues that are troubling you.

◆ **Join the eBay PowerSellers News Group.** While this public forum is open to anyone (you don't have to be a PowerSeller to join), it features the latest news affecting the PowerSeller program. Just hit the "Join Group" button at http:// groups.ebay.com/forum.jspa?forumID=100011305 to receive PowerSeller news via e-mail.

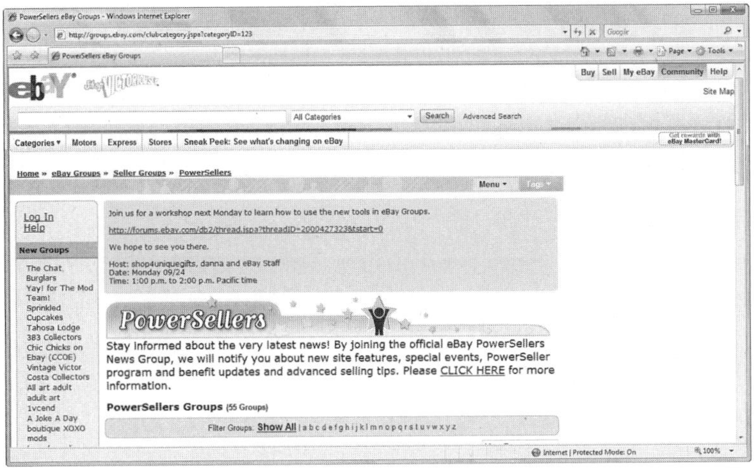

Figure 17.3

Join the PowerSeller News Group

◆ **Join a special trade organization.** PeSA (Professional eBay Sellers Association) at www.gopesa.org is the world's largest trade association dedicated to top eBay sellers—Platinum and Titanium, and for high-volume low-price sellers. Founded in 2003, its members sell over $400 million in merchandise on eBay each year. Members must adhere to high standards in their trading activities; their listings appear in a special directory and they can participate in semi-annual events. Membership costs $199 a year for the United States, and $249 for PeSA Australia.

◆ **Subscribe to the PowerSeller Report.** This independent online publication (www.tprweb.com) contains articles, tips, wholesale lists, and links to help you make more money on eBay. A one-year subscription costs $99; a three-month auto-renewal subscription costs $27.95.

◆ **Participate in special events.** You can attend exclusive meetings and activities at eBay Live! (the annual convention). You are also invited to special events through eBay University as it tours the country or to attend special webinars on eBay. Occasionally, there are special events and promotions. For example, in the fall of 2006, there was an eBay PowerSeller Challenge where participants were given their own sales goals; those who met their personalized target received a one-time eBay listing fee credit equal to 1 percent of the difference between the target and the final value of eligible sales during the challenge period, and all participants were entered for a chance to win one of ten $5,000 cash prizes.

The Least You Need to Know

◆ Becoming a PowerSeller requires you to have a certain number of feedbacks, sales, and revenue, and meet other requirements fixed by eBay.

◆ Becoming a PowerSeller is an important marketing tool to grow your business even more.

◆ PowerSeller status entitles you to special customer assistance and other benefits through eBay.

◆ Joining the PowerSeller community opens up a world of special communications and events.

Chapter 18

Multi-Channel Selling

In This Chapter

- ◆ Setting up an eBay Store to complement your auction activities
- ◆ Using live auctions in association with eBay
- ◆ Increasing your revenue by becoming an eBay affiliate or a Trading Assistant
- ◆ Multi-level marketing for eBay
- ◆ eBay alternative sales venues

Selling on eBay isn't limited to auctions—you can open an online store-front to sell items at fixed prices. You can also make money through eBay by becoming an eBay affiliate. And you can make money by becoming a Trading Assistant to handle the sales of others. All of these options are methods to increase your income and boost your sales.

In this chapter, you'll learn about eBay Stores and how you can use them to grow your business. You'll see how and when to use live auctions that you conduct yourself or sell your items at live auction houses. You'll find out other ways you can make money through eBay.

For selling tips on improving your listings and managing multiple auctions, see Chapter 7. For marketing strategies, see Chapter 10.

eBay Stores

eBay Stores aren't bricks-and-mortar locations for your business. They're online storefronts at which you create an online catalog to sell items through fixed price (Buy It Now) listings. Your eBay Store becomes part of the vast eBay mall. eBay Stores were started in 2001 as a way to augment auction sales for customers who prefer fixed pricing. You can find eBay Stores through the eBay home page (the individual stores are listed at http://stores.ebay.com/*the name of your store*).

Having an eBay Store is a way to bring your business to the next level—the majority of eBay Store sellers said that operating an eBay Store increased their overall sales. It not only opens up another way in which to make money on eBay, but it also creates an image for your business, giving you credibility that can enhance both store and auction sales.

An eBay Store is made up of customized pages that you create using HTML or eBay-provided templates to list the items you have for sale. Obviously, you need to have a number of items to stock your store shelves, or it doesn't pay to start your store.

Power Point _____

You do not need a professional to set up a store—just follow the eBay instructions. However, if you have the money and want to polish your look, consider working with a company that can upgrade your store's appearance. For example, PixClinic, the eBay Store remodelers (www.pixclinic.com/ebay-stores-design.html), creates logos, custom headers, multiple storefront pages, and professional pictures.

Figure 18.1

eBay Stores provide an outlet for fixed-price selling.

Do you need an eBay Store if you have your own website? There's no fixed answer; nothing prevents you from having both. But if you maintain a website, you have more flexibility in selling your other items, and, best of all, you save on eBay fees. For example, you can create an online catalog of your items for sale at your website, compared with a simple listing at an eBay Store. On the other hand, eBay fees are minor compared with the cost of setting up and maintaining your own website.

Having an eBay store can entitle you to claim a Store Referral Credit, which is a credit you receive for successfully driving buyers to your eBay Store directly from a location outside of eBay (such as your own website). The Store Referral Credit is a 75 percent credit on your Final Value Fees.

Power Point

As an eBay Store owner, you receive *free* monthly sales reports. Data enables you to assess your sales efforts. Information is broken down by listing format and category. If your sales are not doing well or you want to make room for new inventory, you might consider putting items on sale. This can be easily done using Markdown Manager (http://pages.ebay.com/help/specialtysites/items_on_sale.html), an eBay tool that lets you cut prices by a fixed percentage or dollar amount that you choose.

A comprehensive multi-channel management tool is available through Infopia (www.infopia.com). This will help you manage multi-channel inventory, marketplace listings, and fulfillment. There are special tools for PowerSellers. You must call for pricing at 1-888-337-6352.

Stores Versus Auction Format

Having an eBay Store isn't mutually exclusive with running auctions. You can—and probably should—run auctions and also maintain storefronts (through either eBay or your own website) if your selling activities are at a high enough level. Each complements the other. Your store drives people to your auctions, and your auctions drive people to your store.

When you see copy on auction listings that says "Buy More Great Items from This Seller," this can mean the seller has an eBay Store. If the seller has an eBay store, a door icon will be present after the user ID.

Having a store and conducting auctions that each refer to the other is called cross-promotion—one thing drives another. There is a cross-promotional tool that you can use to simplify your cross-promotions. The tool is free for anyone with an eBay Store.

> **An Educated eBay Seller**
>
> Take the Cross-Promotion Tutorial (www.ebay.com/stores/cross-promotions/tutorial) to learn how to increase your sales by listing store items on your auctions.

Before you fully commit to running an eBay Store, you can test the waters by taking advantage of the eBay 30-day free-trial period for your store. At the end of this period, if you don't see things working out, you can decide against continuing the store and won't incur any costs.

Let's say you decide that a storefront would be a great complement to your eBay auctions. You *don't* have to go with an eBay storefront. Many eBay sellers do because of the synergy this creates. But you can set up a storefront of your own so that you don't have to pay eBay listing and Final Value Fees. For example, Vendio Stores (www.vendio.com/my/shop/promo_st.html) is a popular alternative. Here you pay a flat monthly fee of $14.95 for an unlimited number of items in your store, plus a lower Final Value Fee of $0.10 per item sold.

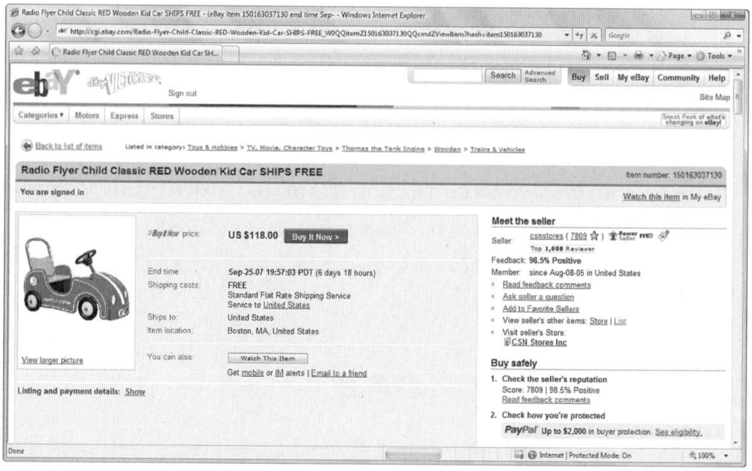

Figure 18.2

Your cue that a seller has an eBay Store.

Opening Your Store

As with listing items for auction, opening and maintaining an eBay Store is easy. eBay provides all the instructions you need to proceed. Eligibility requirements for becoming a store owner are negligible: you only need to have a feedback score of 20 or be ID Verified. The ID Verify Program is run by a third party that checks your credit history (cost: $5). Being ID Verified gives you an icon for this status, which lasts until you change your address or phone number.

Before you start, be sure to select a name for your store. Make the name representative of what you sell. For example, Mile High Comics has been in the business of selling comic books in four retail stores in Colorado for 30 years and maintains an eBay Store. Its main website is www.milehighcomics.com, but at eBay Stores, you can find it through Mile-High-Comics, a name that is descriptive of the products it sells.

Power Point _____

Your store opening is a marketing opportunity. Let your existing customers and the public know about your new store through a mailing, a press release, and other announcements. Create visibility for this event.

Your eBay Store is your unique location on this site. You get your own URL and can register your own unique portion of this URL as your domain name. For example, Bodiddy, a store selling various items, including Shabby chic collectibles, has an eBay address at http://stores.ebay.com/Bodiddy. This business could obtain a domain name under Bodiddy (assuming such name has not been previously registered by someone else).

Once you decide to open an eBay Store, decide on the store level you want. You have three options:

- **Basic Store.** This is the basic storefront with the lowest "monthly rent" in the form of a monthly subscription fee (explained shortly).

- **Premium Store.** This is the next step up, to double the size and increased exposure on eBay pages, for about three times the cost of the Basic Store.

- **Anchor Store.** This is the deluxe storefront, with triple the regular size but added customer support and more, for 30 times the cost of the Basic Store.

Store Fees

One fee does _not_ cover all. Several different costs are associated with maintaining an eBay Store. A complete list of fees can be found at http://pages.ebay.com/help/sell/storefees.html.

The main charge is your subscription fee, which you pay each month. Think of this as your monthly rental cost for store space. The higher the rent is, the more space (pages) you get (the first 30 days of any level you select are free).

- **Basic.** This store level is designed for beginners with low-level sales. It will get you going; you can upgrade later. You get five pages for your listings. Cost: $15.95 per month, plus a free subscription to Selling Manager (which is regularly $4.99 a month).

- **Premium.** This store level is for small to medium-size sellers who want to be more aggressive. The higher price buys you 10 pages of listings, plus a free subscription to Selling Manager Pro (which normally costs $15.99 per month) and eBay Marketplace Research Basic (normally $9.99 a month), increased exposure on eBay store pages, dedicated 24 hour support, and more. Cost: $49.95 per month.

- **Anchored.** This store level is for large, high-volume sellers. The price includes 15 pages of listings, free subscriptions to Selling Manager Pro (normally $15.99 a month) and eBay Marketplace Research Pro (regularly $24.99 a month), plus everything available through the Premium store, including 24/7 dedicated live customer support from eBay. Cost: $299.95 per month.

def•i•ni•tion

If you want an item to be in your store until it's sold or you want to remove it from your inventory, insert it as **Good 'Til Cancelled.** You pay a fee for this as if you are listing it over and over again every 30 days.

Your second main cost is insertion fees for your listings. Think of this cost as a stocking fee for filling your shelves. You have the space, but you pay for each item you put on your shelf by listing it. Unlike auctions that can run a maximum of 10 days, store items can be listed virtually forever. You can even list items as *Good 'Til Canceled* (GTC).

The insertion fee covers any quantity of items with a single listing (for example, the same fee applies to 1 or 100 cameras, as long as they are all the same). The following table lists the insertion fees for the store inventory format.

Store Inventory Format Insertion Fees

Starting or Reserve Price	30 days	Good 'Til Canceled
$0.01 to $24.99	$0.05	$0.50
$25 and above	$0.10	$0.10

As you can see, the insertion fee for eBay Store inventory is much lower than for eBay auctions. The third main cost of having a store is the fee you pay to eBay when something sells. Just as in the auction format, the amount of the fee depends on the cost of the item sold (called its closing or final value). The fee for eBay Store sellers is higher than for eBay auctions. The following table lists the fees.

Final Value Fees

Closing Price	Final Value Fee
Item not sold	No fee
$0.01–$25	10 percent of the closing price
$25.01–$100	10 percent of the initial $25 ($2.50), plus 7 percent of the remaining closing value balance
$100.01–$1,000	10 percent of the initial $25 ($2.50), plus 7 percent of $25.01–$1,000 ($5.25), plus 5 percent on the remaining closing value balance
Over $1,000	10 percent of the initial $25 ($2.50), plus 7 percent of $25.01–$1,000 ($5.25), plus 5 percent on $100.01–$1,000 ($45.00), plus 3 percent of the remaining closing value balance

Power Point

Store Referral Credits are credits that store sellers are eligible to receive by driving traffic to their stores through non-eBay sources, such as their own website or e-mails sent to prospects, so that the buyer comes to eBay from an outside source (not from within eBay). The buyer's browser must accept cookies, a small text file placed on the buyer's computer to denote that he or she came from an outside source. If the buyer purchases the item from your store during this browser session, you will get the credit, which is 75 percent back on your Final Value Fee. For details, see http://pages.ebay.com/storefronts/referral-credit-faq.html.

As with auction listing upgrades (explained in Chapter 7), eBay offers various enhancements you can use to highlight the listings in your store. Each feature you use costs, and, collectively, they can add up to serious money. The amount you pay for each enhancement depends on the features you select and the listing period (for example, 30 days or 120 days). If you opt for GTC, you pay the 30-day fee every 30 days that the item remains listed. The following table shows the listing-upgrade fees.

Listing-Upgrade Fees

Feature	30 Days
Gallery	$0.01
Item subtitle	$0.02
Listing designer	$0.10
Bold	$1.00
Border	$3.00
Highlight	$5.00
Featured Plus!	$19.95
First Picture	Free
Each additional picture	$0.15
Supersize pictures	$0.75
Picture show	Free
Picture pack	$0.76

Being a Trading Assistant

High-powered sellers who have mastered eBay sales techniques can put their knowledge to good use by selling for others. eBay has a program called Trading Assistant, in which you can become a Certified Trading Assistant. This status enables you to be listed in the eBay Trading Assistants Directory for free so that anyone interested in having another person handle the sale of his or her items can find you.

Do you feel qualified enough to handle someone else's sales? This is a question only you can answer. But eBay has minimum requirements for you to act as a Certified Trading Assistant. You must meet all three tests:

◆ You've sold at least 10 items in the last 3 months.

◆ You have a feedback score of 100 or higher.

◆ More than 97 percent of your feedback is positive.

What can you charge for your work as a Trading Assistant? This is entirely up to you; eBay does not set any guidelines or rules. Obviously, you can charge only what the traffic will bear (essentially, what other Trading Assistants are charging). You can charge a fixed rate per sale, a percentage of the final sale price, or a combination of both. It's up to you to negotiate the terms on which you'll act as someone's agent.

If you become a Trading Assistant, be sure to take the following actions:

- ◆ Use a written contract for each sale. After having a discussion with the person you are selling the item for, put the terms on paper.

- ◆ Take possession of the item before you list it. Don't rely on a picture to create a listing for the item; there may be flaws not readily apparent.

- ◆ Guard against stolen goods. Do your own research on the item (e.g., check serial numbers with local police for consumer electronic items that could possibly have been stolen). Look at the person's driver's license for identification and, when paying him for a completed sale, use a check made payable to him at the same address.

- ◆ Agree with the person what the minimum selling price should be. Then set this as the reserve. Decide in advance what happens if the item doesn't sell.

To learn more about being an eBay Trading Assistant, review the discussion in Chapter 1 and also go to http://pages.ebay.com/tradingassistants/learnmore.html#requirements.

Using Live Auctions

eBay now provides an opportunity to hold your auctions in real time through an eBay-approved auction house—live on an auction floor in a bricks-and-mortar auction house. Here you'll see items for sale such as Americana arts and crafts, Persian rugs, antique toys, and nineteenth-century European furniture. If you have high-end antiques and collectibles to sell and think that using a world-famous auction house such as Bonhams and Butterfields in San Francisco may draw a crowd that will bid your item higher, you may want to use this eBay-based selling format. Or you may want to buy something through this auction method.

If you want to *buy* at a live auction, eBay makes it easy for you to do so. You can view upcoming live auctions at www.liveauctions.ebay.com. You can use eBay to place an absentee bid at a live auction. Here's what to do.

- **Register to participate.** In addition to being a registered eBay user, you must separately register for each auction you want to participate in. Registration means you agree to follow the auction house's rules and requirements. Even if you do not want to bid on anything but just want to observe the action, you must register.

- **View the auction catalog online.** Browse each lot to be auctioned off. Live auction catalogs are posted on eBay at www.liveauctions.ebay.com/listings.

- **Place your absentee bid.** Submit the amount of the bid you want.

- **Stay tuned during the auction.** This is crucial so you can revise your absentee bid if you want to. The auction times are posted in Pacific time; adjust your clock accordingly so you don't miss the event.

If you want to *sell* an item at a live auction, eBay has nothing to do with the process. You must contact the auction house directly and discuss the terms and conditions for its auctions. View the live auction listings to see which auction houses are currently running sales to see the types of items they handle.

 Auction Alert

Check on the seller's commissions at the auction houses—the amount you must pay to the auction house for selling your item. Typically, commissions range from 10 percent to 17.5 percent, depending on the auction house (but it could be more). So if your item sells for $1,000 and you owe a 15 percent commission, you'll net only $850 on the sale. Also check on other fees, such as those for photographing your item or insuring it in shipping.

If you have the facilities, experience, and the right kind of items to auction off, you can become an eBay live auction seller and run your own live auction on eBay. As any well-established auction house does, you can create an online catalog of items for sale and hold a live auction conducted by a licensed auctioneer at which eBay bidders can participate. You must apply to become an eBay live auction seller and pay eBay certain fees (including a $1,500 insertion fee to post your catalog and a 5 percent final value fee on all items that are sold). You must complete an online application to become an eBay live auction seller. One of the requirements is that you are either a licensed auction house or are using a licensed auctioneer to control the bidding. If neither of these are true, you cannot become a live auction seller.

For details, go to http://pages.liveauctions.ebay.com/help/forsellers/forsellers.html.

eBay Sales Enhancements

It's in the interest of eBay to help you grow your sales. The more business you do, the more eBay profits from your efforts in the fees it collects. Toward this end, eBay provides an array of tools and resources you can use:

◆ Affiliate program

◆ Preferred listings

◆ Cross-selling

eBay Affiliate Program

If you have your own website, you can become an eBay affiliate to create another revenue stream for your business. eBay has an affiliate program designed to bring in new subscribers to its site. This may be a selfish motive for the program, but you can derive benefits from it as well. The top 25 eBay affiliates average above $100,000 monthly in commissions. The eBay affiliate program has paid on average over $1 million per year to its top 50 partners. There's no cost to you to become an affiliate, but you must be registered with eBay and have bought or sold something on eBay within the past 30 days.

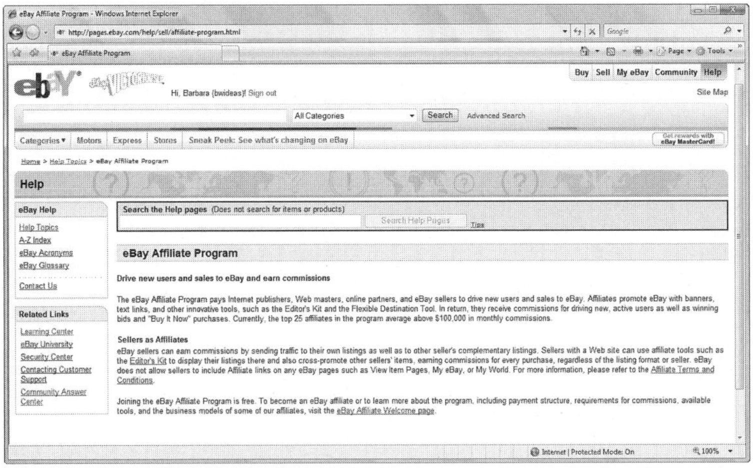

Figure 18.3

Become an eBay affiliate.

Many benefits can be gained from becoming an eBay affiliate:

◆ Earn rewards for driving traffic to eBay from your own website.

◆ Use an eBay banner on your website. Use of this banner is limited to eBay affiliates.

◆ Get special help from eBay. Because eBay wants you to succeed, you can qualify for unique assistance—tools, applications, and practices to grow your business, as well as customer assistance to you.

Affiliate Pricing Structure

Monthly New Active Users (ACRUs)	Monthly Revenue Share Tiers	Total ACRUs recruited	Compensation per ACRU	Total Revenue generated	% of Revenue
1–49	$25		$0 to $99.99		50%
50–1,999	$28		$100 to $4,999.99		55%
2,000–29,999	$31		$5,000 to $199,999.99		60%
30,000+	$35		$200,000 to $699,999.99		65%
			$700,000 to $2,999,999.99		70%
			$3,000,000+		75%

To enroll in the eBay affiliate program, or just to learn more, go to http://affiliates. ebay.com.

Preferred Listings

You can get your auction and store listings featured, but it will cost you money. Home Page Featured and Featured Plus! are listing enhancements you can use to bump your items to the front of the line, so to speak, so that you'll get noticed. In most cases, the added cost is probably not worth it. But you may have a special item that you think can benefit from using these listing options.

For details on these and other listing enhancements for auctions, go to Chapter 7; listing enhancements for eBay Stores are discussed earlier in this chapter.

Cross-Selling

You've already seen earlier in this chapter what cross-selling is all about. One way to do it is by combining auctions with an eBay Store or your own website. This enables you to build your customer base by leveraging each sales venue you use.

◆ Tell visitors at your eBay Stores about ongoing auctions.

◆ Tell bidders at your auctions what other items are for sale in your store.

Multi-Level Marketing for eBay

Tupperware and lingerie parties are a fun way to market plastics and panties. This *multi-level marketing* format has now been adapted for eBay.

Host a party to get friends, relatives, and acquaintances to bring their items to you for sale—they benefit from part of the proceeds and you keep the rest. You can also sign them up to do the same thing—and you get a cut of what they earn (hence, the multi-level marketing). Currently, this selling format is available only through Zippi (www.zippi.com). The starting sales package is $49.95; the more comprehensive package is $499.95.

This format started in 2007 and it remains to be seen whether it will catch on for eBay sellers.

> **def•i•ni•tion**
>
> Make money on many levels by using **multi-level marketing**. You earn money on your direct sales efforts, as well as a portion of the efforts of those you bring on board.

eBay Selling Alternatives

It has been reported that growth of sales through traditional eBay venues—auctions and stores—has slowed substantially as the number of alternative selling venues has exploded. eBay sellers should expand their horizons to include some other selling venues.

The Other eBay

By now you're certainly very familiar with eBay auctions—the core of eBay's business—as well as eBay Stores for online catalog sales. But there's more to eBay.

◆ eBay Express (www.express.ebay.com) lets you list items that are displayed in an Amazon-like format complete with a shopping cart.

◆ Half.com (www.half.ebay.com) lets you list books, music, and video games at a fixed price.

Power Point _____

"eBay to Go" is a widget that promotes eBay—add it to websites, blogs, and social networking sites, such as MySpace. This widget enables you to feature up to 10 items or a favorite search. For installation details, go to http://togo.ebay.com.

Beyond eBay

eBay is not the be-all and end-all of online selling venues. Use other sites in conjunction with your eBay activities to increase your sales. Certainly your own website is a prime example of another place to sell from.

Consider specialty sites, such as those geared for books, stamps, or comic books, if you primarily sell only in these categories. To find specialty sites of interest, do a Google search.

Another site, Craigslist (www.craigslist.org) is an online classified site. eBay now owns 25 percent of it. There are no listing fees for selling on Craigslist, a site well suited if you want to sell locally.

eBay has recently launched its own classified ad site in 220 U.S. cities, called Kijiji (www.kijiji.com). Like Craigslist, this venue is well suited for selling items that would otherwise be difficult to ship, such as a dining room set. At least for now, listings are free in the United States.

The Least You Need to Know

◆ Having an eBay Store is a great way to complement your auction activities.

◆ Using live auctions may be a better way to sell high-end items than using regular eBay auctions.

◆ Using eBay sales opportunities, such as enrolling in the affiliate program and becoming a Trading Assistant, goes a long way toward growing your business.

◆ Look beyond traditional eBay selling venues to expand your sales.

Chapter 19

Taking on Help

In This Chapter

- Taking on co-owners to share the work and increase business

- Hiring employees to free up your time for more productive work

- Engaging independent contractors on a short- or long-term basis to handle certain jobs for you

There are only so many hours in the day. No matter how many software tools or outside companies you use to save time, the reality is that you can't grow your business to the next level all by yourself. If you're a serious eBay seller, you need to work with others. You have several choices on how to expand the number of people working with you: you can take on a partner to share the efforts and the profits, you can hire employees, or you can use independent contractors—individuals who can provide help in doing certain business tasks.

This chapter explores each of the personnel options. You'll see the benefits and drawbacks of taking in a partner. You'll learn about the costs of creating a payroll and how to go about finding and keeping good employees. And you'll see when and how to use outside workers to complement your activities.

Doubling (and Tripling) Your Efforts with Partners

The old expression that two heads are better than one often works well to describe how to expand your business. That's why it's been estimated that 6 in 10 small businesses on eBay have two full-time employees. When you've reached the limits of what you can do personally, before hiring anyone, consider taking in a partner (or two). These are the advantages of inviting a co-owner to join you:

- **Skills.** You may be great at some aspects of running your eBay business, such as handling the sales, but fall short in other areas, such as the mundane tasks of bookkeeping and follow-up work. It's common to see pairs at work on eBay. That's what we do—Malcolm sells and Barbara packs the items for shipping.

An Educated eBay Seller

Many partnerships are husband-wife teams. According to the U.S. Census Bureau, there were 3.8 million husband-wife companies in 1997 (the latest year for statistics). The Small Business Administration says this number increases by about 5 percent each year. Husband-wife sole proprietorships are now called "couplepreneurs" and can opt to avoid the complications of partnerships.

- **Responsibility.** Running a business can be a 24/7 endeavor. No matter how much you like working on your eBay business, you probably want time off to vacation with your family, make a doctor's appointment, or just hang out. Leaving a partner in charge in your absence can give you peace of mind and ensure that your business runs smoothly.

- **Capital.** If you want to expand your business, you need money to invest in new merchandise. Of course, you can borrow the money, but if you don't have great credit or are already borrowed to the limit, bringing in someone with cash can be the answer.

Although there are benefits to taking in a co-owner, there are some drawbacks you should not overlook:

- **You must share the profits.** But hopefully, with the addition of someone else working with you, profits will grow, providing more money for both you and your partner.

- **You must share control.** If you're a control freak, you'll have to get used to letting someone else make decisions on some things, or the relationship will fail.

What the Relationship Means

Before you agree to take in a partner, make sure you understand what the arrangement means from a practical and legal perspective. Some of this is explained in Chapter 13, but here are key points to factor in when getting more help and deciding between partners and employees.

As a practical matter, if you take in an equal partner, each of you has a say in how the business operates. You can't always be in the driver's seat, even if you're used to it. You have to communicate and compromise to make the arrangement work.

From a legal perspective, there are different ways in which to handle your new relationship:

- **Partnership**. The easiest way to arrange the business is by forming a partnership. No legal filing or agreement is required (although it's highly advisable, as explained shortly). As long as two or more people come together with the intention of making a profit, a partnership comes into existence. Taxwise, the partnership isn't taxed. Instead, the income and expenses of the business flow through to the partners and are reported on their personal returns.

 Auction Alert

While a partnership may be easy to form, it may not be your best choice. The reason: each partner is jointly and severally liable for the debts of the partnership. This means that if your partner orders merchandise and the partnership bank account doesn't have the funds to pay for it, you can be on the hook for the entire amount. The vendor can come after your home and other personal assets, if need be, to satisfy the debt.

- **Limited liability company (LLC).** This type of business offers you the same tax treatment, but personal liability protection. If the company fails to pay for merchandise, the vendor can look only to the LLC, not to its owners (called members) personally. To set up an LLC, you must follow the rules of your state.

- **Corporation**. Like an LLC, this type of business gives you personal liability protection (only the corporation is responsible for its debts). But taxwise, it is a separate tax-paying entity unless the corporation elects to be treated as an S corporation. In an S corporation, the corporation is not taxed, and income and expenses flow through to the shareholders, to be reported on their personal returns. Like LLCs, corporations are formed under state law.

Creating Understanding

Whatever type of business formation you select, be sure that you put your understanding in writing. As with a marriage, you always go into a joint-business venture with the best of intentions. But as often happens in a marriage, communication breaks down, one person isn't keeping up his or her end of the bargain, or one person just wants out. Make sure that any partnership or shareholder agreement spells out how you want the arrangement to work and what happens when it doesn't go that way.

◆ **Management**. Who's going to run things? How will you resolve differences of opinion? What type of vote do you require on certain actions, such as selling out or closing down (unanimous)? Will you agree to binding arbitration to resolve important matters that you can't settle on your own?

◆ **Services.** Who's going to do what for the business? Will each of you work full-time or part-time? Will you get paid for your services or only take a share of profits?

◆ **Allocation of profits.** Are you equal co-owners, or should profits be shared in some other way (60/40, or 75/25)? This might be appropriate if one person puts up all of the money, even though both of you work for the business.

◆ **Changes in ownership.** Under what circumstances will you agree to bring in additional owners? What happens if one owner wants out? Will you include a noncompete agreement to bar a departing owner from setting up a competing business? What happens if one owner becomes disabled or dies?

> **Power Point**
>
> Use a lawyer to set up the business organization and the owners' agreement. Setup fees are a one-time thing (usually a few hundred dollars), and you don't want to make mistakes. Although there are many online resources to help you incorporate or form an LLC and write an owners' agreement, spend the extra money for professional help.

The practical and legal consequences of forming your business to expand the number of people participating in it are explained in Chapter 13.

Getting Someone to Work for You

If you're overworked, you can't take your business to the next level unless you bring in more people to work with you. Hiring an employee or three may be your answer. You can free up your time to concentrate on owner-type tasks, such as dealing with vendors, deciding on new lines, and planning for future expansion. Use employees to do the more routine work of your eBay business.

Taking on an employee isn't a simple decision. Hiring costs money, maybe even more than you think. You'll have to pay a competitive wage—what another company would pay for similar work. The pay must be at least the minimum wage in your area.

Currently, the federal minimum wage is $5.85 an hour from July 24, 2007 through July 23, 2008; $6.55 from July 24, 2008, through July 23, 2009; and $7.25 starting on July 24, 2009, but many states and localities already have higher minimum wages. For example, in San Francisco, starting January 1, 2007, businesses with fewer than 10 employees have a rate of $9.14 an hour (indexed for inflation). The minimum wage rate in Oregon for 2007 is $7.25 an hour and is indexed annually for inflation.

Auction Alert _____

Make sure your local zoning laws permit you to have employees in your home who do not live there. Some cities and towns have restrictions on the number of nonresident employees, as well as parking limitations, so check with your local zoning authorities before you hire anyone.

You also have to think about space—can you accommodate another body in your home office? Can you work with someone else around? If not, you can let your worker work from his or her home—a worker doesn't have to occupy your space to be your employee.

An Educated eBay Seller

Make sure you understand all of the laws you must comply with and all of the things you need to do. Some rules apply to all businesses, regardless of size, while others apply only to companies with 10, 20, or more employees. You can get help by visiting the Department of Labor website for employers at www.dol.gov/dol/audience/aud-employers.htm.

Hiring Outside Help

Decide what you need done so that you can seek the right person for the job. Do you want someone to photograph your items? Then look for someone with experience in digital cameras. Do you need someone to write your listing descriptions? Then you need to find someone with writing and typing skills. The following list details what you need to know when hiring outside help.

- **Job description.** You're used to writing up your listings for items you post for sale on eBay. Use the same approach to write up a good job description detailing the work you expect to be done.

- **The search.** You can advertise the position in your local newspaper or post it on local help-wanted boards. One of the best ways to find reliable and interested employees, however, is through word of mouth. A friend of a friend is always a good source for interested candidates. Online postings for "eBay help" are another way to find the help you need if you can work with distant employees or use a job placement website that's local (for example, www.craigslist.org).

- **The interview.** An interview is an opportunity for you to assess an applicant, and for an applicant to question you. You want to be sure that the applicant understands what you expect on the job. You don't want constant turnover, requiring you to go through the hiring process over and over again. But as your payroll grows, beware of what you ask the applicant: under the Equal Opportunity in Employment law, you can't ask about marital status, children, national origin, or religion—although you're free to share any information you want about yourself. For more information on discrimination rules you need to abide by go to www.eeoc.gov/employers/overview.html.

- **References.** It sounds obvious, but no matter how great a person seems, be sure to check out references. Be aware that former employers, afraid of lawsuits, won't tell you any more than the dates of employment and the job title (you won't learn whether the work was good or bad). Still, a phone reference check can help you read between the lines to learn the real story if you listen closely.

 Auction Alert _____

Always do a background check of anyone you hire—especially someone who may be in your home. The cost is modest compared with the risks you face for not doing the check. Go online to Kroll (www.infolinkscreening.com) or Abso (www. absolutebackgrounds.com). The cost for a basic social security number, address verification, and county criminal search is about $25.

Finding employees is only step 1. Then it's up to you to train them on how you want things done, supervise their activities, and keep them interested so they won't look elsewhere for work. Some eBay owners have complained that they have difficulty motivating workers who do tasks such as boxing and shipping. It's usually not about money. Often just making your work environment a fun place—a relaxed atmosphere, perhaps with music—can go a long way in worker satisfaction.

Using Family Members

Because of the difficulty in keeping employees, it may make sense to keep things all in the family, where possible. You may be able to put a spouse, children, or other relatives to work for you. The benefits include these:

♦ **Keeping the money all in the family.** The money that the business makes stays in the family. If you are already paying your teenager an allowance, putting her on the payroll can turn that payment into a business deduction and relieve you of some of the work.

♦ **Reaping intangible benefits.** Working together may give your family benefits that can't be reduced to numbers. It can strengthen the bonds of your relationship with relatives that work with you. It can be a way to teach children about business matters—your teenager is surely as capable on the computer (or more so) as you and can probably help you when it comes to new software tools and resources.

♦ **Enjoying tax breaks.** Paying your child a salary can be a tax-free benefit to him as well as a tax savings to you. In 2007, a child can earn up to $5,350 tax free. If your business isn't incorporated, the wages you pay to your child under age 18 aren't subject to FICA (Social Security and Medicare taxes); wages paid to your child under age 21 aren't subject to FUTA (federal unemployment taxes, explained later in this chapter). Wages paid to your spouse (of

Auction Alert

When hiring any family member, keep good records of the work done and what you paid. The IRS looks very closely at any family relationships tied to business deductions—it may suspect that expenses are made up, so you need records to show otherwise.

any age) are subject to FICA but not to FUTA. Check for possible state unemployment exemptions as well. There are no breaks for wages paid to other relatives, but any salary and employer taxes you pay on behalf of anyone are fully deductible, reducing the amount of profits on which you pay your own taxes.

The drawback (and it's a big one): you can fire your cousin, but you can't remove him from the family. When things don't work out, you can create bad feelings within the family that may be difficult to overcome.

Your Employer Responsibilities

Whether you hire an outsider or a family member or work for your own corporation, you are an employer. Being an employer means handling a number of federal and state-imposed responsibilities. You have to ...

- **Verify eligibility to work.** Don't assume that someone who applies for work is eligible to work in this country. Any employee you take on must prove to you that he or she is permitted to work in the United States. The employee must complete U.S. Citizenship and Immigration Services Form I-9 (you can download the form and instructions from www.uscis.gov/files/form/i-9.pdf). You don't need to file the form with the government; retain it in your files.

- **Obtain an employer identification number.** You use this EIN to report your payroll taxes. Details on getting your number are found in Chapter 13.

- **Pay state and federal unemployment insurance for your employee.** It's called insurance, but it's collected like a tax. The federal tax is called FUTA. Contact your state department of labor for further details.

- **Pay the employer share of Social Security and Medicare (FICA) to the federal government.** This information is included on your quarterly employment tax return.

- **Withhold income tax and the employee's share of FICA.** These taxes come from the employee's wages.

Auction Alert

Withheld income tax and the employee's share of Social Security and Medicare (FICA) taxes from the employee's wages are called "trust fund" taxes for which you remain 100 percent personally responsible, no matter how you set up your business. If the company fails to deposit the funds, the government comes after you.

Power Point

If you handle your own payroll deposits, you can simplify the way in which you get the money to the government by using the Electronic Federal Tax Payment System (EFTPS). You can schedule and make payments online by directing withdrawals from your bank account, ensuring timely deposits to avoid late payment penalties. For information, go to www.eftps.gov. You must file quarterly employment tax returns to tell the government what you've collected and deposited. Details of your employment taxes can be found in IRS Publication 15-A, Circular E, "Employer's Tax Guide," at www.irs.gov; contact your state tax, finance, or revenue department for rules on state employment taxes.

You must deposit the trust fund amounts with the federal government (and deposit any state income tax withholding with your state)—deposit deadlines depend on the size of your payroll.

The following table shows the calendar of your employer tax filing responsibilities.

Employer Tax Filing Responsibilities

Deadline*	Form	Description
January 31	Form W-2	Give your employee a statement of annual compensation and taxes withheld.
	Form 940	File your annual unemployment return (or 940-EZ) with the IRS (the deadline is February 10 if the tax is deposited in full and on time).
	Form 941	File the fourth quarter of FICA and income tax withholding with the IRS (the deadline is February 10 if the tax is deposited in full and on time).
February 28	Form W-2 (copy A) and Form W-3	File with the Social Security Administration to report annual wages and FICA.
April 30	Form 941	File the first quarter FICA and income tax withholding (the deadline is May 10 if the tax is deposited in full and on time).
July 31	Form 941	File the second quarter FICA and income tax withholding (the deadline is August 10 if the tax is deposited in full and on time).
October 31	Form 941	File the third quarter FICA and income tax withholding (the deadline is November 10 if the tax is deposited in full and on time).

If any deadline falls on a Saturday, Sunday, or legal holiday, the deadline is extended to the next business day.

Once you establish your employer status (for example, by depositing payroll taxes for the first time), you don't have to request employment tax forms. The IRS as well as the state sends the forms automatically.

Being an employer requires you to keep records—time slips, wage statements, and employment tax returns. Keep all employment-related records (including job applications) for at least four years.

Many small business owners find the tax-related chores of being an employer overwhelming. They're time consuming and require a broad understanding of many different rules. Some small business owners prefer to have their accountants or payroll companies, such as ADP (www.adp.com) and Paychex (www.paychex.com), handle employment tax work. You decide for yourself which way to go.

Keeping Employees Happy

Ask any small business owner—on eBay or elsewhere—what his or her number one problem is, and many will say finding and keeping good employees. It is a challenge for eBay business owners to find people who are willing and able to do the tasks you need done.

You can't always pay what larger companies can offer—higher wages and a menu of fringe benefits. To compete in the employment marketplace, you need to offer your employees something that they can't get elsewhere, such as flexible work hours and perhaps a work-from-home arrangement.

Hopefully, as you grow your business, you may be able to swing higher salaries and offer some fringe benefits, including health insurance and retirement plans, to your employees. There are ways in which you can offer these benefits while shifting some or all of the cost to employees, yet still generate goodwill among workers for having the benefits. To learn more about employee benefits, see IRS Publication 15-B, "Employer's Tax Guide to Fringe Benefits," and IRS Publication 560, "Retirement Plans for Small Business," at www.irs.gov.

Looking Outside for Help with Independent Contractors

Instead of taking on an employee, someone who remains on your payroll indefinitely (until you let the person go), you can opt to work with another business owner who can provide services for you. This person, called an *independent contractor*, is not under your direct control but merely is required to complete the work you need done at a particular time.

def•i•ni•tion

An **independent contractor** is a worker who contracts to do work according to his or her own methods and who's not under your control.

You can hire an independent contractor for a set period, such as busy holiday time, or indefinitely. You can take on a contractor to do one job and, if you're satisfied, ask him to do more.

Make sure you classify your workers correctly: as employees or independent contractors, as the situation dictates. One of the hottest tax issues continues to be proper worker classification. The reason for all the interest: billions of dollars in taxes (more than $20 billion, at last count) go uncollected because of misclassifying workers. The IRS raises the question when it examines business returns.

The question also comes up when a former worker you've discharged goes to collect unemployment benefits. He'll tell the state unemployment department that he was an employee (not an independent contractor) who is entitled to benefits—because you didn't pay any state or federal unemployment taxes, you can be liable for back payments as well as interest and penalties.

◆ The IRS prefers that you classify workers as employees so you'll collect and pay withholding and FICA taxes, and report this compensation to the IRS.

◆ The state prefers that you classify workers as employees so it can collect unemployment insurance from you.

◆ You usually prefer to classify workers as independent contractors so that they're responsible for their own taxes (they aren't eligible for unemployment benefits). Your only reporting obligation is to file an information return, IRS Form 1099-MISC, to let the government know that you've paid $600 or more to an independent contractor.

You can't simply pin a label on your worker's chest to create an independent contractor. The issue of worker status boils down to a matter of control. Who has the right—you or the worker—to say when, where, and how the work gets done? If it's you, then the worker is your employee, no matter what you want to call him.

Why does it matter so much? If you've been treating a worker as a contractor and the IRS or your state successfully reclassifies the worker as an employee, you can owe back taxes, interest, and penalties that can be huge!

Certain actions can help to shape the situation more clearly in your favor.

◆ Have the worker sign an agreement acknowledging independent contractor treatment and that he or she understands the tax responsibilities. The agreement doesn't ensure that the government will recognize your treatment, but it doesn't hurt. You can have an attorney write the agreement or write your own—use one of the many preprinted forms available online (for example, www.toolkit.com/tools/downloads/indepcon.rtf).

◆ Talk to your tax professional. Because a mistake can be costly, you want all the advice you can get.

- Be consistent—if you hire one person to do your description writing and treat her as an employee, you can't take on a second worker to do the same type of work and treat him as an independent contractor.

- File appropriate returns. You must report compensation paid to a contractor of $600 or more during the year on IRS Form 1099-MISC. Give the contractor his copy of the form no later than the end of January following the year of payment; file the other part of the form with the IRS no later than the end of February following the year of payment. You can gain an additional month to file with the IRS if you file electronically.

> **Auction Alert**
>
> The laws can be confusing and inconsistent. You can have a worker who is an independent contractor under federal law but who must be treated as an employee for state law purposes.

Letting a worker operate from his own home, using his own computer, doesn't guarantee contractor status. Again, you must thoroughly consider the overall picture and answer the question of control.

Hiring someone who's in business for himself, though, is a way to prove independent contractor status. The person does work for other people beside you, advertises himself as a business, and stands to profit (or lose) from the deals he makes.

The Least You Need to Know

- Bring in a co-owner to share with you the financial burden and the workload.

- Hire employees to free up your time for more strategic work for the business.

- Look to family members as potential employees—they keep the money in the family, are conveniently located, and may provide tax breaks, to boot.

- Pay attention to your employer responsibilities so you stay out of trouble.

- Use independent contractors where possible to minimize your payroll costs.

Chapter 20

Using Auction-Management Tools

In This Chapter

◆ Growing your business with eBay tools and resources

◆ Getting answers to your questions from eBay

◆ Using general third-party auction-management tools

◆ Using third-party tools to handle specific functions

To grow your eBay business, you have to maximize your time. It isn't cost-effective to spend an hour on a single listing that returns only a few dollars on a winning bid. To make selling on eBay a thriving business, you have to be able to efficiently list multiple sales at one time and run them simultaneously. You need the ability to do your market research and mailings easily. You need the means to complete all your administrative tasks, including contacting winning bidders; invoicing, where necessary; and completing bookkeeping with a few keystrokes.

In this chapter, you'll learn how to put software and web-based tools to work for you in doing all the things that need to get done in the quickest, most efficient way. You'll see what eBay has to offer for tools, resources, and help to increase your sales. You'll see which resources are currently popular with eBay sellers for different tasks (new tools are being developed every day). Many of these resources have been mentioned throughout this book. This chapter pulls them all together so you can assemble your arsenal of selling weapons and go to work. It doesn't cover every tool available; there are too many to mention.

eBay Tools Can Save You Time and Hassle

Because eBay is web-based, practically every aspect of your sales activities can be handled online. Why not use software and online tools and resources to handle these various aspects for you?

eBay wants you to succeed and provides you with many resources, some free and some for a charge, that you can use to make your life easier and to grow your business to the next level.

Your eBay Options

Once the number of your sales reaches a critical mass, you can't manage them manually (at least, not without losing your mind). You need to automate the tasks associated with your listing and auction management. This enables you to run multiple auctions simultaneously without dropping the ball.

eBay tools for this purpose include …

Power Point

Turbo Lister can be integrated with your inventory-management software and accounting programs, saving you additional time entering information into these programs to keep track of your sales.

- **Turbo Lister.** This tool, designed for medium- to high-volume sellers, enables you to easily create multiple listings. You can use it alone or in combination with other software tools. Easily format your text and schedule your auctions. Cost: free. Download it from http://pages.ebay.com/turbo_lister.

- **Blackthorne Basic.** You can create professional-looking auction listings with this easy-to-use, all-in-one tool provided through eBay. Insert information on shipping, tax, and payment terms, and create e-mail for customer correspondence to easily follow up with winning bidders. This product is best suited if you're listing about 25 items a month. Cost: $9.99 per month (30-day free trial period). Subscribe at http://pages.ebay.com/blackthorne/basic.html.

- **Blackthorne Pro.** With this tool, you get everything you have through Blackthorne Basic, plus many more features. These include scheduling listings, automating repetitive processes, tracking buyer information, bulk printing shipping labels, monthly profit and loss reports, and submitting feedback automatically. This product is best suited for medium- to high-volume sellers. Cost: $24.99 per month (30-day free trial period). Subscribe at http://pages.ebay.com/blackthorne/pro.html.

◆ **Selling Manager.** Also designed for medium-volume sellers, this tool assists you in managing listings and post-sale activities. You can use it to manage pending items to be listed on eBay at a future date; track active eBay listings; monitor unsold listings; and manage feedback, payments, and other post-sale activities. Cost: $4.99 per month (30-day free trial period) and free for Basic Store subscribers. Subscribe at http://pages.ebay.com/selling_manager.

◆ **Selling Manager Pro.** Use this handy online tool to track your inventory, pending, and active listings; relist unsold items in bulk; send invoices, e-mails, and feedback in bulk; track payments; and generate profit and loss reports. Cost: $15.99 per month (30-day free trial) and free to Premier and Anchor Store subscribers. Subscribe at http://pages.ebay.com/selling_manager_pro.

Getting Answers on eBay

In the course of your sales activities, a question (not answered in this book) may come to mind. Can you list a Civil War rifle for sale, in light of the eBay policy against selling firearms? Can you reach a living human being to talk with at eBay if you have a problem you can't solve on your own? You may get the answer you need on eBay—if you know where to look.

The first place to look for answers is through the eBay site map. Click the link beneath the navigation tabs at the top of the home page to view a three-column display of topics ranging from Buy and Sell to Community. You're likely to find answers using the Sell and Selling Tools links.

 Auction Alert

Don't use the eBay Search box or click the Search tab to find answers to your questions. This box and tab are only for locating items for sale on eBay. To find answers to questions, press the Help tab.

If this approach doesn't yield satisfactory information, click the Help tab at the top of any eBay screen. Doing this reveals a search box (called Search Help) in which you can put your question. For effective help searches, keep it to as few words as possible (not complete sentences) because answers will be responsive to all of the words you've included. Don't worry about using capital letters; the help search isn't case sensitive.

You can also try the eBay Answer Center, at http://pages.ebay.com/community/answercenter/. Here you can scan question-and-answer boards on various subjects, such as international trading, PayPal, and Turbo Lister. Some questions are answered by eBay users; others are answered by eBay staff (known as "Pinks" because there is a pink highlight across the top of any of their posts). Usually hundreds of answers are posted for each subject.

Power Point

All PowerSellers have access to more prompt customer support to answer questions and obtain help. All PowerSellers above the Bronze category have a toll-free number to call for assistance. Those in the Gold, Platinum, and Titanium categories have their own account managers to answer questions directly.

If you can't find a satisfactory answer through your searches, try contacting eBay customer support. Go to http://pages.ebay.com/help/contact_us/_base/index_selection.html and complete an online contact form that is then e-mailed to eBay. eBay says it will respond to your question within one to two days.

Want to use eBay's Live Help? Guess what! There is no phone number to connect you to customer service (unless you are a PowerSeller). You can, however, send an e-mail for assistance by clicking on the Live Help button found on the home page and several other pages.

Third-Party Auction-Management Tools

Although eBay provides you with various tools that can help you adequately manage your sales activities, you may want to use third-party products. This is especially true if you also sell through your own website; third-party tools can integrate all of your sales activities.

- **AuctionHawk** (www.auctionhawk.com) offers custom management and check-out services, including feedback capabilities and photo storage. Cost: Basic plan is $12.99 per month, Power plan is $21.99 per month, Professional plan is $29.99 a month, and the Unlimited plan is $44.99 per month (21-day free trial period).

- **Auctiva** (www.auctiva.com) is an easy-to-use complete auction listing package. There are templates, free image storage, and scheduling. It's our favorite! Cost: free.

- **ChannelAdvisor** (www.channeladvisor.com) is a marketing tool to help buyers find you. You have to call 1-866-264-8594 for pricing.

- **eHarbors** (www.eharbors.com) offers virtually everything you need to run auctions, including creating auction ads, sending e-mail to buyers, inventory maintenance, image hosting, and relisting unsold items in bulk. Cost: free.

- **Ink Frog** (www.inkfrog.com) offers a wide range of services, such as image hosting, counters, sales, and inventory management tools. Cost: $9.95 a month.

- **Marketworks** (www.marketworks.com) is a tool for large sellers who want a store format, extensive research, and other sophisticated selling tools. Cost: starting at $29.95 a month (14-day free trial).

- **Spoon Feeder** (www.spoonfeeder.com) is a comprehensive auction management tool. Cost: $19.95 to $199.95 for the setup fee, plus $10 to $40 per month service charge.

- **Vendio** (www.vendio.com) offers a wide range of tools, from listing and auction management assistance to research and image hosting. Cost: prices vary, depending on whether you choose a monthly fixed rate, variable plan, or pay as you go.

- **Zoovy** (http://zoovy.com) has auction-management tools that have been around for a while and are easy to use. Cost: you must call 1-877-966-8948 for a free consultation.

> ### An Educated eBay Seller
>
> eBay encourages third-party businesses to create tools and resources for the eBay community. Toward this end, the eBay Developer Program (http://developer.ebay.com/businessbenefits/aboutus) allows developers to tap into the eBay platform. New products are being introduced all the time.

Other Third-Party Auction Tools for Specific Tasks

eBay doesn't provide you with everything useful to your business. Many other tools and resources are designed to work with eBay auctions and can help you deal with various tasks.

Research

It's important to know what items are selling and which ones are not so that you maximize your sales efforts on items more likely to prove profitable for you. But how do you know this? The answer is research—checking auctions to see how much bidding took place and how much items actually sold for. Because you don't have all day to sit and view this information yourself, you need to rely on software tools that can do this for you.

eBay sellers use these popular tools to determine what items are hot and how to value them:

- **Hammertap3** (www.hammertap.com) gives you sell-through rates, average bids per item, average sales price per item, and much more. Cost: $19.95 per month (with a 30-day free trial period). Note: this is the leading seller for market research on eBay.

- **TeraPeak** (www.terapeak.com) offers advanced research tools geared for eBay, such as best listing times, what's hot, and best pricing for your items. Cost: some features are free; basic service (Insight) is $14.95 a month; advanced service (Advantage) is $24.95 a month.

- **Vendio** (www.vendio.com) gives product line details to help you determine price. Cost: $14.95 for Vendio Research.

- **What's Hot** (www.vendio.com) reports on the hottest items selling in each category on eBay. Cost: $3.95 per month.

Popular tools that eBay sellers use to value antiques and collectibles include these:

- **Collect.com** (www.collect.com). Cost: free, but registration is required.

- **InstAppraisal.com** (www.instappraisal.com). Cost: free.

- **Kovel's Online** (www.kovels.com), a database of more than 600,000 items. Cost: free, but registration is required.

- **Maine Antique Digest** (www.maineantiquedigest.com). Click on Price Database. Cost: free.

- **WhatsItWorthToYou.com** also called Eppraisals.com and wiw2u (www.whatsitworthtoyou.com), with appraisals for each item you submit. Cost: $9.95 per appraisal.

Counters

Do you know how many people have visited your listings? You will if you use a counter to keep track of your visitors. You can use viewable counters that visitors to your listings can see, or you can opt to hide the information from sight. There are *numerous* counters available from third parties, including counters from:

♦ **Counterguide.com** (www.counterguide.com) is a resource that links you to counters for eBay.

♦ **Freelogs.com** (www.freelogs.com) offers dozens of counter styles. Cost: free.

♦ **Sellathon's ViewTracker** (www.sellathon.com) not only tracks visitors, but it lets you know what keywords led them to you, if they're planning on sniping, and more, and provides data you can use to make your listings more effective. Cost: from $4.95 per month for the basic version to $19.95 per month for the most sophisticated version (with a 30-day free trial).

♦ **Vendio** (www.vendio.com) gives you two counter types to choose from. Cost: basic counter is free; a pro version that enables you to track hourly and daily traffic is $3.95 per month.

Sniping

The person with the final highest bid is the winner of an auction. How can a person ensure that he or she is this winner? Today, with the help of software tools, when you're in buying mode, you can *snipe* so that your last-minute bidding will probably make you a winner. Sniping doesn't guarantee that you'll win, but it certainly increases the chances of success.

Is the practice illegal or somehow immoral? eBay doesn't forbid it, although it doesn't encourage it, either—you won't find eBay tips on how best to snipe. It's been estimated by some that about 5 percent of all eBay auctions are won through sniping. You can't block out sniping from your auctions.

def•i•ni•tion

> **Sniping** refers to the practice of waiting until the very last second before the auction closes to place your bid so that you'll be the final and highest bidder in order to win.

When you are in buyer mode, decide whether you want to use this technique to lock in your purchases. You can't be prevented from sniping. The advantage is that you won't have to be online when the auction is closing if you use a sniping program— you tell the sniping program what item to bid on, and it takes it from there.

Images

Pictures are a vital way to entice someone browsing for items to take a closer look at what you have to sell. In the past, you had to be a pro to get great pictures, but today digital cameras and software tools make it easy for anyone to look like a pro. eBay enables you to supersize your images so that viewers can get a better look at your items. But you can use many different types of tools to create better images by adjusting lighting, cropping them, or otherwise manipulating the images. Here are some tools you can use:

◆ **3cim** (www.3cim.com), primarily used for real estate, enables you to offer a slide tour format that includes magnification combined with an audio presentation. Cost: free for 5 MB to $99.95 a year for 250 MB.

◆ **Adobe Photoshop Elements** or **Adobe Photoshop** (www.adobe.com/products/photoshop) enables you to resize images, change backgrounds, adjust lighting, and more. Cost: $99 for Photoshop Elements and $649 for Photoshop (often free with the purchase of a camera or other photography equipment).

◆ **Auctiva** (www.auctiva.com) offers free image hosting.

◆ **Fast Photos Auction Photo Editor** (www.pixby.com) is a photo editor designed specifically for auction sellers. Add watermarks and borders, and create eBay gallery thumbnail shots easily. Cost: $24.95 (free 21-day trial period).

◆ **FotoKiss** (www.fotokiss.com), designed for people with no photo experience, lets you crop, add frames, and write text on your images for listing on auctions and catalogs. Cost: $39.95 (30-day free trial period).

Image hosting, through eBay and third parties, is discussed in Chapter 7.

Make Your Listings Come Alive

Your eBay listings don't have to be flat, two-dimensional vehicles for selling. You can involve the viewer more by using various enhancements, such as sound and the opportunity to communicate with you in real-time online. Here are some tools you can use:

◆ **AuctionVideo** (www.auctionvideo.com) is an eBay-approved vendor that enables you to add video clips to your listings. You create the 30-second clips to show your items or yourself. Cost: $9.95 a month for low-volume usage.

◆ **Boldchat** (www.boldchat.com) enables bidders to ask you questions through live chat. Cost: $25 setup for the Basic Edition and then $29 per month; $42 setup and $49 a month for the Pro Edition.

◆ **Vhost SitePal** (www.sitepal.com) provides video and audio hosts for your listing. Cost: starts at $9.95 per month for basic version (bronze), to $49.95 for the advanced version (gold), with a 15-day free trial.

 Auction Alert _____

The more elements added to your listing, the longer the download time. For the most part, buyers don't want to wait to view your auction, so weigh the benefits of these listing enhancements against the potential viewer turnoff. What's more, they're annoying to many viewers.

Bulk Mailing

Want to reach out to your customer base quickly and easily? To do this, you need a tool that can create e-mail from your customer database. Most of the comprehensive auction management tools will help you with this. One dedicated tool for bulk mailing:

◆ **BayMail** (www.sharewareconnection. com/baymail.htm) enables you to send messages to up to five people at one time; the Pro version can send to large groups at once, providing powerful management of mailing lists—yours or those you buy or rent. Cost: free.

Auction Alert _____

E-mails that you send out in bulk shouldn't violate federal antispam rules. You must have an honest subject line and provide a way for recipients to opt out of further messages from you. For details, go to www.ftc.gov/bcp/conline/pubs/buspubs/canspam.shtm.

Customer Management

You can choose who you want to do business with on eBay. You can be as selective as you want. eBay has free tools that let you block unwanted bidders and create an exclusive list of bidders and buyers. But third-party tools can also be used to identify problem customers and block unwanted bidders. For example, BidderBlock (www.hammertap.com/products/#bidderblock), available through Hammertap3, helps you create a detailed list of customers you want to block from bidding at no cost.

Miscellaneous Tools

If you think of something that needs to be done, you can bet that someone else has, too, and there's probably already a product out there to help. For example, wouldn't it be great to learn when an item you've been looking for comes up for auction? Well, there's an online tool for this very purpose.

Auction Alert

Be selective about the tools you really need to use in running your business. The costs can add up quickly (especially those with ongoing monthly subscription fees) and can severely cut into your bottom line.

◆ **Auction Checkout** (www.auctioncheckout.com) enables you to accept credit cards and process transactions using your own merchant account (you don't need to have a separate website). Cost: basic service $24 per month, plus 10¢ per transaction.

◆ **Auction Navigator** (www.auctionnavigator. com) enables you to find and track auctions, as well as bid and snipe with one product. Cost: $29.95 (free-trial version).

◆ **Auction Sieve** (www.auctionsieve.com) lets you find bargains and items you're looking for on eBay. Cost: free.

◆ **FeeFinder** (www.hammertap.com/DownloadFeeFinder.html) calculates all your eBay fees for regular and Dutch auctions, including all your listing enhancements, and links to shipping calculators. Cost: $12.99 (free trial).

◆ **Prospector Professional** (www.bayprospector.com) helps you find items you're looking for on eBay from a watch list you create. Cost: $39 (free lite version is restricted to 30 searches a day).

The Least You Need to Know

◆ To handle multiple listings and volume sales, you need to use software and online tools to automate your sales activities.

◆ eBay has several avenues to explore in seeking answers to your questions; PowerSellers command greater customer service.

◆ Third-party tools for auction management can be more useful than similar eBay tools if you also sell through your own website.

◆ Use specific third-party software and online tools to handle specific functions, such as market research and sniping.

Chapter 21

Raising Money to Grow Your Business

In This Chapter

♦ Deciding on a type of business financing

♦ Borrowing from family and friends or commercial sources

♦ Taking in investors to raise money and share the workload

♦ Using credit cards prudently to grow your business

The great thing about *starting* an eBay business is that it can be done on a shoestring budget, using a computer and other equipment you already own and unwanted items you have lying around your home. But to *grow* your business to the next level, you need to add money as you would in any other business.

In this chapter, you'll learn about different types of financing options and the advantages and disadvantages of each. You'll see where to borrow money with the least hassle and assess whether to take in investors.

Sources of Financing

Let's say you've arrived at a crossroads: you can continue to do business as usual (and make about the same money you've been earning) or expand your business so that you can make more money. If you choose to grow your business, you may need funds to buy more inventory, to advertise your business, to purchase new equipment such as a laptop to complement your desktop computer, or to hire employees. Unless you are independently wealthy or are willing to tap into funds from a second mortgage, you probably don't have a fat bank account bulging with money that you can use for expansion. You'll need to look beyond your immediate resources for new capital.

You can find money to put into your business in three basic ways:

- ◆ Borrow money (called debt financing).

- ◆ Find investors to provide money (called equity financing).

- ◆ Reinvest business earnings, which is essentially setting aside profits for future use (called retained earnings).

There is no "right" way to add capital to your business. You need to look at the positives and negatives of each alternative. And you aren't limited to making a choice; you can combine two or all methods to find the money you need.

Borrowing to Build Up

The concept of borrowing isn't hard to understand—someone lends you money for a set time, and you pay it back with interest. In this arrangement, you become the debtor; the lender is the creditor. Most small businesses need to borrow money to stay in business and expand operations. According to the Small Business Administration, the dollar amount of small business loans from all sources totaled $601 billion (as of June 2005).

Borrowing is a finite arrangement. You enter into a relationship with the lender that lasts only for the term of the loan. Once you've satisfied all the conditions of the loan by repaying the money you've borrowed, plus interest, on a timely basis, your relationship ends. You can always choose to renew acquaintances if you need to borrow more money.

The creditor usually has no say in how you run your business. All the lender wants is repayment, and as long as you're sticking to your bargain, the lender is happy.

The main downside to borrowing money is the ongoing cost of repayment. You not only have to come up with cash (usually each month) to pay interest, but you're also repaying the balance (the money you borrowed). Although interest rates are low today, they could be higher and more costly when the time comes for you to borrow money.

Another issue about borrowing is creditworthiness. You must be of a certain standing to be able to borrow money (usually someone with a FICO score—a credit rating developed by Fair Isaac & Co. decades ago—under 620 will not be able to borrow money at favorable interest rates because they are classified as a bad credit risk). The business's credit rating and your personal credit rating are key factors in your ability to borrow money from a commercial lender.

Auction Alert

As a small business owner, you are usually on the hook personally for any money loaned to your business. A commercial lender *always* requires the owner to personally guarantee a business loan (unless it can be secured by real estate or certain other property). Your personal guarantee exposes your personal assets to possible seizure by the lender if the business or you fail to repay the loan—even if the business is incorporated or is a limited liability company.

Your Personal Resources

You may be sitting on money you can tap into and don't even realize it. You may take for granted certain assets you've accumulated over the years and don't think of as cash cows. These are some resources to consider:

- **The equity in your home.** If you've owned your home for a while and paid down the mortgage, or if the home's value has appreciated since you bought it, you may have built up *equity* that you can now tap into.

def•i•ni•tion

If you sell your home today, the money that you net out (after repaying any outstanding mortgage) is your **equity**.

Home equity loans are determined solely on the equity available in the home, not on your personal credit rating. You can borrow from the bank holding your main mortgage or any other lender offering home equity loans. There are different types of borrowing arrangements; some require immediate repayment of principal and interest on a monthly basis, while others require only interest to be repaid now, with principal repayment deferred to some future time. Usually, repayment can be made over a term of up to 15 years. Interest rates on these loans fluctuate along with changes in interest rates in general.

Auction Alert

If you leave your employer, you must repay the outstanding balance of the loan. If you don't, that amount is treated as a distribution from the plan and you're taxed on it. And if you're less than age 59½, there is also a 10 percent penalty on the amount still outstanding.

◆ **Retirement plans.** If you have a day job, your savings in your employer's 401(k) or other retirement plan may provide you with needed capital. (You can't borrow from an IRA.) The plan may permit you to borrow from it at highly favorable interest rates. The loan can usually be arranged with your plan administrator in a day or two. The maximum loan amount is 50 percent of your account balance or $20,000, whichever is smaller. You must immediately begin repayment in level amounts over a period of no more than five years.

◆ **Life insurance.** If you've owned a whole or universal life insurance policy for some time, you may have built up cash value that you can borrow against with favorable terms. You can arrange the loan by calling the insurance company and can usually receive a check in a day or two. Interest rates are low, and you don't have to repay principal at any set time; the interest just continues to build up. Of course, if you die, your beneficiaries will collect only the face of the policy *minus* the outstanding loan, so you may be leaving heirs short of money they counted on.

Borrowing from Friends and Relatives

If you don't want to use your personal resources and don't want to (or can't) get a commercial loan, your family or friends may help you with a private loan. Maybe your rich uncle or a neighbor is in a position to help you. The upside to borrowing from a friend or relative is that you probably don't need to show the lender your financials or complete a complicated loan application, and you may be able to obtain more favorable terms than you would with an unrelated third party.

But if things turn sour and you can't repay the loan, consider what this might do to your relationship. Discuss "worst case" scenarios with your lender to make sure he or she understands the risk.

An Educated eBay Seller
While your Aunt Em may be eager to lend you what you need, be sure to follow all of the formalities of the arrangement that you would with an unrelated third party. Sign a promissory note that should include all the terms of the loan (the amount borrowed, the interest rate, and the repayment term). This will let Aunt Em write off the loan on her tax return if you fail to repay it. Without this loan agreement, the IRS may disallow the write-off, claiming that the loan was really a gift to you.

Commercial Loans

In the past, banks found it financially rewarding to make only big loans to large corporations and wouldn't even talk to the little guy. Today, however, as banks compete for small business customers, you can more readily find small loans called *microloans*, usually starting at $5,000 (although some lenders offer microloans as small as $500). Check with local commercial banks for their small loan policies. Banks such as Commerce Bank (www.commerceonline.com) and Wells Fargo (www.wellsfargo.com) are aggressively looking to lend to small businesses and capture them as customers for other bank services. Usually, the banks require only a simple one- or two-page loan application for loans up to $50,000 or $100,000. The application must be accompanied by the business's tax returns for the past two years, but you usually don't have to submit a formal business plan or other documents typically required on larger loans. Of course, you must personally guarantee the loan. This means that your ability to obtain a business loan depends on the credit rating of both the business and you.

You may also qualify for an SBA loan, which is a commercial loan guaranteed by the Small Business Administration. Don't be misled by the term; the SBA doesn't make the loans directly, and you don't apply to the SBA for the loan. The SBA only protects the lender in case of your default. (The fact that the SBA guarantees 75 percent or 85 percent of the funds loaned by the bank does not relieve you of your personal guarantee for the entire loan amount.) Different types of loans are given for different purposes, such as equipment purchases, working capital, and revolving lines of credit. Repayment terms depend on the nature of the loan. Generally, SBA loans must be repaid within seven years. For details on SBA loan programs, go to www.sba.gov/services/financialassistance.

Microloans of up to $35,000 (the average loan is $13,000) are available through the SBA, which makes funds available to nonprofit community-based lenders called intermediaries (www.sba.gov/services/financialassistance/sbaloantopics/microloans).

You can borrow funds and get a check for the entire amount, or you can take out a line of credit that you can tap into when and to the extent that you need the money. Either way, you must follow the same loan process. However, with the line of credit, you pay interest only on the amount you've tapped into, cutting your borrowing costs. When you repay the portion of the credit line, you can reborrow that amount. When the revolving line of credit expires, you can work with the lender to renew it.

To seek out lenders online, you can go to iBank, at www.ibank.com, to submit applications to several lenders at one time. iBank works with about 325 lenders nationwide that make loans to small businesses. Also check on local loan programs that may be available in your area through development corporations and other economic assistance programs.

Power Point

PayPal enables buyers to finance their purchases using its Buyer Credit program. By telling your buyers about Promotional Financing through PayPal, you can boost sales. As long as you are a qualified seller (PayPal determines this), you can offer customers 3-, 6-, or 12-month deferred-interest financing, or 12- or 24-month fixed interest financing. For details on this program, go to https://www.paypal.com/us/cgi-bin/webscr?cmd=xpt/cps/buyercredit/BCMKTSellFNC-outside.

Also, there may be an "angel" eager to sit on your shoulder, a private lender who makes small loans to worthy small businesses. Angel investors can be found through various means, including an online search and checking with the directory of the Angel Capital Association (www.angelcapitalassociation.org).

GE Capital Financial has teamed up with eBay to offer a line of credit and secured financing (http://pages.ebay.com/businesscredit). The unsecured line of credit (no collateral is required) is up to $100,000 (lines can range from $5,000 to $100,000) and grants access to the line through a credit card. Secured financing (with collateral) can exceed the $100,000 credit line limit, but the minimum is $50,000. You can access the capital through GE direct payment to your suppliers. Because of the eBay-GE connection, there are no application fees, account opening fees, or first-year annual fees if you apply through eBay.

Taking in Investors

Instead of borrowing money that you have to pay back, consider bringing in co-owners who bring money to the table. For their cash investment, they receive an ownership interest in your business. Instead of being a 100 percent owner, you may have to reduce your share of the business in order to grow. Just do the numbers to see that it's better to own, say, 60 percent of a business grossing $1 million (your share of which would be $600,000) than 100 percent of a business grossing $200,000.

The upside to this financing strategy is that you aren't required to make any repayment. You don't have to use company funds each month to service debt, giving you more money to run the business. Of course, investors want to see a return on their money at some point, and you must plan for this up front. When do you expect to be able to distribute profits to an investor? How much do you foresee? You also don't have to show a great credit rating, as required for loans.

The downside to bringing in investors, aside from having to share the wealth, is that investors usually have a long-term relationship with you. They aren't out of the picture at a specific date, as is the case with lenders once the loan is repaid. Investors often want a say in how the business is run and may think they know how to do things better than you. Depending on the size of their ownership interest, they may be entitled to participate in certain decisions or may simply be silent, minority owners. Be sure to understand the dynamics involved in taking in partners before you get started.

An Educated eBay Seller

Whether you're incorporated, an LLC, or an unincorporated business, be sure to draw up an agreement with any new investor. Set down on paper the terms of the arrangement so there won't be any misunderstanding on who has control over things and what type of consent is required to take certain actions, such as borrowing money. This will help the business run smoothly now and create an exit strategy if you want to part ways.

What Investors Can Do for You

The fact that investors may want a say in your business can be a plus for you. An investor may bring skills and expertise that you lack. For example, an investor may be a knowledgeable financial person who can suggest ways in which to cut costs and become more profitable. An investor may have contacts with vendors and suppliers, banks, and other businesses that can benefit the company.

An investor may also become a working partner to share the chores of running your business. This gives you another person to bounce ideas off of and someone to hold down the fort when you are away—for a few hours or a well-deserved week's vacation.

Where to Find Investors

Investors, sometimes called "angels" (like those who invest in Broadway plays) if they're putting in small sums, are all around these days. The Small Business Administration estimates that there are about 250,000 active angels funding about 30,000 small businesses nationwide. Potentially, there are about two million people in the United States who have the means to make angel investments.

Just as you might start by asking family and friends for a loan, consider asking them to become an investor in your business and become your angel. If you can demonstrate that you know what you're doing and how you expect to reward them for their investment, you may have found your funding.

An Educated eBay Seller
How can you recognize an angel? According to a study by the Center for Venture Research at the University of New Hampshire conducted a few years ago, the "average" angel is 47 years old with an annual income of $90,000 and a net worth of $750,000. He or she is usually college educated, has been self-employed at some time, and invests $37,000 in a small business. Most angels invest close to home, usually within 50 miles.

If you need to look beyond your immediate circle of family and friends, you'll have to do some digging. It's best to network for an investor than try to find one through the Internet or a newspaper ad—the chances of finding a legitimate investor through networking are much higher.

Financing by Credit Card

A 2006 report from the Small Business Administration's Office of Advocacy noted that aside from car loans, the most frequently used type of credit was credit card borrowing: 46 percent used personal credit cards, and 34 percent used business credit cards to help finance the needs of small businesses.

For the most part, interest rates on credit card financing are higher than other financing alternatives. However, for short-term money needs, credit card loans are easy to arrange—just buy what you need or take a cash withdrawal. Repayment terms are basically up to you if the credit card company provides this flexibility; you can repay the loan all at once or over time (as long as you make minimum payments each month).

When It Might Make Sense

If you have an immediate need to buy something, such as a computer or merchandise to sell on eBay, you may not want or need to seek commercial loans or take in investors. You can swing the extra cash by using your plastic. Use credit card borrowing when …

♦ The need for cash is modest. Remember that your credit cards have borrowing limits.

♦ The need for cash is short term. If you expect to repay the funds quickly—in a month or a few months—the convenience of credit card borrowing makes this financing option preferable to other longer-term arrangements.

♦ The need for cash is specific to a particular purchase. If you need cash to buy a new and better digital camera, your cash needs are modest and the interest cost for financing the purchase is also small.

Keeping Credit Card Costs Down

You probably use a separate credit card for your business (or, if you don't, you should do so to help you keep track of your business expenses). Which card is best for you? It depends on what you're looking for—low interest rates, travel discounts, or rebates on purchases? The following cards, all with no annual fees, are worth exploring (although free introductory periods, rebate amounts, and other terms may change):

♦ **Advanta** (www.advanta.com) has a number of different business credit cards that offer not only benefits, but also detailed expense-management reports to track your business spending.

♦ **Chase Business Card** (www.chase.com, and click on Business Credit Cards) offers special discounts and rewards for various types of cards.

♦ **CapitalOne Visa Business Platinum Card** (www.capitalone.com and click on Credit Cards—Small Business) lets you personalize your card with your company name, add cards for employees at no cost, and, depending on the card, receive cash back or earn frequent flyer miles.

♦ **eBay MasterCard** (www.mastercard.ebay.com) lets you earn one point for every dollar you spend in purchases that can be redeemed when shopping on eBay or to save on shipping and seller fees. The card can easily be tied to PayPal so you can view and manage eBay MasterCard activities on an existing PayPal account. There's no annual fee. You can add your eBay user ID to the face of the card.

♦ **Open from American Express** (http://home.americanexpress.com/home/open.shtml) offers various small business credit cards that let you save money on gas, office supplies, and wireless services.

♦ **PayPal Plus Credit Card** (www.paypal.com/cgi-bin/webscr?cmd=xpt/cps/general/PPPlusCC-outside) offers a MasterCard that includes a rewards program.

Reinvesting Business Earnings

Like the ant in Aesop's fable, you can set aside funds you earn when times are good so you have them to spend if sales are slow or you have a need for cash. You build up a war chest of funds, which you keep in liquid investments (such as money market accounts or short-term Certificates of Deposit). This enables you to earn income on your business savings while growing a ready fund of money to have for emergency or planned expansion.

The Least You Need to Know

♦ In deciding whether to borrow money, factor in the ongoing repayment cost involved.

♦ When looking to borrow money, check your own resources first, as well as exploring your options with family and friends.

♦ Raising money by seeking investors means having to share the profits and perhaps answer to another person.

♦ Credit card financing can make sense in some situations, provided that you find low-interest cards.

Social Commerce: Learning, Growing, and Staying Connected

In This Chapter

- ◆ Using online tutorials, workshops, and local adult education programs
- ◆ Matriculating in eBay University
- ◆ Keeping up with changes and developments
- ◆ Participating in the eBay community
- ◆ Attending conventions and conferences

Reading this book isn't the final answer on how to start and grow an eBay business. New ideas and resources are cropping up all the time, and you have to stay alert to change. It's up to you to keep up with new developments, such as changes on eBay and new resources to aid you in your business.

In this chapter, you'll see where to go on eBay to learn how to master different techniques. You'll find out how eBay University can help you widen your horizons. You'll also learn about other resources that can help you stay up on developments and opportunities to grow your business and enjoy your eBay experience.

Tutorials and Online Courses

You can learn basic and advanced sales techniques through eBay and elsewhere. These learning opportunities give you pointers and tips that you might otherwise miss or take years to discover through your own experiences.

eBay has free tutorials at the eBay University Learning Center to explain certain tasks. For example, use its tutorial to learn how to add a photo to your listing (http://pages.ebay.com/education/selling/Photographytips.html), or follow a checkout tutorial on how to complete the payment process (http://pages.ebay.com/help/sell/checkout_tutorial.html). There isn't a general listing of all eBay tutorials; you can search for one using the Help tab.

eBay also offers courses from eBay University (explained later in this chapter); you can take both online and classroom courses.

Although eBay is probably a great starting point for your educational experience, you may want to take other online or local courses to expand your knowledge of eBay and develop other business skills to grow your company.

Online and Local Courses

A growing number of online courses are offered to instruct you on how to become an eBay seller and start an eBay business. Community colleges and continuing education schools sponsor eBay courses to teach buying and selling and starting an eBay business.

For example, to learn about selling, a 12-lesson course on buying and selling, titled "How to Buy and Sell," is offered through ed2go at www.learntobuyandsell.com. The instructors, Kara Gordon and Shirley Muse, are accessible for answering students' questions online. To sign up, you are connected with a school (often a community college) near you and take the course online (prices vary with the school).

Check with your local adult education program and community college brochures to see about upcoming courses. Here you can gain hands-on experience with courses hosted in the school's computer labs.

Power Point _____

Become a Certified eBay Education Specialist so you can teach others how to buy and sell on eBay. Or become a Certified Business Consultant so, in addition to teaching others how to buy and sell on eBay, you can help businesses with a successful eBay business model. Courses are available through Power U (www.poweru. net/ebay/index.asp), which is not affiliated with eBay.

Workshops

eBay conducts free online workshops, hosted by eBay staff or outside experts, to help you learn about new features and products on eBay that enhance your selling experience. For example, one workshop is on "Using Research to Maximize Your Profits." Each workshop covers a single topic. For example, eBay has run a workshop on its Customer Services the eBay Way.

The workshops usually run for an hour. You can view a calendar of upcoming eWorkshops at http://pages.ebay.com/community/workshopcalendar/current.html.

eBay University

You don't need to matriculate or submit SAT scores to enroll in a study course to learn selling basics or advanced selling techniques. You won't find a rolling campus green with ivy-covered buildings. And the courses you take won't give you credits that can be applied toward a college degree.

Figure 22.1

Sharpen your seller skills at eBay University Learning Center.

But you can take the courses you want from eBay University, regardless of your level of formal education. The dean of eBay Education is Jim "Griff" Griffith, who was the first eBay customer service representative (there are now thousands of them). Incidentally, he is also the host of eBay Radio at www.wsradio.com/ebayradio.

There are three ways to learn: online from the convenience of your home, by purchasing a DVD for self-study, or by attending classes held around the country.

- **Online courses.** Watch a free online video; there are two online courses for eBay sellers:

  - **Selling Basics.** Learn how to set up an account, do research, monitor listings, and complete transactions.

  - **Beyond the Basics of Selling.** This course covers choosing the right listing format, using listing tools, marketing your business, packing and shipping, and using PayPal.

- **Self-study.** You can purchase a DVD of *Selling Basics* for $7.95 and *Beyond the Basics* CD for $19.95.

- **Live seminars.** One-day (9 A.M. to 3:30 P.M.) classes are held in different cities around the country. You can find the schedule by going to http://pages.ebay.com/university. Cost: $59.

Staying Up on Developments

eBay is always changing the rules, adding new features, and creating new alliances with third parties to enhance eBay selling opportunities. Just ask any eBay old-timer from the 1990s how different eBay is today.

Fortunately, there are many ways to keep up on developments and learn new tricks to help you sell on eBay and grow your business. Some of these venues are through eBay; others are from third parties.

The Chatter

eBay publishes a blog called *The Chatter* for its community. Various eBay employees post about topics such as success stories, helpful hints, community news, and more. View it at www.ebaychatter.com.

There's a special eBay newsletter for sellers, called *PowerUp Seller Newsletter* (http://pages.ebay.com/sellercentral/newsflash.html). Here you get the latest details on free listing days and discounts, tips and resources, and more.

AuctionBytes

eBay isn't the only way to learn about auction developments. You can sign up for an online newsletter that alerts you to new tools, resources, and industry trends related to online auction activities. There are two alternatives (we use both):

♦ **AuctionBytes-Update,** an e-zine started in 1999 that comes out two times a month

♦ **AuctionBytes News Flash,** which started in 2001 and provides snippets of news items four to five times a week

To subscribe to one of these free newsletters, that are independent and impartial trade publications for merchants, go to www.auctionbytes.com.

The PowerSeller Report

Once your selling activities have reached the level at which you join the inner circle and become a PowerSeller, you may want additional information—beyond what eBay provides. The newsletter *The PowerSeller Report* gives you tips, product sources, and auction selling secrets.

To subscribe, go to www.tprweb.com; it costs $99 per year for 12 issues (or try a 3-month membership for $27.95). You can also sign up for a free weekly *Hot Sheet* with a tip for PowerSellers.

Big Ideas for Small Business

The features on eBay may be the core of your business, but there are many other aspects to running and growing your company. You need to stay abreast of developments on insurance, taxes, personnel, marketing, technology, and other subjects. Barbara Weltman's monthly online newsletter *Big Ideas for Small Business*® (www.barbaraweltman.com and click on "Big Ideas for Small Business"), which started in 2002, provides easy-to-read vital information to help you stay ahead of the curve. In addition to articles on various topics, there are answers to reader inquiries, reviews of new business books, and a calendar of upcoming events and small business-related dates.

You can also receive a free daily e-mail with a brief Small Business Idea of the Day[SM] to help you better run your business (www.barbaraweltman.com and click on "Idea of the Day").

The eBay Community

The buzz word today is *social commerce*. It's the way information is being spread on the web. In an instant, anyone around the world can learn about something—a great new product, a bad buyer, or an interesting new website. This type of information-sharing is ideal for the eBay community.

The eBay community isn't a geographically bound area. It's a state of mind, encompassing all buyers and sellers who use eBay.

eBay has created a set of community values by which users are supposed to govern themselves. All members are encouraged to use open and honest communication and follow five fundamental values:

def•i•ni•tion

Today we are in the age of Web 2.0, where **social commerce** rules. Word-of-mouth marketing has been taken to a new level, through YouTube, MySpace, blogs, and other online personalized sites.

"We believe people are basically good."

"We believe everyone has something to contribute."

"We believe that an honest, open environment can bring out the best in people."

"We recognize and respect everyone as a unique individual."

"We encourage you to treat others the way you want to be treated."

An Educated eBay Seller

eBay has opened up a social network for a diverse group of individuals. It's been estimated that 20 percent of all visitors to the site are age 55 or older; many use eBay to make friends and keep busy. Some find the site after being laid off or retiring and use eBay to create a new career.

---

eBay has created a number of ways that you can connect to other members of the eBay community to talk, get answers, and learn more. Although eBay gives you the party line on what's happening, you may want to get the inside scoop from other eBay sellers.

Your options for making connections include these:

- Discussion boards
- Chat rooms
- eBay groups
- Blogs
- Answer Center

Power Point _____

Looking for someone in particular within the eBay community? You can do a search to find anyone with an eBay user ID. Learn about the person and read his or her About Me or My World page and feedback profile by clicking on Community and then entering the user ID in the Find a Member box.

Discussion Boards

Discussion boards are venues for posing your questions to the eBay community for anyone to answer. The responses you get may not be helpful or even accurate (though they usually are).

eBay has five types of discussion boards:

- General discussion boards where you can air your pet peeves, relax with friends, or share your views with others.

- Community help boards on topics ranging from auction listings to trust and safety. Here you can post your concerns and receive answers from other eBay users (or answer posted questions yourself).

- eBay Tools boards for discussing tools such as Blackthorne, Selling Manager, Picture Services, eBay Toolbar, and so on.

- Category-specific discussion groups on topics from animals to vintage clothing and accessories.

- eBay Giving Works board, where buyers, sellers, and nonprofit organizations join in building "a marketplace for change." This is a place for charity-minded people to learn how they can use eBay to advance their philanthropic desires.

Auction Alert _____

Revisit the discussion boards often—new categories are added from time to time. Postings don't remain there forever, either, and are continually replaced by newer responses.

To access any of the discussion boards, you just click the link for the board that interests you. But even though you are a registered user of eBay, you must also register at any discussion board you post to by entering your eBay user ID and password.

Chat Rooms

Chat rooms are real-time communication devices in which you enter your questions or statements, and those logged into the chat room can immediately respond to you. You can stay for as long or as short a time as you want and can visit as frequently as you want. There are general chat rooms as well as category-specific chat rooms. For example, if you plan to attend eBay Live! and want to find low-cost accommodations, meet up with people, or get the inside scoop on convention activities, you'll find this all through a chat room.

> **Power Point**
>
> Participation in chat rooms is a marketing tool. You can post a link to your store or items whenever you post a message. Also see Chapter 10 for more ways to use chat rooms in marketing your eBay business.

If you join a chat room, you are supposed to adhere to eBay policies on board usage. For instance, you're required to refrain from using profanities or trying to sell things there. You'll find these policies at http://pages.ebay.com/help/policies/everyone-boards.html.

As with discussion boards, to post a message, you need to register. This is simply a matter of entering your eBay user ID and password.

> **Auction Alert**
>
> The messages posted in chat rooms and on discussion boards are strictly the opinions of individuals. Take everything you read with a grain of salt (for every person who complains about a particular eBay policy, you'll find others who love it). eBay takes no responsibility for misinformation.

eBay Groups

The eBay Groups center helps connect you with other eBay members who have interests similar to yours. There are public groups where any eBay member can join; there are private groups where a member must send a request to the group leader or receive an invitation to participate. You have a number of ways to form a connection:

◆ **By region.** Find people in your area to connect with. Some groups have a handful of members; others have hundreds.

◆ **By collectible interest.** Find people who are interested in the same items as you.

◆ **Selling groups.** Join other sellers on certain topics, such as running an eBay store or being a trading assistant.

◆ **Special interest groups.** Meet other people who share your unique interests in subjects such as art, music, or families.

> **Power Point**
>
> Disabled individuals who are sellers on eBay may find it helpful to join the Disabled Online User's Association (DOUA) run by eBay PowerSeller Marjie Smith.

Blogs

eBay web logs—blogs—give you an opportunity to voice your opinion. You can create and monitor your personalized eBay blog by going to http://blogs.ebay.com.

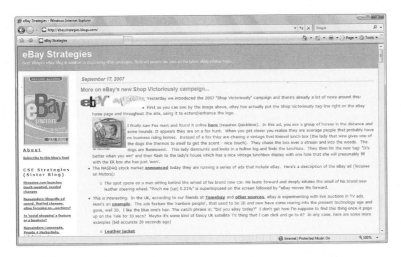

Figure 22.2

Read eBay seller Blogs

Answer Center

View the answers to frequently asked questions at eBay's Answer Center (http://pages.ebay.com/community/answercenter). This member-to-member page is another way to connect to the community. Ask your questions or view responses to those posed by others, or just share information here.

Listen Up!

Instead of turning your dial, you can use your computer to connect to the radio and listen to eBay-related information. There are numerous small-business radio shows to help you learn about various aspects of running your business, including *Small Business Advocate* at www.smallbusinessadvocate.com.

eBay-specific shows can also help you hone your selling skills and learn about new developments and resources. These include *eBay Radio* and *Entrepreneur Radio*.

eBay Radio

Every Tuesday, from 11 A.M. to 2 P.M. (Pacific Standard Time), you can listen to eBay Radio, hosted by Jim "Griff" Griffith, Dean of eBay University. Griff brings in experts in various fields to talk on topics of interest to listeners and to field call-in questions. Barbara Weltman has been a guest on the show numerous times, and there's always a lively discussion.

Griff also hosts *eBay Radio PowerSeller Show*. You don't have to be a PowerSeller to listen!

To connect, go to www.wsradio.com/ebayradio.

You can sign up to be notified of upcoming broadcasts and access a calendar of prior and upcoming events at http://groups.ebay.com/forum.jspa?forumID=1278. You need audio capacity on your computer to be a listener.

You can also listen to archives of past radio shows anytime you want. Go to www.wsradio.com/eBayradio.

World Syndications Biz Radio

World Syndications Biz Radio sponsors an Internet-based radio show and offers weekly segments hosted by Lee Mirabel (www.wsradio.com/internet-talk-radio.cfm/shows/World-Syndications-Biz-Radio-Magazine.html). With the help of guests, such as Barbara Weltman, the show discusses all aspects of starting and growing a business, from business plans and how to manage employees, to home-based business issues and more.

Getting Together at Conventions

Although eBay is essentially an online activity, there is an opportunity to meet other eBay sellers in person. You can exchange your stories about your experiences, get your questions answered, and make connections that you can use to grow your business.

eBay Live!

For the past six years, eBay has held a nationwide three-day convention where thousands of eBay sellers and potential sellers get together to hear presentations, learn, and share experiences.

In 2007, eBay Live! was held in Boston; more than 10,000 people came to find out how to maximize their eBay potential. Topics for classes and discussion groups ranged from basics (such as beginning photography) to advanced sales techniques and business strategies for PowerSellers (such as selecting a retirement plan for your business).

Beyond the structured instructional segments, there are opportunities to meet with vendors of tools and resources for your business and to connect with other eBay sellers to share war stories and develop friendships.

One of the major benefits of attending eBay Live! is getting to meet with the "Pinks" (eBay employees). This is the one time of the year that you can talk face-to-face with the head of a department. So come primed with questions. If you've got an on-going issue, you'd be amazed at how quickly it gets fixed if you talk to the right person at eBay Live!.

 Power Point

Can't attend the convention? You can attend webcasts of select eBay Live! seminars and catch up on the news as reported by the many AuctionBytes reporters in attendance.

In 2008, eBay Live! will be held on June 19–21, 2008, in Chicago, Illinois at McCormick Place (West). Try to attend for an educational and extremely enjoyable experience.

Conventions for Your Items

If you sell collectibles and antiques, there's bound to be an organization or club of like-minded people. For example, there's a McDonald's Collectors Club for those who appreciate McDonald's premiums, and the Society of Inkwell Collectors for people who collect antique inkwells. These groups usually hold meetings and often annual conventions where you can get together with your fellow members to share information and stories.

You can find a club for your items by visiting Collectors.org (www.collectors.org; click on Join a Club).

eBay Groups Summits

Top sellers on eBay are part of an elite group that has access to not only special assistance on eBay, but also special events. PowerSellers have special registration and activities at eBay Live!.

Some PowerSellers have formed groups to discuss topics and arrange meetings. For example, the Chicago Area PowerSellers organized in September 2003 and is a public forum on eBay. For details, go to http://groups.ebay.com/forum.jspa?forumID=8364.

PeSA, the Professional eBay Sellers Alliance for eBay high achievers, holds summits in spring and fall, as well as hosting an event during eBay Live! (www.gopesa.org/index.cfm?page=events). The Fall 2007 summit was held in San Francisco.

The Least You Need to Know

♦ Use eBay tutorials, classes, and workshops to walk you through a specific activity, such as including pictures with your listings, or learning advanced sales techniques.

♦ Subscribe to online and print newsletters to keep up on developments that affect eBay and your business operations.

♦ Engage in social commerce by joining the eBay community through discussion boards, Answer Center, chat rooms, groups, and blogs to find answers to your questions, meet other sellers, help others, and share your opinions.

♦ Attend conventions such as eBay Live! and other conferences to meet other eBay people in person, learn what's new, and make friends for life.

eBay and Third-Party Tools

Whatever task you have to perform, there's probably software or an online tool to help you do it better, faster, and often cheaper. The options you select depend, of course, on your personal needs, what the tool can do for you, and how much it costs.

This appendix includes resources you can use to help you run your eBay business. Many of them have been discussed throughout this book. I've listed them here for your convenient reference, categorized alphabetically according to the task you want to do.

Accounting and Record Keeping

Keep track of your sales and expenses—it's required by law, and it helps you know how you're doing. Use software and online tools to simplify this daily task.

◆ **Intuit QuickBooks** (www.quickbooks.com). This is the leading small business recordkeeping software. Cost: $199.95, or $399.95 for the Pro edition. There are also online editions.

◆ **Intuit Simple Start and Simple Start Online** (www.quickbooks. com). This simplified bookkeeping software is so easy to use that there is no user's manual. Cost: $99.95 for software; $9.95 a month online.

- ◆ **IRS** (www.irs.gov). Download IRS Publication 583, "Starting a Business and Keeping Records."

- ◆ **Office Accounting** (http://office.microsoft.com/en-us/accounting/). Microsoft's desktop bookkeeping tool, which enables you to save money on credit-card processing and contains eBay and PayPal tools. Cost: varies.

- ◆ **Office Accounting Express** (http://office.microsoft.com/en-us/accountingexpress/). This is Microsoft's accounting tool. Cost: free.

- ◆ **Peachtree First and Pro Accounting** (www.peachtree.com). Basic and advanced accounting tools. Cost: $69.95 for First; $169.99 for Pro Accounting.

- ◆ **SageFire** (www.keepmore.net/ebay). Simple online accounting tool, with an automatic export feature for eBay transactions. Cost: $14.95 a month.

Appraisals

Find out what your items are worth so you can price them right when you list them for sale.

- ◆ **American Society of Appraisers** (www.appraisers.org).

- ◆ **Antique Appraisals Online** (www3.sympatico.ca/appraisers). Cost: $9.95 per appraisal.

- ◆ **Appraisers Association of America** (www.appraisersassoc.org).

- ◆ **Collect.com** (www.collect.com). Cost: free, but registration is required.

- ◆ **InstAppraisal.com** (www.instappraisal.com). Cost: $14.95 per appraisal.

- ◆ **International Society of Appraisers** (www.isa-appraisers.org).

- ◆ **WhatsItWorthToYou.com** (also called Eppraisals.com; www.whatsitworthtoyou.com). Cost: $9.95 per appraisal.

Auction Management

Manage the listing process and follow your sales using online tools.

- ◆ **AuctionHawk** (www.auctionhawk.com). Obtain custom management and checkout services, including feedback capabilities. Cost: Basic plan $12.99 per month, Power plan $21.99 per month, Professional plan $29.99 per month, Unlimited plan $44.99 per month (21-day free trial period).

- **Auctiva** (www.auctiva.com). Easy-to-use comprehensive auction management tool. Cost: free.

- **Blackthorne Basic** (http://pages.ebay.com/blackthorne/basic.html). Designed for listing 24 items or more, this tool helps you create listings and manage sales. Cost: $9.99 per month (30-day free trial).

- **Blackthorne Pro** (http://pages.ebay.com/blackthorne/pro.html). Designed for high-volume sellers, this tool provides complete sales management, bulk listing, and post-sales assistance. Cost: $24.99 per month (30-day free trial).

- **ChannelAdvisor** (http://channeladvisor.com). Marketing tool to help buyers find you. Cost: call for pricing at 1-866-264-8594.

- **eHarbors** (www.eharbors.com). Enables you to create auction ads, send e-mail to buyers, maintain inventory, host images and relist unsold items in bulk. Cost: free.

- **File Exchange** (http://pages.ebay.com/file_exchange). High-volume sellers can transfer their files from their computer to eBay. Cost: free for qualified sellers.

- **HammerTap3** (www.hammertap.com). This is a comprehensive auction-management tool. Cost: subscriptions starting at $19.95 (10-day free trial period).

- **Ink Frog** (www.inkfrog.com). Image hosting, counters, sales, and inventory management tools. Cost: $6.95 a month for image hosting only, or $9.95 a month for all features.

- **Selling Manager** (http://pages.ebay.com/selling_manager). Designed for medium- to high-volume sellers, this tool helps you manage listings and post-sale activities. More specifically, you can use it to manage items to be listed on eBay at a future date; track active eBay listings; monitor unsold listings; and manage feedback, payments, and other post-sale activities. Cost: $4.99 per month (30-day free trial period); free for Basic Store subscribers.

- **Selling Manager Pro** (http://pages.ebay.com/selling_manager_pro). Use this handy online tool to track your inventory, monitor pending and active listings; relist unsold items in bulk; send invoices, e-mails, and feedback in bulk; track payments; and generate profit and loss reports. Cost: $15.99 per month (30-day free trial period); free for those using Blackthorne Pro and Anchored Store subscribers.

- **Spoon Feeder** (www.spoonfeeder.com). Comprehensive auction management tool. Cost: $19.95–$199.95 for set up, plus $10–$40 a month.

- **TurboLister from eBay** (http://pages.ebay.com/turbo_lister). Designed for medium- to high-volume sellers, this tool enables you to easily create multiple listings. Use it alone or in combination with other software tools. Easily format your text and schedule your auctions. Cost: free.

- **Vendio** (www.vendio.com). Obtain customer manager, sales manager, and store manager tools. For example, the sales manager tool lets you automate the listing process. Cost: varies, depending on whether you choose a monthly fixed rate or variable plan, or you can pay as you go or choose an annual plan. Your sales volume affects your plan choice.

- **Zoovy Auction Package** (www.zoovy.com). A variety of auction management tools. Cost: call for pricing at 1-877-966-8948.

Bonding

Gain insurance protection for items you purchase.

- **BuySAFE** (www.buysafe.com). Large insurance companies—Liberty Mutual, Travelers, and ACE USA—guarantee protection to buyers up to $15,000. Cost: 1 percent of the final transaction price.

Counters

Keep track of visitors to your eBay store or other websites.

- **Auctiva** (www.auctiva.com). Add a free counter to your listings.

- **Counterguide.com** (www.counterguide.com). Check out your counter options by using this resource to link to counters for eBay. Cost: free.

- **Freelogs.com** (www.freelogs.com). Choose from dozens of counter styles. Cost: free.

- **Sellathon ViewTracker** (www.sellathon.com). Tracks visitors, what keywords led them to you, whether they're planning on sniping, and more. Cost: from $4.95 per month for the basic version to $19.95 per month for the most sophisticated version (30-day free trial).

- **Vendio** (www.vendio.com). You have a choice of two counter types. The basic counter is free; a pro version, which enables you to track hourly and daily traffic, is $3.95 per month.

Customers

Keep track of customers so you can market to them. Also bar "bad" customers from participating in your auctions or buying at your stores.

- ◆ **BidderBlock** (www.hammertap.com/bidderblock). Create a detailed list of customers you want to block from bidding. You can easily share this information with others. Cost: free.

- ◆ **Blocked Bidder/Buyer List from eBay** (http://pages.ebay.com/services/buyandsell/biddermanagement.html). Set up a list of bidders who can no longer bid or purchase your listings. You can add or delete bidders at any time (you don't have to give eBay a reason for doing so). Cost: free.

- ◆ **Preapproved Bidder/Buyer List from eBay** (http://pages.ebay.com/services/buyandsell/biddermanagement.html). Create an exclusive list of bidders or buyers you want to participate in your sales—those not on the list can't buy from you unless they contact you so that they can be placed on your list. Cost: free.

Customs

When shipping outside the United States, you may have to complete certain documents and pay certain duties or fees.

- ◆ **A&A Contract Customs Brokers Ltd.** (www.aacb.com). This Customs broker will handle your export documentation. Cost: varies.

- ◆ **AESDirect** (www.aesdirect.gov). This is the automated export system sponsored by the U.S. Census Bureau that enables you to file the Shippers Export Document electronically instead of using a paper form. Cost: free.

- ◆ **FedEx International Resource Center** (http://gtm.com/us.international/irc). If you log on with a FedEx account, you can read about Customs rules.

- ◆ **International Business Training** (www.i-b-t.net). Free online discussion groups where you can post your questions about Customs.

- ◆ **International Federation of Customs Brokers Associations** (www.ifcba.org).

- ◆ **National Customs Brokers and Forwarders Association of America** (www.ncbfaa.org).

- **Shipping Solutions** (www.shipsolutions.com). Software enables you to quickly produce export documents, file your Shipper's Export Declaration (SED) form electronically, and monitor all your shipping costs. Cost: $499 (there's a free demo).

- **U.S. Postal Service** (www.usps.com/global/customsforms). Complete necessary shipping documents online. Cost: free.

Dispute Resolution

You may have problems with a buyer, or a buyer may have problems with you. It's always a good idea to work things out, if possible, and certain online sites can help.

- **SquareTrade** (www.squaretrade.com). There are two types of dispute-resolution options: direct negotiation or resolution using a mediator who can bring parties together in an effort to amicably resolve problems. Both parties must agree to the process. The mediator facilitates discussion; he or she is not a judge or jury. Cost: direct negotiation process is free; the mediation process costs $20 to the party filing the case.

Drop Shippers

Instead of buying inventory, use an arrangement in which you sell items for wholesalers who provide the goods and, usually, the storage and shipping, at your direction.

- **Drop Ship Access** (www.dropshipaccess.com).

- **Drop Shippers** (www.dropshippers.com).

- **Ezdropship.com** (www.ezdropship.com).

- **Shopster** (www.shopster.com).

eBay Stores

Customize your eBay store to attract customers.

- **PixClinic.com, the eBay store remodelers** (www.pixclinic.com/ebay-stores-design.html). Create logos, custom headers, multiple storefront pages, and professional pictures. Cost: depends on services you select.

Escrow Services

Currently, only one service is approved by eBay for the United States; four companies are approved for international sales.

- **Australia** (eBay.au users)—**Escrow Australia** (www.escrowaustralia.com.au). Here you deal in the Australian dollar ($A) and track items via international trade partners with local knowledge and experience. You must register to use this service (registration is free). Cost: $A9.90 and up.

- **Belgium, Denmark, France, Netherlands, Norway,** and **Sweden** (eBay.com.be, eBay.com.dk, eBay.com.fr, eBay.com.nl, eBay.com.no, and eBay.com.se users)—**Triple Deal** (www.tripledeal.com). Currently, this escrow service operates in 10 countries and projects worldwide operations soon. Cost: an item less than €250 has a fee of €.50; other fees apply to higher-price items (determined on a per-transaction basis so that if you sell several items to the same buyer in one transaction, the fee is determined accordingly).

- **Germany** (eBay.com.de users)—**iloxx Safe Trade** (www.iloxx.de, but go to Google first to obtain a translation of the site by clicking on Language Tools if your German isn't adequate). Fees are based in euros and depend on the value of the item. Currently, only those with a bank account in Germany or Austria can use this service. Cost: starting at €.50 for an item valued at less than €250.

- **Italy** and **Spain** (eBay.com.it and eBay.com.es users)—**Escrow!** (www.escrow-europa.com). Fees are based in euros (there is an international currency converter on the site to help you see the fees in U.S. dollars). Cost: for items up to €5,000 or $5,000, the fee is 3.8 percent when charged to a credit card or 2 percent when paid with a bank transfer (the minimum cost is €8); lower rates apply to higher-priced transactions.

- **United States** (eBay.com users)—**Escrow.com** (www.escrow.com). This company is approved for domestic eBay sales. Cost (which can be split between buyer and seller): 3.5 percent on the first $5,000 to 0.89 percent on amounts over $25,000. Higher fees apply to premier service, which includes additional buyer ID verification and fraud screening.

Financing

Borrow money or help customers finance their purchases with these tools.

- ◆ **Advanta** (www.advanta.com). Borrow on your business credit card. There are a number of different credit card programs. Cost: varies.

- ◆ **CapitalOne Visa Business Platinum Card** (www.capitalone.com and click on Credit Cards; Small Business). This lets you personalize your card with your company name.

- ◆ **Chase Business Cards** (www.chase.com and click on Business Credit Cards). Find special discounts and rewards for various types of cards.

- ◆ **Commerce Bank** (www.commerceonline.com). Small-business-friendly bank.

- ◆ **eBay Business** (http://business.ebay.com). Find merchant solutions for your business on eBay.

- ◆ **eBay MasterCard** (www.mastercard.ebay.com). Earn points for dollars spent on eBay purchases that can be redeemed when shopping on eBay or to save on shipping and seller fees.

- ◆ **GE Capital Financial** (http://pages.ebay.com/businesscredit). GE Capital Financial has teamed up with eBay to offer a line of credit and secured financing.

- ◆ **PayPal** (www.paypal.com). Mention to customers that they can obtain credit through PayPal Credit Program. Cost: varies.

- ◆ **SBA loan programs** (www.sba.gov/financing). Find out about SBA loan programs if you need to borrow money. Cost: free information.

- ◆ **Wells Fargo** (www.wellsfargo.com). Small-business-friendly bank.

Franchises and Multi-Level Marketing

If you want to buy a prepackaged business that provides structure and support, become a franchisee. Alternatively, consider multi-level marketing arrangements.

- ◆ **QuikDrop** (www.quikdrop.com). Franchise opportunity.

- ◆ **Zippi** (www.zippi.com). Multi-level marketing arrangement.

Fraud Protection

Fraud is a big problem on eBay, especially when selling to overseas buyers, so you have to be vigilant and take all available steps to protect yourself.

- ◆ **Better Business Bureau Online** (www.bbbonline.org/Idtheft/business.asp). Six proven ways to prevent business ID theft.

- ◆ **Department of Justice** (www.usdoj.gov/whatwedo/whatwedo_if.html). File a complaint if you've been victimized.

- ◆ **eConsumer** (www.econsumer.gov). Two dozen governments share information ("cross-border complaints") here.

- ◆ **Federal Trade Commission** (https://rn.ftc.gov/pls/dod). Report scams you've experienced to the federal government. Cost: free.

- ◆ **Interpol** (www.interpol.com). Get help with international fraud.

- ◆ **U.S. Postal Inspection Service** (www.usps.com/postalinspectors). Report suspected mail fraud.

- ◆ **U.S. Secret Service** (www.secretservice.gov/ectf.shtml). Report suspected fraud to this electronic task force.

- ◆ **VeRO from eBay** (http://pages.ebay.com/help/tp/vero-rights-owner.html). If someone infringes on your intellectual property rights (for example, uses your photo), stop the practice. Cost: free.

Fulfillment Companies

These businesses can store and ship your inventory at your direction.

- ◆ **Innotrac** (www.innotrac.com). A publicly owned company that's a full-service fulfillment provider.

- ◆ **FFP Global** (www.fulfillmentplus.com). An outsource business process solution provider.

- ◆ **Fulfillment by Amazon** (www.amazonservices.com/fulfillment). This allows eBay sellers to have their items stored, packed, and shipped by Amazon.

- ◆ **VendorSeek** (www.vendorseek.com). Get competitive bids from fulfillment companies. Cost: free search.

Insurance

Protect your business from unexpected disasters by carrying adequate insurance protection.

- ◆ **American Red Cross** (www.redcross.org/services/disaster/0,1082,0_606_,00. html). Free disaster-planning guide for business.

- ◆ **Flood Smart** (www.floodsmart.gov/floodsmart/pages). Find out about flood insurance.

- ◆ **Guardian** (www.disabilityquotes.com/occupations/homebasedbusiness.cfm). Disability policies for home-based business owners.

- ◆ **The Hartford** (www.thehartford.com). Business owner's policy (BOP). Cost: varies.

- ◆ **Institute for Business and Home Safety** (www.ibhs.org/business_protection). Obtain a free disaster-planning guide.

- ◆ **Insurance Information Institute** (www.iii.org). Find general insurance information as well as a disaster planning guide.

- ◆ **Insure U** (www.insureuonline.org/smallbusiness). Insurance information for small and home-based businesses.

- ◆ **National Federation of Independent Business (NFIB)** (www.nfib.com). Members can get insurance coverage for less than they could on their own.

- ◆ **Safeco Insurance Company** (www.safeco.com). Business owner's policy (BOP). Cost: varies.

- ◆ **Travelers Insurance** (www.travelers.com). Business owner's policy (BOP). Cost: varies.

- ◆ **Zurich North America** (www.zurichna.com). Business owner's policy (BOP). Cost: varies.

Inventory

Find inventory through liquidations, bulk sales, and cheap inventory sellers.

- ◆ **Auction Sieve** (www.auctionsieve.com). Find bargains and items you're looking for on eBay. Cost: free.

- **Cannylink's Flea Market Guide** (www.cannylink.com/fleamarketguide).

- **Department of Defense** (www.drms.dla.mil). Buy items at this government auction site.

- **Flea Market Guide of U.S. Flea Markets** (www.fleamarketguide.com).

- **Government Liquidation.com** (www.govliquidation.com). This is a one-stop source of surplus inventory sold in bulk by government agencies.

- **Government surplus** (www.usa.gov/shopping/shopping.shtml). This site lets you buy office equipment, furniture, and industrial equipment that the federal government no longer needs. This site is a gateway into buying surplus from the government. You can also find government surplus sold through auction at Liquidity Services (www.govliquidation.com).

- **GoWholesale** (www.gowholesale.com). Provides very extensive sourcing for a wide range of products.

- **Liquidation.com** (www.liquidation.com). This is a one-stop source of surplus inventory being sold in bulk from manufacturers, wholesalers, retailers, and service providers.

- **Lost Auction 6.2** (www.vbbitman.com). Find items on which there may be few or no bids because of typos or spelling errors. Cost: free.

- **OutletsOnLine** (www.outletsonline.com). Locate outlet centers nationwide.

- **Overstock.com** (www.overstock.com). This is an online outlet for clothing, electronics, and more. Check the clearance bins for buying opportunities.

- **PawnShops.net** (www.pawnshops.net). Locate a pawn shop near you.

- **Salvation Army Thrift Stores** (www.satruck.com/FindStore.aspx). Locate local Salvation Army thrift stores.

- **Thrift Shopper** (www.thethriftshopper.com). A nationwide thrift store directory.

- **Ubid** (www.ubid.com). This is another online auction place and a bargain hunter's dream site. Here you can often buy cameras, stereos, and other items at very attractive prices.

- **U.S. Treasury** (www.ustreas.gov/auctions). Buy items at this government auction.

- **Wholesale Distributors Net** (www.wholesaledistributorsnet.com). This site calls itself the center of the wholesale universe because it is visited by 34,000 businesses each month. This site is another directory to domestic and imported wholesale lots.

- **Wholesale Lots** (http://pages.ebay.com/catindex/catwholesale.html). Find wholesale items offered by merchants and distributors.

- **Worldwide Brands, Inc.** (www.worldwidebrands.com). This product-sourcing service, founded by Chris Malta (the product-sourcing expert for eBay Radio), sells a wholesale directory for light bulk, which means buying in affordable quantities (generally less than $500 per order). Cost: $69.95 (including updates).

Legal

If you want to incorporate your business or set up a limited liability company (LLC), follow the law.

- **BizFilings** (www.bizfilings.com). Set up a business entity in any state.

- **Legal Zoom** (www.legalzoom.com). Set up a business entity in any state.

- **MyCorporation** (www.mycorporation.com). Set up a business entity in any state.

Listing-Enhancement Tools

Make your listings stand out from the crowd by using special tools.

- **Boldchat** (www.boldchat.com). Lets bidders ask you questions through live chat. Cost: free for the simple plan, $39.95 for the Pro version.

- **Onstream Auction** (www.auctionvideo.com). Add video to your listings. Cost: $9.95 per month for low-volume usage.

- **Skype** (www.skype.com). Add the ability to talk by phone or instant message with customers by adding this free service to your listings. Cost: free for calls to and from Skype users; varies for additional usage.

- **Vhost SitePal** (www.sitepal.com). Add video and audio to your listings with this host site. Cost: about $9.99 per month for the basic version (15-day free trial).

Market Research

What's selling and for how much? Check the competition so you know what will sell and what price it will bring.

- **Auction Navigator** (www.auctionnavigator.com). Enables you to find and track auctions, as well as bid and snipe with one product. Cost: $29.95 (free trial version).

- **Hammertap3** (www.hammertap.com). Gives you sell-through rates, average bids per item, keyword sales data, best day and time of the week based on number of bids or final price, average sales price per item, and much more. Cost: $19.95 per month (10-day free trial period). Note: this is the leading seller for market research.

- **PriceIt!** (www.gale.com/PriceIt). A comprehensive antique and collectibles pricing tool. You can request a free trial or call for pricing at 1-800-877-GALE.

- **PriceMiner** (www.priceminer.com). A comprehensive pricing tool to help you access eBay market data. Cost: $9.95 per month for computer access; $14.95 per month for wireless access.

- **TeraPeak** (www.terapeak.com). Reports the hottest items selling in each category on eBay. Cost: $14.95 a month for Insight, $29.95 for Advantage (some research is free). Terapeak also offers research for international sites and eBay Motors Parts and Accessories (called P&A) for an extra fee.

- **Vendio Research** (www.vendio.com). Offers an online pricing tool to help you set opening and reserve prices. Cost: $14.95 a month.

- **What's Hot** (www.vendio.com). Reports on the hottest items selling in each category on eBay. Cost: $3.95 a month.

Marketing

Devise your marketing strategies in an organized way to help grow your business to the next level.

- **BayMail** (www.sharewareconnection.com/baymail.htm). Send messages to up to five people at one time. The Pro version can send to large groups at once, providing powerful management of mailing lists—yours or those you buy or rent. Cost: free.

- **ClickXChange.com** (www.clickxchange.com). Develop your affiliate program. Cost: varies.

- **Marketing Plan Pro from Palo Alto Software** (www.paloalto.com). Create your own marketing plan. Cost: $179.95.

- **MyStoreRewards.com** (www.mystorerewards.com). This program encourages repeat buying by having buyers accumulate credit on each purchase. Cost: $7.95 a month, plus 1¢ for each invitation and 10¢ for each rebate issue.

- **Small Business Administration** (www.sba.gov/smallbusinessplanner/manage/marketandprice/SERV_MARKETINGPLANS.html). Cost: free.

Merchant Services

Take credit cards, verify checks, and accept other forms of payment without worry.

- **Auction Checkout** (www.auctioncheckout.com). Accept credit cards and process transactions using your own merchant account (you don't need to have a separate website). Cost: Gold service has a fee of $29 per month, plus 29¢ per transaction (there are other prices for other levels of service).

- **BidPay** (www.bidpay.com). A credit card payment processing alternative to PayPal. Cost: 50¢ transaction fee and 2.5 percent for U.S. buyers; 50¢ transaction fee and 2.9 percent for out-of-U.S. buyers.

- **PayPal** (www.paypal.com). Accept payment online with this company through either credit card or bank transfer. Cost: depends on your volume (most U.S. sellers pay 2.9 percent plus 30¢ per transaction if the buyer is also in the United States).

- **Security Check** (www.security-check.net). Verify that a check is good so you won't get stuck for money. Cost: varies with volume of business.

- **TeleCheck Check Verification Service** (www.telecheck.com). Verify that a check is good so you won't get stuck for money. Cost: monthly fee of about $100, depending on the types of items you sell, plus 30¢ per check.

- **VeriCheck** (www.vericheck.net). Verify that a check is good so you won't get stuck for money. Cost: $99 initial fee, plus 20¢ for each check verification.

News and Information

Stay on top of developments and educate yourself about business and eBay opportunities.

- ◆ **AuctionBytes** (www.auctionbytes.com). Free e-mail alerts and newsletter, and "cool tools" at the site.

- ◆ **Big Ideas for Small Business** (www.barbaraweltman.com). Free monthly e-newsletter from Barbara Weltman for small business owners.

- ◆ **eBay Radio** (www.wsradio.com). Internet-based radio featuring Jim ("Griff") Griffith, who provides insightful eBay information.

- ◆ **Entrepreneur Magazine Radio** (www.wsradio.com). Internet-based radio show with information for small business owners.

- ◆ **Idea of the Day** (www.barbaraweltman.com). Free daily e-mail from Barbara Weltman with a tip for small business owners.

- ◆ **PowerUp Newsletter** (http://pages.ebay.com/sellercentral/newsflash.html). Free newsletter for eBay PowerSellers.

- ◆ **The Chatter** (www.ebaychatter.com). eBay's blog about the company and community.

- ◆ **The PowerSeller Report** (www.tprweb.com). Newsletter for PowerSellers. Cost: $99 a year.

Photos

Create and display great images using software and online tools.

- ◆ **Auctionpix** (www.auctionpix.co.uk). Image storage. Cost: free.

- ◆ **AuctionSuite** (www.auctionsuite.com). Image storage. Cost: from $1.50 monthly.

- ◆ **Auctiva** (www.auctiva.com). Image hosting. Cost: free.

- ◆ **Cloud Dome** (www.clouddome.com). Photo tent kit. Cost: under $159.

- ◆ **Deadzoom** (www.deadzoom.com). Image storage. Cost: $3 per month for 5MB.

- ◆ **EZ Cube** (www.ezauctiontools.com). Light tents and table top photo setups. Cost: Tents start at $79.

- **Fast Photos Auction Photo Editor** (www.pixby.com). This is a photo editor designed specifically for auction sellers. Add watermarks and borders, and create eBay gallery thumbnail shots easily. Cost: $24.95 (free 21-day trial period).

- **FotoKiss** (www.fotokiss.com). Designed for people with no photo experience, this tool lets you crop, add frames, and write text on your images for listing on auctions and catalogs. Cost: $39.95 (30-day free trial period).

- **InkFrog** (www.inkfrog.com), also found as SpareDollar (www.sparedollar.com). Image storage. Cost: $6.95 per month for 300 MB (14-day free trial).

- **Onstream Auction** (www.auctionvideo.com). Add video to your listings. Cost: $9.95 per month for low-volume usage.

- **Photoshop by Adobe** (www.adobe.com). This is the premier program for improving the quality of your digital images. Cost: $99 for the basic version (Photoshop Elements); $649 for the professional version.

- **Ranchoweb** (www.ranchoweb.com). Image storage. Cost: $11.95 per month for 50 MB.

- **Sharpics** (www.sharpics.com). D-Flector portable studio. Cost: prices start at under $70.

- **SlideTour** (www.slidetour.com). Upload, display, and manage your images. Cost: free for 5MB or an annual rate starting at $24.95 for 50 images.

There are also shareware alternatives to many commercial applications.

- **Download.com** (www.download.com). Find user ratings and ratings by CNET (a tech site company).

- **Tucows Inc.** (www.tucows.com and enter "Photography" in the Search box). Find popularity and ratings for each application.

Price Guides

Determine the price of antiques and collectibles using appraisers, price guides, or prior appraisal results.

- **Collect.com** (www.collect.com). There are two online guides: one for sports cards and the other for antiques and collectibles. Cost: free.

- **Kovel's Online** (www.kovels.com). Prices are listed for more than 600,000 antiques and collectibles. Cost: free.

◆ **Maine Antique Digest** (www.maineantiquedigest.com) and click on Price Database. Cost: free.

Seal Programs

Let buyers know about your authenticity and reliability by displaying a recognizable sign or symbol.

◆ **BBB OnLine** (www.bbbonline.org/reliability/apply.asp). This is the electronic version of the Better Business Bureau. More than 34,000 websites now participate in the BBB OnLine Reliability Seal Program. Cost: pricing varies, depending on the size of the business.

◆ **NetCheck** (www.netcheck.com). Members can display a company profile listing contact information, what customers say about that company, and other information. This includes what NetCheck has to say about the business, including whether any customer complaints have been filed. Cost: $95 per year.

◆ **SquareTrade** (www.squaretrade.com). This seal program is used on three million eBay listings to denote that the buyer can be trusted. SquareTrade verifies sellers as trusted and continually monitors their activities to see that they meet certain standards. Cost: $9.50 per month (30-day free trial period).

◆ **VeriSign** (www.verisign.com). This seal program attests that your site is secure. This gives buyers a sense of security when paying with a credit card. Cost: free trial period.

Shipping and Packing Supplies

When sending out your items, keep costs down and merchandise safe by using the right tools for the job. Free supplies are noted; for all other sources, prices vary. Here's where to find what you need.

◆ **eSupplyStore** (www.esupplystore.com). Discount shipping supplies.

◆ **Fast-Pack.com** (www.Fast-Pack.com). Colored bubble wrap and colored packing tape.

◆ **FedEx** (www.fedex.com, click on Order Supplies under Manage My Account). Boxes. Cost: free.

- **FP International** (www.fpintl.com). Buy your own machine and supplies to produce six different types of bubble wrap.

- **Office Depot** (www.officedepot.com). Various shipping and packing supplies.

- **Office Max** (www.officemax.com). Various shipping and packing supplies.

- **Pakmail** (www.pakmail.com). Professional packing solutions.

- **PostNet** (www.postnet.com). Professional packing solutions.

- **Staples** (www.staples.com). Various shipping and packing supplies.

- **U.S. Postal Service** (http://shop.usps.com). Boxes (including those with the eBay logo at www.ebaysupplies.usps.com). Obtain free co-branded supplies.

- **UPS** (www.ups.com, Click on Order Supplies in the Quick Links box). Professional packing solutions. Cost: free.

At U-PIC (www.u-pic.com), a division of UPS, you can obtain insurance that's good for any shipper you use—USPS, UPS, or FedEx, at up to 80 percent lower than other shipping insurance solutions.

Shipping Calculators

Determine what it costs to ship a package—domestically or internationally—without leaving your computer screen. All of the calculators are free

- **DHL** (www.dhl-usa.com/ratecalculator/HandlerServlet?CLIENT= RATES_REQUEST_DISPLAY&nav=GetRates). Get shipping rates by entering origin, destination, and information about what you're shipping.

- **eBay shipping calculator** (http://pages.ebay.com/services/buyandsell/shipping. html and click on Shipping Calculator). Use this to figure shipping costs at USPS and UPS.

- **FedEx** (www.fedex.com/ratefinder/home?cc=US&language=en). Obtain a shipping quote and determine the expected delivery date.

Shipping Companies

Send out and insure items cheaply so you can pass savings on to your customers.

- **DHL** (www.dhl.com). Drop off or arrange for pickup. Cost: varies.

- **DSI** (www.dsiinsurance.com and click on Auction Sellers and Buyers). This full-service shipping company boasts the lowest insurance rates (promising savings of up to 90 percent on shipping insurance). Cost: varies.

- **FedEx** (www.fedex.com). Ship at your local Kinko's, from 46,000 drop-off locations, or request a pick up from your location. Cost: varies.

- **UPS** (www.ups.com). Ship at your UPS store or request a pickup from your location. Cost: varies.

- **U.S. Postal Service** (www.usps.com). Ship at your local post office or request a pick up from your location. Cost: varies.

- **Yellow** (www.myyellow.com). Use this small carrier when shipping specialized goods, such as temperature-sensitive items. Cost: varies.

Taxes

Burdensome as it may be, use online tools to make things easier.

- **ADP** (www.adp.com). Outsource employment tax filings to this payroll company.

- **Business Owners Toolkit** (www.toolkit.com). Link to your state for forms.

- **EIN** (http://sa1.www4.irs.gov/sa_vign/newFormSS4.do). Obtain your employer tax identification number (your federal business ID) online. Cost: free.

- **IRS** (www.irs.gov). Obtain forms and schedules online.

- **PayChex** (www.paychex.com). Outsource employment tax filings to this payroll company.

- **The Sales Tax Clearinghouse** (http://thestc.com/STrates.stm). Find information and rates on your state's sales tax.

eBay Icons

eBay listings are peppered with icons conveying a lot of information for those who can decipher the little pictures. Here's a glossary of eBay icons.

eBay Help

Help Topics
A-Z Index
eBay Acronyms
eBay Glossary

Contact Us

Related Links

Learning Center
eBay University
Security Center
Contacting Customer Support
Community Answer Center

Was this page helpful?
 Yes   No

How can we improve this page? (optional)

700 characters left

Submit Comment

Search the Help pages (Does not search for items or products)

Search Help Pages   Tips

Icon Glossary for Listings

eBay listings include many little pictures or icons that give you additional information about the listing. The following is a description of each icon.

Icon	Description
	The camera icon means that a picture is included with the listing. Click the icon to see the picture.
	The PayPal logo means that the seller accepts PayPal as a payment method for the listing.
Skype	The Skype logo means that members using Skype can contact each other. This may include chatting with or calling the other member.
	The rising sun icon means that the item has been listed within the last 24 hours.
	The auction paddle icon means that the item is part of eBay Live Auctions. Click the paddle to go to eBay Live Auctions. Learn More.
Buy It Now	The Buy It Now icon means that an item has a set price for which you can purchase it without going through the auction process. Learn more.
	The wrapped present or gift icon means the seller of this item wanted to highlight it a potential gift item. Learn more.
	The frame icon indicates that the item is visible in eBay's picture gallery. This means you can see this item's photo in search results and category listings.
	The ribbon icon means that the vehicle has been inspected.
	The blue and yellow ribbon icon means that the seller has elected to donate a percentage of their final sale price to charity. Learn more about eBay Giving Works.
me	The About Me icon means that the member has created an About Me page to tell you more about themselves. Click on this icon to open the About Me page. Learn more about creating an About Me Page.
	The eBay Stores icon means that the seller has an eBay Store. Click on this icon to go to this member's eBay Store. Learn more about eBay Stores.
Power Seller	The Power Seller icon means that this seller has sustained a consistent high volume of monthly sales and has a high level of feedback (98% positive or better).

eBay icons.

Index